Art on the Edge

ART ON THE EDGE
Creators and Situations

HAROLD ROSENBERG

MACMILLAN PUBLISHING CO., INC.
New York

Macmillan Publishing Co., Inc.
866 Third Avenue, New York, N.Y. 10022
Collier Macmillan Canada, Ltd.

Library of Congress Cataloging in Publication Data

Rosenberg, Harold.
    Art on the edge.

    Includes index.
    1. Art, Modern—20th century. 2. Art—Tech-
nique. 3. Artists. I. Title.
N6490.R5915   709'.04   75-16128
ISBN 0-02-604900-7

First Printing 1975

All the chapters in this book appeared originally
as essays in *The New Yorker*, except for
"Criticism and Its Premises," which was
commissioned for "A Seminar in Art Education
for Research and Curriculum Development"
at Pennsylvania State University, and is
reprinted with the permission of
Edward L. Mattil, Project Director.

Printed in the United States of America

For Ben Raeburn

Contents

SITUATIONS

Illustrations

Foreword

This book is about evenly divided between studies of outstanding artists and analyses of situations—intellectual, institutional, financial—typical of today's art world. The works and ideas of the artists stand as possibilities for the future. The situations are for the main part adverse, obstacles to creation that at times seem to foreclose the possibility of valid art in the years to come.

It is generally agreed that the modernist art movements of the past one hundred years have exhausted their premises. In any case, modernism in art is no longer a Cause furthered by an international élite. Internationalism in art today is predominantly represented by the world market on which masterworks of all periods and cultures are traded.

The decline in modernist enthusiasm is offset in the opinion of some by the tremendous expansion of public interest in and official support of the arts. Constantly growing museum attendance, staggering prices at auctions, millions poured into museum programs by the National Foundation for the Arts, by State Arts Councils and private foundations, plus commissioning of painters and sculptors by public agencies, banks, and business firms provide statistical promise of a new Golden Age.

Yet this prolific support of art and hyperanimation of the art scene themselves carry the danger of propelling painting and sculpture over the edge that separates them from the crafts, commercial design, and the mass media.

In the deepest sense, ongoing developments in painting and sculpture are testing the cultural direction and creative capabilities of the United States, now that this country is no longer under the guidance of Europe and has assumed leadership in these arts.

If art is to survive as an important language, it will be through the persistent will of artists and through models chosen from among themselves. Each of the masters dealt with in the first section of this book—from Duchamp and Miró to Steinberg and Giacometti—takes his departure from a unique insight into the actuality of art in this century. And each has evolved responses to that actuality that form the substance of his work and the style of his life.

Indeed, one may say that art today is the realization in materials of strategies for making art possible—and that art is needed in order to make artists possible.

In the end, antagonistic factors in a culture tend to produce the kind of mind and personality (for example, Aleksandr Solzhenitsyn in the Soviet Union) that is equipped to combat them. Perhaps the situations described here indicate that the time has come for a new type of artist to arise and replace the individualist dandy of the modernist epoch.

H. R.

East Hampton, New York,
August, 1974

I. CREATORS

1

Duchamp: Private and Public

Duchamp began his conversation with Pierre Cabanne* by congratulating himself on never having worked for a living, even as an artist. "I haven't known," he said, "the strain of producing, painting not having been an outlet for me, or having a pressing need to express myself. I've never had that kind of need—to draw morning, noon, and night, to make sketches, etc." Duchamp's dislike of work was probably a matter of temperament, but it became one of principle, too. When his interviewer listed the products of what was evidently Duchamp's most fruitful time, 1912–13, in which a dozen of his most important creations emerged, among them *The King and Queen Crossed by Swift Nudes*, *Virgin No. 1* and *Virgin No. 2*, *The Passage from the Virgin to the Bride*, *The Bride Stripped Bare by Her Bachelors, Even*, Duchamp's only response was "Ugh!" Contrasting himself with his followers among young vanguardists today, he emphasized that he had always done "as few things as possible"—an effective antidote to the "easy art" that some of his innovations have inspired.

Duchamp's strategy in regard to work involved a complex evaluation of the nature of art in our time. People like to think that art is the mystery of creation, but, Duchamp pointed out, the artist, as a person active in society, is a "man like any other. It's his job to do certain things"—in the case of the painter, "things on a canvas, with a frame."

* Pierre Cabanne, *Dialogues with Marcel Duchamp*, ed. Robert Motherwell (New York: Viking Press, 1971).

Duchamp said that he had always been drawn to the notion of the artist as a craftsman—a term more venerable than "artist." This was a reversion to the traditional idea of making, and it provided him with a stand against the romanticism of his friends the Surrealists. But he then brought into play a fact that totally undermines any identification of modern art with medieval craft. The contemporary artist, he noted, "doesn't make things for people; it's the people who come to choose things from among his production." Collaboration between the creator and his patron has been dissolved. The collector today can decide what he will acquire, but the artist has the prior decision about what he will make. He can, if he chooses, prepare an inventory for the art market, or he can make works for himself, as if he were a patron in the old style. He can, as well, decide not to produce—a freedom he may exercise in our time without ceasing to be an artist.

Duchamp calls the liberation from dealing with patrons "the artist's revenge." For his own part, he appears to have leaned toward patronage, however, as evidenced by his continuing tie to Walter Arensberg. He would have no objection, he explains, to producing things for friends—as he made the birdcage containing marble sugar cubes for Katherine Dreier's sister—as long as "they let me do what I wanted." Normally, though, the modern artist fabricates not for individuals he knows but for an anonymous and ever-changing public. If as a maker he resembles the craftsman of the past, in relation to society he is more akin to the manufacturer of a trademarked commodity. The situation of the free artist seems simple, but one who offers art for buyers to choose from is confronted by a swarm of ambiguous possibilities. There is nothing to prevent him from increasing his output by resorting to improved tools, including machines, or by assembling under his signature objects reflecting his mood but never touched by his hand. ("'Readymades' cover the globe!" cries Dali in a preface to *Dialogues*. "The loaf of bread fifteen yards long has become a loaf of fifteen miles!") The artist can determine the physical character of what he makes or selects, but its existence as art depends on the public; Duchamp remarks that it is posterity that will keep objects in the Louvre. *Art is defined not by its technique of production, manual or other, but by the inner shape of the society in which it appears. To follow Duchamp's reasoning is to translate art into archeology.* It is as if one looked back on the artifacts of the twentieth century from a point far enough in the future to make all of them seem equal.

Duchamp's lazy-man's questioning of why he and other artists should

Marcel Duchamp, *Ready-Made, Why Not Sneeze Rose Selavy?* 1921,
marble blocks in shape of lump sugar, thermometer, wood, and
cuttlebone in a small birdcage, 4½″ h. x 8⅝″ l. x 6⅜″ d.
PHILADELPHIA MUSEUM OF ART, LOUISE AND WALTER ARENSBERG COLLECTION

do what they are doing when they do anything opened art to a universe of non-art that duplicated art in all definable aspects. The
thought of making by hand brought up by implication the power of
the machine to duplicate human activity, which is the theme of
Duchamp's major creations, from the *Nude Descending a Staircase*,
through the *Large Glass* ("The Bride and the Bachelors"), to the various categories of readymades. Duchamp's response to the hand and its
mechanical equivalents was one of profound ambivalence—a conflict
of feeling that he could not surmount through his dispassionate ration-
alism and that led him from paradox to paradox. His most influential
innovations and significant attitudes are offshoots of his inability to
choose between a glorification of manual skill and a dismissal of
handiwork as tiresome routine. He shies away from the "manual servi-
tude" of the artisan and suggests to Cabanne that his break with painting was stimulated by its requirement that the artist "work by hand."
Among the technical reasons he gives for using glass instead of canvas
for *The Bride* is his feeling that glass "took away any idea of 'the
hand.'" In his *Optical Discs* and *Rotoreliefs*, he experiments with
visual effects obtainable through physical movement via mechanical
devices. And as a final rival to art he conceives the readymade—a
product of the factory which requires only to be signed, titled, and
exhibited.

The readymade exceeds art intellectually in concentrating into itself
the riddles, contradictions, correspondences, and negations that arise
from the modern mixing of art and reality. It carries to a logical
conclusion the principle of Cubist collage that painted forms, machine
products, and natural phenomena can be made aesthetically interchangeable by locating them within the same picture frame. The
integration of art and non-art is the essence of twentieth-century
vanguardism in art. And for fifty years artists have sought new ways to
push the unification closer, notch by notch. But in the readymade a
total fusion of art and non-art had already been achieved—a fact that
may account for the progressive thinning out of vanguardism since
Duchamp showed store-bought goods in art galleries.

The emergence of Duchamp's non-manual, or semi-manual, objects
automatically discredited the craft-based values of excellence in conception and execution by which art had been dominated. In a statement
that anticipates the de-aestheticized aesthetics of the anti-form movement of the sixties, Duchamp stipulates that the readymades represent

not a shift in art standards but the total elimination of such standards. "A point which I want very much to establish is that the choice of these 'readymades' was never dictated by an aesthetic delectation. This choice was based on a reaction of *visual* indifference with at the same time a total absence of good or bad taste . . . in fact, a complete anesthesia" (his italics).

Having identified art with making, Duchamp concludes that making has lost its attractiveness. The readymades are not art but a kind of infra-art that goes along with art as the minus sign of its qualities. In a speech on the readymade, he imagines "reciprocal readymades" that would "expose the basic antinomy between art and readymades." But, having set art and readymades in opposition to each other, he moves on to a semi-comic summing up in which he declares all paintings to be in essence readymades. "Since the tubes of paint used by the artist are manufactured and readymade products, we must conclude that all the paintings in the world are readymades aided [Duchamp's term for readymades that are changed by adding details] and also works of assemblage."

The notion that a painting or sculpture is a bringing together of manufactured items found in art-supply stores is a materialistic dwarfing for farcical effect, in the tradition of Rabelais's reduction of a scholars' debate to the gesticulations of the speakers. The deliberate absurdity of Duchamp's proposition has not, however, prevented it from providing a rationale for works that consist of moving or displacing materials from one site to another—boulders in Arizona or ticker tape from the floor of the New York Stock Exchange to the artist's roof. The artist, as I have noted elsewhere, is transformed into a porter, and sculpture consists of any disturbance of the environment by delivery or by taking away—a cow munching grass is a readymade aided by adding to himself and by subtracting from the meadow. Moving materials from one site to another is a function of technology as well as of organisms, so Duchamp's blending of machinery and bodies in the *Nude* and *The Bride* survives in the earthworks mode of the readymade.

The logic of Duchamp's innovations contemplates getting rid of "the hand" or radically reducing its role. Yet Duchamp has a nostalgia for craft and an antipathy for the machine. His emphasis on the "antinomy" between art and readymades carries a depreciatory overtone with regard to the latter. Applying his principle that art is craft, he insists that making *The Bride*, like choosing the readymades, amounted to a "renunciation of all aesthetics . . . not just another manifesto of new painting." He praises Tinguely but adds the reservation that "he's more of a mechanic." Instead of using a movie camera, Duchamp conceives of turning the film by hand, and he denounces the cinema for failing, as does photography, to "go much further than a mechanical way of making something. It can't compete with art. If art continues to exist. . . ."

Suddenly, the image of Duchamp the arch anti-artist gives way to the image of a person troubled by the crisis of art in this era of mechanical duplication, and giving form to his doubts in visual-verbal riddles, puns, and enigmas as well as in a critical detachment from the vocation of artist. Duchamp declares to Cabanne his antagonism to modern painting for having devoted itself, since Courbet, to appeals to the eye—what Duchamp calls "retinal" painting. "Before, painting had other functions: it could be religious, philosophical, moral." Apparently, this avant-gardist secreted a strain of belief that "real art" belonged back in the Renaissance, or even earlier. Since those centuries of greatness, the art object has become fundamentally unsettled, as the relation between the artist, his product, and the spectator entered into a process of transformation whose end is not in sight. Attempts to establish continuity between modern works and masterpieces of the past inevitably return to the ideal of the well-made picture that satisfies educated tastes. But this effort toward continuity cannot escape turning into parody when the standard of making is the art market and the modern Medici is the millionaire whose collecting follows market trends.

In an epoch of making for sale, the alternative for the artist who refuses to work for money is making-as-criticism (parody, irony, subversion) or making-for-oneself, that historically indestructible patron. Occasionally, a work carries the hint of an idea; all the rest is manufacturing. Duchamp made no secret of the fact that art attracted him less than did artists; few contemporary works had meaning for him and he rarely attended exhibitions. "The individual, man as man, man as a brain, if you like, interests me more than what he makes, because I've noticed that most artists only repeat themselves. . . . They have that old habit which inclines them to do one painting a month, for example. Everything depends on their working speed. They believe they owe society the monthly or yearly painting." The tradition of art as work survives as the self-enslavement of the artist and the reduction

Marcel Duchamp, *Ready-Made, Girl with Bedstead*, 1916–17, painted
tin advertisement, 9¼″ x 13¼″.

of the art object to a mechanical reproduction, even when it is executed by hand. The professional artist is a machine for making art, and his possibilities as a person are more interesting than the readymades in which he repeats himself. "Arman," said Duchamp generously of the extremely successful assemblage-maker, "is very capable of changing, however."

Duchamp's stubborn anti-professionalism kept him at a safe distance from the schools of aesthetic absurdity fostered by some of his gestures. The artist freed of making works for patrons could fulfill himself only through resisting the obsessive self-repetition of the artist as supplier of the market. Modern technology exposes the futility of manual copying and forces the artist to reconsider his vocation. Art in the age of readymades ought to consist exclusively of acts of origination. Avoiding the manual multiplication of objects, it can restrict itself to a search for the new. Those incapable of grasping this fundamental alteration in the function of art have condemned Duchamp as a novelty-monger. Duchamp, however, was always the last to exploit Duchamp. Gide asserts that the difference between a novelist and his characters is that the novelist enjoys the privilege of not acting on his ideas; having conceived the "gratuitous act," Gide could leave it to his protagonist Lafcadio to shove a stranger off a moving train. Artists are permitted to act as provocateurs, but they must be on guard against falling into the trap of becoming their own disciples.

What was inimitable in Duchamp was the discipline by which he kept himself on the edge of art—neither of it nor out of it, a fringe personage, a permanently borderline case. As he himself said, speaking about a Surrealist exhibition he helped to organize, art occasionally "borrowed" him from the world. When Cabanne intimated that certain young artists "are a little like your children," Duchamp was quick to point out that though he was delighted to fill their need for a "prototype," there was no great resemblance between him and them, since he "did as few things as possible, which isn't like the current attitude of making as many as you can, in order to make as much money as possible." To be a professional producer of anti-art or non-art art objects is a meaningless role, if not a degraded one; it converts radical criticism of the place of the art object in contemporary society into a hoax by supplying other objects which take its place. In the dialectic of the aesthetic and the counter-aesthetic in which the art of this century is engaged, every art object can be matched by an anti-art or a non-art object. By erasing a de Kooning drawing and displaying it under the title of *Erased de Kooning Drawing, Robert Raus-chenberg*, Rauschenberg performed a proper Duchampian gesture, in that his exhibit diverted the spectator from the visual experience of a sheet of soiled drawing paper to the mental concept of a negated work of art. But this concept cannot bear repetition. For Duchamp, it was a quasi-ethical principle that the art-cancelling readymades should be strictly limited in number. If too many aesthetically "neutral" objects appeared, they would turn into art in the minds of spectators, for whom art is "a habit-forming drug," and the critical function of the readymade would be defeated by reverence for art belonging to a new category.

Instead of practicing art as either a craft or a profession, Duchamp established himself as a squatter in the outskirts of art and devoted himself to one-shot projects that happened to arouse him. The *Large Glass*, his most extended and complex undertaking (except for the twenty-year "underground" construction, *Given: 1. The Waterfall, 2. The Illuminating Gas*, unveiled after his death), was not the realization of an idea but the sum of separate experiments, observations, analogies, puns, metaphors, analyses, and technical decisions collected over a decade with what Marcel Jean has eloquently characterized as *"per-sévérance négligente."* Hundreds of pages of recondite exegesis, includ-ing interpretations based on psychoanalysis, Hindu mythology, alchemy, linguistics, and the influence of Rube Goldberg, continue to be devoted to this work and to Duchamp's accompanying notes, assem-bled in the *Green Box* and distributed as a work of art in a different medium. "The *Large Glass*," conjectures. Octavio Paz, in his *Marcel Duchamp, or the Castle of Purity*, "is the design for a piece of machinery, and the *Green Box* is something like one of those instruc-tion manuals for the upkeep and running of a machine." As an almost random set of illustrations picked from a mass of unsystematic calcula-tions, recollected images, symbols, and made-up scientific formulas, the *Glass* is, of course, intellectually impenetrable, a joke that relates to its being transparent as material. Its historical significance lies in its being a painting that is no longer an object but an objectified segment of the artist's mental and emotional life during a given portion of time —a kind of second self projected by him into the art world, compara-ble to such Duchamp aliases as Rrose Sélavy, R. Mutt, and Mr. Salt Seller. Like a life, the *Large Glass* was never finished but simply came to an end. It "held me," Duchamp said, "until 1923, the only thing I

Marcel Duchamp, *Ready-Made, 50cc, Air de Paris*, 20th century, glass
bulb, 2½″ in diameter.
PHILADELPHIA MUSEUM OF ART, LOUISE AND WALTER ARENSBERG COLLECTION

was interested in, and I even regret not finishing it, but it became so monotonous, it was a transcription, and toward the end there was no invention. So it just fizzled out." Here, as in the readymade, "transcription" is the antithesis of art and marks its expiration.

Duchamp liked to explain that he did things because he found them "amusing"—a position not dissimilar to that of Valéry, that other great twentieth-century holdout from creation, who described poetry as a "game." In presenting art as an activity of the mind that he indulges in for pleasure, the artist evades the need to resolve the ambiguities of contemporary art-making by assuming the guise of a dilettante. Yet, despite his detachment and his contributions to the myth of himself as anti-artist, Duchamp's casualness about art was a pose. His dandyism, clowning, and disintegrative wit provided a brilliant formal vocabulary for dealing with the art situation as it is, but his hopes for a new profundity in art had to be passed over quickly to avoid falling into commonplaces. "The painting," Duchamp summed up for Cabanne, "is no longer a decoration to be hung in the dining room or living room. We have thought of other things to use as decoration. Art is taking more the form of a sign. . . . This is the feeling that has directed me all my life." Art as a sign is primarily art for the artist acting as his own patron, and thus both free and answerable in ultimate terms for the fact of its existence. In signifying art, as exemplified by the *Large Glass* or certain Action paintings, the aim is not an art object but a continuum of mental and psychic events of which the painting survives as an evidence. It is making for its own sake and for the sake of the maker. Duchamp found it rewarding to spend the last twenty years of his life at this kind of "craft," without the intervention of "people who come to choose things."

With his retrospective at the Museum of Modern Art of more than two hundred pieces, a three-hundred-and-fifty-page illustrated catalogue, and the concurrent distribution of his notes, diagrams, and observations,* knowledge of Duchamp has reached a plateau on which it is likely to remain for some time. Indeed, there is an inclination to believe that all relevant material has been rounded up. "I have tried to add something to what has been said about Duchamp," writes Matta, one of his most basically indebted disciples, "but I think that everything has already been said." Another invitation for everyone hence-

---

* Michel Sanouillet, *The Complete Writing of Marcel Duchamp: An Updated English Version of Marchand Du Sel* (New York: Oxford University Press, 1973).

forth to hold his peace is issued by Rauschenberg, a mimic of
Duchamp's bearding of the Mona Lisa: "Marcel Duchamp is all but
impossible to write about"—though this does not prevent Rauschenberg from adding that to think of Duchamp makes him feel "sweet"
inside. Lucy Lippard's contribution to the catalogue—a clever colla-
tion of bits of literature gathered from farfetched sources to accompany such celebrated Duchampiana as the bottle rack, the snow shovel,
and the birdcage containing lumps of marble sugar—carries the threat
of ridicule to those still tempted to discover new deep meanings in
these "creations." Given such evidences of satiety, the Duchamp dos-
sier should now be closed. Or, as Michel Sanouillet, co-editor of *Salt
Seller*, puts it, "A myth has been built around that [Duchamp's] existence and that work, and the authenticity of the factors which serve to
support the myth is less important than the collective state of mind
which gave birth to it." Five years after his death, Duchamp is no
longer represented by the sum of his own acts and ideas; instead, he
has been dissolved into public fantasizing. If one is to follow Sanouillet, Duchamp is now a sociological problem, on the same level of
inquiry as, say, how Nixon came to be reelected—the problem of
analyzing the process by which a public image is imposed on an individual life, like a lion mask on a ballet dancer, and makes the individual
inaccessible and, ultimately, even irrelevant. How long has it been
since "the real Duchamp" was in a position to decide what he wished
to contribute to that which Breton called "the great modern legend"
of Duchamp?

To a greater extent than that of any of his contemporaries,
Duchamp's career—after the scandal-success of *Nude Descending a
Staircase* at the New York Armory Show in 1913, when he was
twenty-five—took place on the stage of public opinion; his insistence
in later statements and interviews that the public, not the artist, decides
what is art was a literal description of his own coming into being as a
renowned art-historical personage fabricated by the eccentric mechanisms of myth-making. It was because he was so securely pinned under
the eye of his audience after his arrival in New York in 1915 as a
celebrated representative of the farthest outpost of vanguardism that
he found it desirable to play a part in the vaudeville of the modern-art
cultural takeover and then to go "underground" thirty years later in
order to create an absolutely secret work, *Given: 1. The Waterfall,
2. The Illuminating Gas*, during the last two decades of his life. The
division between public, and private, experienced by all artists in a

free society, was for him sharpened to the utmost degree—there was the art-world comedian and the Symbolist, note-making, visual-verbal poet of the closed room. Thus it became possible to consider that even while he was alive he existed completely in the mirror of what was said about him. Picasso is undoubtedly at least equal to Duchamp as an art-world presence, but when one thinks of Picasso there is a strong inflection toward the objectively interrelated mass of his creations, whereas in regard to Duchamp the works are reflected in the changing silhouette of their creator. Every Duchamp piece is a piece of Duchamp, and derives its meaning from the spectator's total impression of the artist.

It is natural, therefore, that the Duchamp retrospective at the Museum of Modern Art, organized in collaboration with the Philadelphia Museum of Art, should have less the character of an art show than of a display of mementos celebrating a hero and his deeds. A good portion of the exhibition could be described as straight publicity or myth-building. A long corridor leading to the exhibits was placarded with Duchamp memorabilia of the past sixty years. The catalogue and the exhibition itself went back eighty years, to include a photograph of the artist at the age of one; photographs of him with his artist-brothers and with friends and colleagues of different periods (Breton, Man Ray, Brancusi, Picabia, Alfred Barr, Peggy Guggenheim, Richard Hamilton, John Cage); several photographs of his studio, of him in numerous disguises and with a star cut out of the hair on the back of his head, of him on the stage, of him playing chess with a naked girl, taking the air at a chess table in Washington Square Park, of his installations of historic Surrealist exhibitions; drawings, paintings, and sculptures of him or referring to him, by artists from Miró and Pevsner to Nakian, Florine Stettheimer, and Tinguely. Among self-testimonials in the exhibition is a photograph by Man Ray of Duchamp as a devil, with horns and a beard of shaving soap, imprinted on his profit-sharing Monte Carlo bonds; a reproduction of his false check to his dentist; and a picture of Duchamp as Rrose Sélavy on a bottle of toilet water.

To fill out the myth-making of the exhibition, an extraordinary catalogue was assembled by Anne d'Harnoncourt, of the Philadelphia Museum, and Kynaston McShine, of the Modern. It covers every event, almost every moment, of Duchamp's life after he was fifteen. In addition to the usual introductory essay, there is an analysis of his intellectual background, of his relation to the machine, of his use of

Marcel Duchamp, *The Large Glass, or The Bride Stripped Bare by Her Bachelors, Even*, 1915–23, oil and lead wire on glass, 109¼″ x 69⅛″.

language, of his influence on contemporaries and on artistic descendants
—plus symbolic interpretations of *The Bride Stripped Bare by Her
Bachelors, Even* and of *Given*, and an inquest into the fabulous meanings of Duchamp's alter ego, Rrose Sélavy, whom he impersonated in
drag. Above all, the catalogue contains "A Collective Portrait of Marcel Duchamp"—comments and appreciations by some sixty painters,
poets, composers, dancers, photographers, art dealers. Never has a
product been supported by more impressive testimonials.

The Museum of Modern Art apotheosis reflects the appropriation of
the Duchamp myth by the official art world. In fact, however,
Duchamp is today by no means an object of unanimous veneration.
Since their first public appearance, his creations have possessed an
inherent capacity to stir up conflict. Sixty years ago, he entered the
art world by splitting it, and he still stands in the cleft, wearing a
grim smile, as he does in the last photograph in the catalogue—
Duchamp peering out like the Sphinx through the parting of a curtain.
It would be unusual, of course, for a museum to complete the documentation of a retrospective by reproducing writings of the artist's
enemies. In the case of Duchamp, however, the antagonism he arouses
is an essential element of his role, and even, if one wishes, of his greatness and profundity. He may be fulfilled as a myth; he is genuinely
important as an issue. To situate him in the conflict in which he has
been engaged is the only way to draw him back from the otherworld
of public relations into the actual history and outlook of art today, and
from empty worship of a publicity-swollen Name into appreciation
as a force still active in determining the future of culture. The 1913
Armory Show uproar over *Nude Descending a Staircase* was a joining
of battle over the emergence of a twentieth-century consciousness in
the United States. The scandal of exhibiting clusters of bladelike planes
as a human body in motion was matched by the scandal of the bellicose ignorance and smugness of "representatives of the public" with
impermeable, inherited notions of what a work of art should be.
Today, Duchamp, as the most potent leftover of radical thinking and
practice in art between the two wars, continues to personify the problems of art in modern technological society, and to serve as a reminder
that not one of these problems has been solved. For this reason, he
remains the primary target of those critics and artists whose interest
lies in restoring art to a "normal" continuity with the masterpieces of
the past. Fundamentally, the issue is a cultural-political one.

The case against Duchamp may be sketched as follows:

(1) He is held responsible for leading art off the track of evolutionary advance (which implies that art belongs on a track). Instead of extending the formal potentialities of the Cézanne-Cubist tradition, he deviated into eccentricity; the *Nude* initiated no new developments in painting, and such interest as it has relates to the artist's misguided effort to introduce motion into an essentially static medium, and to its upsetting effect upon an uncultivated public. Hence it is contended that Duchamp, far from representing the avant-garde, has been an obstacle to genuine experiment and a reactionary force in the painting of the past half century. He has boasted that he has no use for "good" painting, he has fought against taste, good and bad, and in a message to Alfred Stieglitz he expressed the desire to see people "despise painting." Thus, despite the apologetics of his supporters, he is fundamentally anti-art and a practitioner of aesthetic nihilism. His aggrandizement in the 1960s is an offshoot of New Leftism.

(2) He has built up the importance of the artist's signature at the expense of his product. For him, as he has several times remarked, the artist ranks higher than the work of art—a concept that opened the door to art-world "stars" whose talent consists in attracting attention to themselves, and who have brought about the degradation of the art object (Warhol), and even its total elimination (Conceptual art). In the Duchamp era, one can exhibit one's own body as a "work of art" or make a record of one's temperature or blood pressure as "information" equivalent to a painting.

(3) In adopting the readymade, Duchamp has introduced the deadly rival of artistic creation—an object fabricated by machine and available everywhere, an object chosen, as he put it, on the basis of pure "visual indifference," in order to "reduce the idea of aesthetic consideration to the choice of the mind, not to the ability or cleverness of the hand." In the world of the readymade, anything can become a work of art through being signed by an artist. All particular genres and disciplines become superfluous. The title "artist," no longer conferred in recognition of skill in conception and execution, is achieved by means of publicity.

(4) Duchamp has placed innovative art under permanent suspicion of being a hoax. If in 1913 the *Nude* raised doubts about its seriousness, the readymades validated those doubts in regard to the doings and values of the avant-garde. Were the bicycle wheel mounted on a

stool, the snow shovel, the dog comb inscribed with "a nonsensical phrase" to be taken seriously as works of art?—especially after the artist had supplied a description of "the characteristics of a true ready-made: no beauty, no ugliness, nothing particularly aesthetic about it." And, if it is not art, what is a readymade? A provocation? A sacred relic of an art-world personage? Duchamp's masterwork, *The Bride* (or *The Large Glass*, as it is also called), with its disparate images, reiterated as fetishes throughout Duchamp's career (the water mill and glider, the chocolate grinder, the clothes dummies, a machine suspended from a cloud that has three square apertures), is not likely to supply confidence in the artist's intentions, which were placed in doubt by *Nude* and the readymades. Even Sanouillet, whose worship is unflagging, feels obliged to face the possibility that Duchamp was playing on public credulity: "If it were demonstrated to us that *The Bride* was only a gigantic put-on, the myth of an enigmatic and infallible Duchamp would only be more alive, and a real and fertile interpretation would be found for that now forever senseless work." The admirers of Duchamp, Sanouillet is saying, are a cult of fanatics, closed to evidence and prepared to build a tower of casuistry upon anything associated with their master—which is exactly what they have been accused of by non-believers.

(5) Assuming that it is not a hoax, *The Bride* can be seen as an extended gag not far removed in tone from the visual and verbal wisecracks, often bawdy (for example, the 1968 etchings), that permeate Duchamp's retrospective. Metaphysical symbolism aside, machines and sex are Duchamp's themes from *Nude* onward. Like most artists, he has preferred old machines and imaginary ones to complex, up-to-date technology: one of the few genuinely attractive paintings in the exhibition is the small oil on cardboard entitled *Coffee Mill*. *The Bride* translates erotic love into a hookup of fanciful mechanical and chemical operations. It is a variant on slapstick comedy, in which human beings act as if their feelings and movements were controlled by wheels, pulleys, and gases. "*The Bride* basically is a motor," explains a note in *The Green Box*, the collection of writings on *The Bride*. She is operated through "timidpower," a sort of "automobiline, love gasoline." Another element in *The Bride* is described this way: "A lead weight in the form of a bottle of Benedictine acting normally on a system of cords attached to the chariot, would force it to come from A to B. . . . After having *pulled* the chariot by its fall, the bottle of

Benedictine lets itself be raised by the hook C; it falls asleep as it goes up; the dead point wakes it up suddenly and with its head down. It pirouettes, and falls vertically according to the laws of gravity."

Rube Goldberg's *The Only Humane Way to Catch a Mouse* is a machine-composition contemporary of *The Bride*, and the vertical cloud in it has much the shape of the horizontal one in the upper half of Duchamp's creation. There is also a resemblance in the explanatory text—in this case, appended below the drawing: "Magic lantern (A) throws picture of piece of swiss cheese on screen (B)—mouse, mistaking picture for real thing, jumps at screen and falls in rowboat (C)—he rows around in tub until he gets seasick and wants to end his suffering—he jumps overboard and lands in can of yeast (D)—mouse has high fever which causes yeast to rise and lift him to steel plate (E)—his head presses against steel until he gets softening of the brain and goes crazy—he thinks he is a stream of water. . . ."*

The devil with horns and beard of lather is held accountable for the chaos and frivolousness in which art has finally lost its definition, become "random and accidental," "neutral" (without interest to the artist or spectator), and Conceptual (bodiless). The criticisms I have enumerated are not of equal weight; some are more difficult to answer than others, and the conflict over Duchamp probably cannot be resolved. It is likely, however, that his attitudes were less a cause of the present situation than a response to a deep perception of it. His rejection of taste, for example, is related not only to his observation that taste leads to mechanical repetition in choosing but to the meaninglessness—in the absence of a social élite—of choice based on taste. The idea of a one-person authority on taste is no less absurd than Mona Lisa with a mustache. To a "vanguard" that restricts itself to form in painting and is content to accept the existing cultural situation, Duchamp's denial of values based on the characteristics of any particular genre (color, to name one) is an important affirmation that a vanguard must deal with basic cultural forces; for example, the replacement of the craftsman by the machine. Duchamp's denigration of art, his equalizing it with urinals and dog combs, was a matter of principle; he was determined that art should not be overestimated and that the "art habit" should not produce the reactions of blank solemnity that had once been associated with religion. Composing enigmas is as valid a

* Peter C. Marzio, *Rube Goldberg* (New York: Harper & Row, 1973).

medium as painting, and probably as venerable. Duchamp the comedian was an aspect of his philosophy of aesthetic deflation. He must have realized—and the retrospective has confirmed this—that his most hopeless undertaking was to try to induce the art world not to take art too seriously. His pseudonyms (Sélavy, Mutt), like those of Kierkegaard, were intended not to conceal identity but to advertise that for certain works one had to invent authors of a certain kind. With his lean, resigned features and inward-turned look, Duchamp was a kind of French Buster Keaton; that is, a self-conscious Buster with an ironic theory of history. Like Keaton, he was often passive and moved around by others and by circumstances. Being something of a schoolboy is intrinsic to Dada, with its hostility to middle-class and professional (grownup) postures of dignity. Would it, for example, have been possible for him to refuse to be photographed playing chess with a naked girl? After all, the theme of his most famous work was stripping, and Picasso, too, in his last great series of etchings, had become a Dirty Old Master. Fun and Eros were to the reticent Duchamp qualities as necessary to art as clarity was to Mondrian. Henri-Pierre Roché, an old friend, said that Duchamp's "finest work is his use of time." Yes, but that fine use includes wasting it. A Dadaist cannot be too concerned about how he manages his life. He cannot hoard it, and must let it amble at random; the only consistent program he is allowed is keping free of chains.

Duchamp accepted almost any means to pay his way (he even functioned briefly as an art critic) except that of becoming a professional artist. Enslavement by art, he was convinced, is no different from enslavement by other tyrannies of work. On this path his disciples refused to follow him, thus separating themselves from him on the central issue of art as the unlimited practice of freedom ("I believe," he said to James Sweeney, "that art is the only form of activity in which man as man shows himself to be a true individual"). With his friends and enemies combined in pursuit of professional goals, Duchamp emerges neither as hero nor as wrecker but as the ruminant and solitary note-taker engaged in the constant circling—to bring his past into focus with his imagination—that produced *The Bride*, *Valise*, and *Given*. He did not change the situation of art, but he did explore with the most realistic acuity what art could be, and could not be, in the twentieth century—thus what it was possible for the artist to create without falsifying himself.

2
Miró

I. FERTILE FIELDS

All transformations are possible. . . .
The description of the landscape is of little importance.
—*"Invention," by Paul Éluard*

In the "Walpurgis-Night" portion of Thomas Mann's *The Magic Mountain*, Hofrat Behrens, the director of the sanitarium, introduces a game into the invalids' festivities. It consists of drawing, with eyes closed, the image of a pig on the back of a visiting card. Behrens's drawing is not accurate, but it manages to unmistakably resemble a pig. But when the patients try their hands at the game, the pig disintegrates into a chaos of lines and shapes. "The eyes were outside the head, the legs inside the paunch, the line of the latter came nowhere near joining, the little tail curled away by itself without organic connection with the figure, an independent arabesque." Mann might have been parodying Miró's *Sourire de Ma Blonde*, done the year (1924) that *The Magic Mountain* was published: a detached eye and other "signs" representing parts of the body radiate from the ends of thin lines that project out of a scribbled oval set in the opening of a V in the center of the canvas; from each side of this V protrude an arm and a foot, while below it a floating pennant proclaims the title of the painting in partly obliterated lettering. What Miró has in common with other Surrealist painters, as well as with Behrens's patients, is that his marks on the canvas, no matter how obscure, refer to actual things: this is an ear, this a shooting star, this the embrace of a man and a woman. But reality (the pig) has receded behind the closed eyes, and in the darkened mind phenomena merge with other phenomena and with abstractions (the pig's tail as an "arabesque"). "The sea," wrote Éluard, whose influence contributed to Miró's transformation in 1923 from "realist" into poetic visionary, "has deposited its ears on the beach." It has also deposited words, isolated letters of the alphabet, stick figures, and doodles that in the dream or hallucination have the same substance as persons and objects.

Thus, Miró's paintings are never abstract; each has a scenario, which can be "read," and the artist holds the key to the reading. Although, according to Masson, Miró would not divulge "the inspirational origins of his paintings," he has never been reluctant to explain what his signs stand for and how he happened to think of them. James Johnson Sweeney recalls Miró's saying, in 1948, that a form is "always a man, a bird, or something else. For me, painting is never form for form's sake." It is the translatability of his imagery that differentiates Miró from the American Abstract Expressionists and Action painters, whom he anticipated in important respects—for instance, in developing his pictures in the course of painting ("The form becomes a sign for a woman or a bird as I work") instead of beginning with a subject and carrying it to a conclusion. Miró's figurations remain symbols, while a Rothko or a Pollock is not a sign of anything but an object in itself. Even a de Kooning "woman" has no reference outside the frame; it is a unique "event" that has occurred only on the canvas. Surrealist automatism evokes data of nature and memory; Action-painting spontaneity projects a new world.

Miró's vocabulary of signs has remained mostly stable over the past fifty years—it consists of male and female "personages"; eyes, lips, and other organs; the sun, moon, and stars; animals, birds, and reptiles and emblematic abstractions, such as the crossing of vertical and horizontal lines to represent the human figure—and his paintings and sculptures are legible in various degrees, according to the amount of control exercised upon the artist's hand (much as Behrens's pig was "rather more fanciful than realistic, yet undoubtedly the lineaments of a pig," while Hans Castorp's pig came apart into "some horrible inanity").

In the first phase of his conversion to Surrealism, Miró drew his visions from self-induced hallucinations, in which he was aided by being always hungry. *Portrait of Madame B.* (1924), with its scattered lettering, "iMRA," and its central figure of a woman with satanic eyebrows, a neck nearly as long as her body, and tiny breasts that suggest a double Adam's apple, bears a distinct likeness to drawings by schizophrenics—an impression strengthened by the symmetry of the composition, also characteristic of the art of the deranged. But Miró's innovation consisted in abandoning the psychic automatism of dream and chance combinations exploited by the Surrealists, in order to place his imagination under the guidance of the materials of painting itself; the surface of the canvas or paper was turned into a creative force. In a Miró, the figures are signs, but so, also, is the background a sign, as well as a source: a yellow night, a blue abyss, the tawny earth of the artist's native Catalonia. The painted ground is no longer merely a hue intended to unify the composition; it has become a space, alive with energies, that throws up images, as the field planted with dragon's teeth brought forth warriors. Paintings such as *The Poetess* and *The Nightingale's Song at Midnight and Morning Rain* are geysers of balloons, hourglass shapes, moons, eyes, streamers, dunce caps, kites, stars diffused into the air above surfaces of smudged buff and gray.

Miró's poetic wizardry, distilled from Rimbaud's color-generating vowels and Mallarmé's white void of the writing paper, transforms his painting surface into an equivalent of the unconscious. A line, a dot, a stroke of the brush is sufficient to animate this space and set the image-forming activity into motion. "I even used some spilled black-berry jam in one case as a beginning," Miró told Sweeney. A smudge converts the canvas into a dynamic field that responds actively to the next mark placed upon it. "A touch of the finger on the drum dis-charges all the sounds and begins the new harmony," wrote Rimbaud in "Illuminations." Hans Hofmann, who in general would have noth-ing to do with Surrealism, taught that space "resounds" and that "the plane is the creative element" in painting. Something similar was pres-ent in Pollock's notion of "contact," in which the reciprocal flow of energy between the artist and the surface insured rightness in the painting. William Rubin, in a pre-publication release of a portion of his catalogue for a Miró exhibition to be presented at the Museum of Modern Art, describes in detail how Miró would mess up the surface on which he worked, in order to animate it: in *The Birth of the World* (on view at the Museum of Modern Art) he "began by covering the canvas with glue sizing which was purposely laid on irregularly, in varying densities, so that the painting would take to the canvas unevenly, here consisting of a film atop the sizing, there impregnating

Joan Miró, *The Birth of the World*, 1925, oil on canvas, 8′½″ x 6′
4¾″.

COLLECTION, THE MUSEUM OF MODERN ART, NEW YORK, ACQUIRED THROUGH AN
ANONYMOUS FUND, THE MR. AND MRS. JOSEPH SLIFKA AND ARMAND G. ERPF
FUNDS AND BY GIFT FROM THE ARTIST.

or staining it," and so on. Miró himself has summed it up by saying that a painterly ground stimulates his imagination to invent.

The conversion of the canvas into an active "field" represents a major revolution in the form of painting; Hofmann conceived of the "push and pull" of the surface as the basis for the modernist elimination of perspective. The reverberation of the entire canvas or paper supersedes compositional structure. In his "notebooks for *The Idiot*," Dostoevsky speaks of a "field of action" against which the character of his protagonist would take on a unique splendor. The field of action as dynamic background is the alternative to the traditional plot as a structure of related events; expanding fields of phenomena determine the moods of *The Castle* and *Ulysses*. Instead of moving toward a resolution, the field remains open, to attract an indefinite quantity of data seemingly placed at random. Similarly, Miró's fields produce resplendent effects within his—to quote Douglas Cooper—"basically unstructured composition." Miró's sign-objects locate themselves arbitrarily in the vibrating expanse or settle wherever they have emerged into sight. In this type of automatism, the artist submits to being controlled, but he is controlled, so to say, with his eyes open. Miró speaks of a "second stage" in his paintings, in which, during certain periods in his career, he assumed direction over paintings that originated in his unconscious. His ideas of composition are, however, rudimentary— amounting to little more than equilibrium—and discipline in his painting consists, one assumes, of a revision of the spontaneous positioning of his forms. Cooper's ultimate tribute is that "his sense of placement is faultless."

For Miró, the field has been as endlessly fertile in signs and metamorphoses as the unconscious itself. It is a projected "mind," an externalized dream machine. And Miró early saw that the profusion of images could be dispensed with and that the field, vibrating with textures, lines, spots, and masses of color, would be sufficient in itself to strike profound chords of feeling. Hence, while producing his image-laden canvases, Miró simultaneously made himself the master of the "empty" painting, in which the power of the ground, or field, is emphasized. In the year he began *Carnival of Harlequin* (1924), populated with almost the entire inventory of symbols that he was to dispense in the following five decades (from snakes, eyes, ears, and ladders to nudes, comets, and bars of music), he executed *Le Baiser*, a painting consisting of a recumbent figure 8 within a loose oval on a green ground, and *Sourire de Ma Blonde* and *Le Renversement*, both of them yellow rectangles on which are inscribed faint geometrical line drawings, unobtrusive signs, and words (in *Le Renversement*, "ʜ!!," "ʜꝏ!," and "ᴊᴏᴜʀ"). Perhaps the most radical of Miró's "empty" works is one called *Painting*, which consists of an agitated blue surface with a faint seam or slit above center and a tiny white dot in the upper left corner. In his juxtaposition of fields in different degrees of fertility, Miró has consistently held to the vision of man in a world that is alive, which to him constitutes the continuous revelation brought by modernism in art. "The Impressionists realized," he has said, "that the landscape breathes, that it changes from one moment to the next. . . . We simply have to see it again, that is to say, to find a new form for it." In his sensing of the breathing landscape, of which the canvas is the embodiment, the Catalonian outsider to Europe (Gertrude Stein's conception of Picasso) is an ancestor of the animistic American Action painters, despite deep differences in form, symbolism, temperament, and creative method.

The exhibition at the Guggenheim in 1972 of some sixty Mirós under the inspired title of "Magnetic Fields" (the name of a collection of prose poems by André Breton and Philippe Soupault published in 1920) was a selection of this artist's "empty" canvases done in two widely separated periods—the 1920s and the 1960s. In stressing the importance of the ground in Miró's creation the show called attention to one of the liveliest features of his paintings—their ability to arouse feeling through texture and color alone. Miró's paintings on burlap and such works as *Painting on Celotex* (1937)—a golden surface, roughened in spots, with a figuration of thin crossed lines, and dotted with red, yellow, black, and white splatters—have always had a special appeal to me. The Guggenheim exhibition, however, went beyond a selection based on taste; its aim was to dissociate Miró's field, or "open," paintings from his other works and thus to recast the accepted concept of the artist as the creator of the teeming imagery of *Carnival* and *The Poetess*. In the opening paragraph of the Guggenheim catalogue, Rosalind E. Krauss, co-curator of the exhibition, identified painting with music, dance, and theatre, and claimed the privilege of staging an artist's work in what amounts to a new performance. The curator-impresario has discovered, she contended, a second Miró—one substantially different from, if not opposite to, the artist familiar this past half century. Miró *autre*, as the French might call him, is, like Ms. Krauss and her generation of art critics, "haunted" by the question of space, and proves to be much more American than the original Miró, influenced by Matisse, Picasso, Ernst, and Klee, and by Rimbaud, Mallarmé, Apollinaire, and Breton. Ms. Krauss and her collaborator, Margit Rowell, associate curator of the Guggenheim, remind the reader of their catalogue that in the early fifties Miró saw and was moved by work of the American Abstract Expressionists, particularly Pollock, and that thereafter he returned to producing large-scale color paintings, specimens of which had appeared among the "dream landscapes" of his Surrealist days.

Paintings of the 1920s are thus combined with color-field canvases of the 1960s to produce a Miró remote from automatism and gifted with a high level of "formal intelligence," the chief quality of the American abstractionists of the 1960s. In sum, the Guggenheim Miró is a naturalized formalist who happens to have had an early leaning toward poetry and metaphysical feelings but whose true "concern" has been similar to that of the American color-field structuralists, such as Ellsworth Kelly and Frank Stella. "In *Les Champs Magnétiques*," writes Ms. Krauss, "the concern to create an uninterrupted field of language parallels the concern Miró came to by the mid-twenties: to make painting from an uninterrupted field of color;" she does not explain why the desire to create "an uninterrupted field" should have induced Miró to "interrupt" his surface with irregular densities of glue sizing, as described by Dr. Rubin.

To contrive an American-scale color-field painter out of two segments of their hijacked Surrealist required that the two curators eliminate the great bulk of his paintings, to say nothing of his sculptures, graphics, tapestries, and book illustrations. One critic, Ms. Krauss told me, objected that this reduction of Miró is a distortion. Ms. Krauss, however, held that, as curator, she had the right to replay an artist in the key of her own values, and, besides, an artist's image comes to us already distorted by the accepted way of presenting him. This might be a defense of the Guggenheim show, but it is not a justification of the catalogue, the thesis of which was that a particular group of Mirós represents a principle alien to the artist's creation as a whole. If this premise is accepted, the next step would be to "refine" Miró by getting rid of all his work (i.e., most of it) that does not fit the new idea, as had earlier been done, for example, in eliminating several years of the work of Morris Louis.

In any case, Ms. Krauss misunderstood the concept of the field. It is for its function in Miró's automatism that the field is important, not as the solution of Ms. Krauss's "problem of how to represent space without constructing an illusion of it." If Miró had a "problem," it was how to reach a state of creation unhindered by problems. In that state, solutions arise simultaneously with problems, or else problems and solutions respond to each other as if they were interchangeable. In keeping with her formalist ideology, Ms. Krauss sought to impose an order upon Miró's improvisations by discovering in them "an internal structure, based on color." But color is too fluid and subjective to sustain a "structure," and in discerning currents flowing through Miró's fields Ms. Krauss simply contradicted herself. Color can become a building element only as a static quantity, whether of area or of intensity, as in the color compositions of Stella or Noland. Such measured color is effective as design, but it is alien to the idea of a field capable of "magnetizing" images out of the unconscious. In the effort to reconcile her perceptions of the mobility of Miró's figurations with her color-field ideology, Ms. Krauss resorted to what can only be described as formalist theology: "The areas of lightness which open out behind these marks simultaneously underscore visually and seem to signify the meaning of the pictorial field itself: the tenuous grasp it has on its own opacity"—a type of neo-medieval nonsense that has taken refuge in art criticism.

Ms. Rowell, who in the catalogue did admirable detective work on Miró's poetic sources, and who was aware that his metaphysical sensibility differentiates his canvases from " 'color-field' paintings in the American sense," joined with Ms. Krauss in expressing the fear that the Guggenheim presentation may imply a split between form and content. Yes, and it is a split that formalist casuistry cannot heal. For if there is one thing that should have been learned from Surrealism, as from Freud, it is that the antithesis consciousness/unconsciousness, or form/imagination, upon which the Guggenheim exhibition is based, is unreal, and that it falsifies the manner in which original art is created.

II. AVANT-GARDE MASTERPIECES

The Miró exhibition at the Museum of Modern Art of some forty paintings, sculptures, and collages, plus prints and drawings, presented the Mirós accumulated by the MOMA during the past thirty-five years or promised for the future. At eighty, Miró had become a twentieth-century master of primary rank, the only Surrealist-inspired

Joan Miró, *Dutch Interior I*, 1928, oil on canvas, 36⅛″ x 28¾″.

artist who is on the level of Picasso, Matisse, Braque, and Mondrian. The MOMA exhibition is an official recognition of this status; it is accompanied by a book by the chief curator, William Rubin, issued in commemoration of Miró's birthday, that is described as "a companion volume" to the author's item-by-item analysis of the Museum's collection of Picassos. Both collections are billed as "the finest and most complete" in the world, and the Miró group is said by Rubin to contain "a number of [his] unrivalled masterpieces."

Masterpieces there definitely are in the collection: *Dutch Interior I, Portrait of Mistress Mills in 1750*, the drawing *Self-Portrait I, The Birth of the World, Hirondelle/Amour*, and one of Miro's "big-foot" paintings—*Person Throwing a Stone at a Bird*. Unlike an exhibition based on a single conception of the artist, as was the Miró show at the Guggenheim in 1972, the MOMA display had an emotional tone influenced by the tastes of the various persons who acquired the paintings. The first major Miró came to the Museum through the efforts of Alfred Barr in 1937, almost a decade after the excitement about Surrealism had died down. Reflecting this belated interest (in contrast to such pioneering collecting as that of Picassos and Matisses by the Steins), the MOMA exhibition is visually low-keyed and aesthetically conservative. Miró's "savage" aspect is manifest, of course, but not with the force of an exhibition that could be made up of others of his paintings and a larger proportion of constructions and sculptures. Selection by curators and donors intent on avant-garde masterpieces rather than by adventurous people attracted to innovations has resulted in a tamed Miró. But there are also historical reasons for the tameness.

Miró's paintings, and especially his constructions and sculptures, are exemplary embodiments of what is now called the counterculture. His revolution lay in loosening the shapes of things to the point of liquefaction. "He believes," writes Joan Teixidor, co-author with Alain Jouffroy of *Miró Sculptures*, recently published in France, "that a thing can become something else, and in this game of transformations he finds the major stimulation of his art." Metaphorical displacement (a snail shell representing a woman's heavy braids of hair), continuous metamorphosis (human hands turning into birds, into arabesques), plus arbitrary scale (microscopic torso, enormous tongue) produce the effect of a submarine world which blends into that of the dream. The characteristic two-planed format of his paintings is like water with petals and insects floating on the surface, below which a mottled bottom is vaguely visible; this could represent the surface of consciousness and the unknown underneath. In a universe of unstable identities, shapes of every kind—biomorphic, mechanical, symbolic, representational—are disencumbered of limits, and mix or grow together. Rubin quotes Giacometti: "For me, Miró was synonymous with freedom— something more aerial, more liberated, lighter than anything I had ever seen before." The liberated lyrical spirit perceived by Giacometti is, it must be emphasized, complemented by Miró's avant-garde negativism and its affiliation with the unconscious, the jungle, and anti-art. "Now I am involved with something more brutal," he said recently to the Parisian critic Pierre Schneider, referring to his earlier "sensitivity" to line. But a program of assault on civilized assumptions has always been the basis of Miró's vocabulary of matter-of-fact obscenity, fertility goddesses, bony and melonlike cave-dwellers, showers of birds and fish, huge primitive suns and stars, and—mixed with anatomical parodies—mockeries of art.

Most expressive of his cultural radicalism are three paintings at the MOMA in which works by earlier artists are redone in what Kenneth Burke, referring to a general characteristic of avant-garde art and literature, called "perspective by incongruity." In each instance, Miró chose to liquefy an image of outstanding pictorial and social solidity. *Dutch Interior I* is translated from a colored postcard reproduction of a seventeenth-century Dutch painting. In the Miró version, the picture has become unrecognizable: the artist radically altered the scale and the placement of objects and transposed some, abstracted others, and inserted new matter. In *Portrait of Mistress Mills in 1750*, a heavyset matron enveloped in folds of silk and lace and wearing an enormous feathered hat on a pile of curls has been reduced to a few simple forms endowed with a lyrical grace and balance entirely absent from the original composition. Most amusing is *Portrait of a Man in a Late Nineteenth-Century Frame*, an actual nineteenth-century painting of a gentleman with a mustache and a gold watch, Miróized by scraping its surface to alter its depth and by introducing Miró's signs for the night mind, sex, music, the sun, and monsters. In these paintings, conventional styles of three centuries of Western art and life have been disintegrated and superseded by modernist radical aesthetics.

For Miró, the merit of a work lies in its capacity to disturb the spectator's equilibrium. Schneider reports that during a visit with him to the Louvre he complained of a famous sculpture that "you don't get that little shock. . . . it is too official," and Schneider notes that

Joan Miró, *Portrait of a Man in a Late Nineteenth-Century Frame*,
1950, oil on canvas with ornamented wood frame, 57½″ x 49¼″ (including frame).

Miró's "predilection is for objects of bizarre shape, asymmetrical, tattooed with inscriptions." The violence, mystification, and black humor of Miró's creations amount to a systematic training of the psyche in appropriating the unfamiliar. Together with his anti-art, they serve the avant-garde enterprise of assimilating alien cultures and areas of consciousness. Signs are activators of feeling, whether or not they can be decoded. You don't have to comprehend what a row of medals stand for in order to be impressed by them, or to understand a hydrogen bomb to get a thrill out of confronting one. Miró belongs to the decade of *Finnegans Wake* and *The Large Glass,* works that are impenetrable by direct scrutiny (to the same degree as *Dutch Interior I*) and yet challenge their public to manage, if only temporarily, without footnotes. The solution for the spectator is to take what is directly available to him, including the wonder. As Miró put it, "Above and beyond all, it is the visual shock that counts. Afterward, one wants to know what it says, what it represents. But only afterward."

No doubt half a century of encounters with Miró's sign language has contributed to the reduced emotional impact of the MOMA exhibition. In the seventies, the avant-garde creations of Miró's generation, and even later generations, have established themselves as masterpieces, and they are displayed as treasures. It is in this guise that the Miró's are presented at the museum and inventoried in Rubin's catalogue. When it is accredited as a masterpiece, what a work does matters less than what it is—and the more we know about it the better. Once "shock" has been dissipated, the appropriate reactions are aesthetic recognition and intellectual respect. Can a Miró still set in motion in the spectator that anxious and elated decoding of messages from the unknown that accompanies discovery? If a Miró no longer "works," one will be content to find it pleasing, and Rubin's catalogue can add to the pleasure by satisfying curiosity.

Alain Jouffroy, in *Miró Sculptures,* confronts the issue of the continued *activity* of Miró's creations. In their Surrealist inception they were revolutionary; are they still? Jouffroy indignantly rejects the belief that modern art is, in the last analysis, a revolution without a future, a revolution that new traditionalists constantly succeed in redirecting along the old paths. For him, Miró at eighty is still a Surrealist; indeed, "he was never more Surrealist than he is today." Inventing new objects, he continues to undermine aesthetic criteria and ideologies, and to demonstrate that in the realm of art freedom exists as a possibility for the individual. Jouffroy quotes Miró's remark to Schneider about becoming less lyrical and more "brutal," and sees him as a mental participant in the wars and insurrections of the current epoch. In the heart of the thriving art market, which justifies itself on cultural grounds, art continues to face the possibility of its own abolition. "All of his [Miró's] work tends to prove, by the simplest means, that art is nothing in itself, and that it has no other function than that which can be given to it through frustrating society in the boldest possible manner. All the scholarly and museological gravity that surrounds art today is nothing but a vast social comedy designed to disguise this elementary truth." And Jouffroy concludes that the fact that Miró's creations have become objects of financial speculation has changed nothing: paintings and sculptures ought always to be considered in terms of their original meaning. An economic crisis that at one stroke could destroy the market value of vanguard masterpieces would cause their fundamentally subversive character to reappear.

Jouffroy's argument is a vivifying corrective to the drab historical determinism that dominates thinking about art in the United States today. As far as the individual is concerned, nothing can prevent him, whether as spectator or as artist, from making out of a Miró whatever he wishes. He can dream his way into *Dutch Interior I* as Miró himself did into the original colored postcard, and can loftily disregard the sixty-five items of iconographical identification listed by Rubin in his analysis of the painting. But the individual has this creative liberty in regard to *any* work, past or present, radical or conformist, as Miró demonstrated in transforming his stuffy originals. Whether or not Miró's creations still have a revolutionary role is for society, not individuals, to decide.

In seeing Miró as the personification of an unsinkable radicalism, whose paintings and sculptures need only to be liberated from high prices to begin to agitate again as they did in the twenties and thirties, Jouffroy has postulated a revolutionary essence subsisting outside of time and immune to change. Today, Miró's taste for the bizarre and his prizing of shock have been incorporated into traditional art appreciation, as has his liking for the use in art of brooms, kitchen chairs, and other everyday objects. The radicalism of his ideas and practices belongs to the Surrealist epoch and remains embedded in the physiognomy of that period: in those days it was not even necessary for Miró to have anti-social or anti-art ideas; his intellectual environment could be relied on to inject them into his work. Jouffroy's Miró is revolutionary by interpretation only. Miró Agitator is a subjective image, not a cultural fact. Avant-garde art, resting on a *frisson*, cannot sustain the weight loaded on it when it is recast as a masterpiece. Only a new radical avant-garde could reawaken the transforming energies in Miró's paintings and sculptures—as it could also, however, those in a Poussin or a Cézanne. Art does not live past its day, though it is always susceptible of resurrection.

Rubin's catalogue of the works in the MOMA collection is devoted not to their revival but to a more informed public response. In it, Miró's enigmas are replaced by established fact and opinion. Rubin has assembled all the major available data on each work—its history, its place in Miró's *œuvre*, pertinent comments on it by other writers— and has analyzed its formal features and interpreted its iconography. A painting becomes a jewel box of elucidated signs; *The Hunter*, a small picture, has fifty-eight items, from "sun-eggs" to "sardine spines," that the spectator can check off. Miró turned portraits into mysteries; Rubin turns Miró's mysteries into lists of iconographic features. "Why talk of it?" Miró had asked. "Isn't anything we could say superfluous, imprecise, for the very reason that the precision we aim at is an impossible one? What statement could ever explain these signs, these emblems, these enigmas . . . these chrysalid forms forever undergoing metamorphosis? . . . It is as if the artist were amusing himself behind the mask. In actuality, though, he is escaping, eluding the world in which he lives, and amid those myths that for him are the reflection and reverse of that world, himself becomes myth."*

A spectator who has had enough of bafflement now has the opportunity to return for a second look through the window of authenticated information. Miró himself has collaborated with Rubin in revealing the origins of his works and the intended references of his images. Signs once under dispute have now been firmly codified: a figure in *The Hunter* that was taken by earlier analysts to be a rabbit has been identified as a sardine—no doubt a gain, though one is tempted to ask for whom or for what. A creature whose identity is so indecisive might well have been left in the dark. In painting *The Hunter*, Miró wanted to supply a clue (but only a clue), so he wrote "SARD" in a corner of the canvas, but this only led to further misunderstandings,

* Gyorgy Kepes, ed., *The Visual Arts Today* (Middletown, Conn.: Wesleyan University Press, 1960).

Joan Miró, *The Hunter (Catalan Landscape)*, 1923–24, oil on canvas, 25½" x 39½".

for ingenious exegetists missed *sardina* (sardine) and settled on *sardana*, a Spanish folk dance. Now the fuss is over and we know. One wonders, however, why, if Miró sees the need for keys to his compositions, he did not make them available long ago, as Eliot did for *The Waste Land*. Perhaps the answer lies in Miró's remark about the visual shock's coming first and the understanding afterward. Today, apparently, is "afterward."

3

Mondrian: Meaning in Abstract Art I

A nice question for organizers of retrospective exhibitions is whether the career of an artist such as Piet Mondrian begins when he commences to paint or when he arrives at the concept that separates him from the incoherence of his past. If it be assumed that it is sounder to think of an artist in terms of the creations by which he has identified himself, the retrospective ought to begin with these works and present the earlier ones in an "appendix." A retrospective arranged chronologically automatically promotes the impression of a "development" in which the mature paintings evolved gradually out of those that came before. Thus it supports the prevailing tendency in art criticism to ignore the idea by which the artist has transformed himself. Of course, a dramatic transformation does not always take place. But with Mondrian, arriving at his idea was of exceptional importance. The conception came before the painting; it was the primary act of creation. His Neo-Plastic abstractions are affirmations not of himself and a sensibility refined through practice ("Neo-Plasticism aims precisely at representing nothing that is individually determined") but of a carefully worked-out program regarding art, the artist, society, the past, and the future. Theo van Doesburg, with whom Mondrian worked closely during the formation of his final style, stated the Neo-Plastic position on the relation between the artist's idea and his product: "The work of art must be completely conceived and formed by the mind before its execution. It must not receive any formal impressions from nature, nor from the senses, nor from sentiment. We exclude lyricism, dramatism, symbolism, and so on."

It was the odd though exalted conviction of Mondrian that nature, the individual, and human society could be revolutionized by compositions of planes of color and intersecting straight lines. Form-making— or "plastic representation," as Mondrian called it—was a force by which the mind could impose its order on the world. (In our day, Buckminster Fuller maintains a similar view of the possibilities of design.) History, Mondrian believed, was on the side of the plastic revolution, as was evidenced by the advance in consciousness that had caused painting to break away from imitating nature. "Plastic vision," he wrote, "implies action. . . . The pure plastic vision should set up a new society . . . a society composed of balanced relationships." Like Marx, Mondrian anticipated the end of the tragedy of history and the attainment of "the great repose" of philosophy. A new type of man, selfless and indifferent to particulars, would see through the "capricious forms" of nature to the motionless center of being, abstract and universal.

Mondrian's program could not be stated in his paintings; at most, it could only be implied. For by its edict the new canvases were to be constructed of purely plastic elements and were to signify nothing but themselves. The universal human society of the future was to be signalled by compositions exclusively concerned with such qualities as flatness, balance, correct placement, angularity. Hence, nothing of the grand, radical purpose of Neo-Plasticism was visible in the large retrospective at the Guggenheim Museum celebrating the hundredth anniversary of Mondrian's birth. (It is always a surprise to realize that modern art comes from men born that long ago.) More than half of the 132 paintings in the show were "early"—that is, pre–Neo-Plastic —pictures (Mondrian was just short of fifty when he conceived his ultimate geometric format), of trees, churches, dunes, and the sea, plus the attractive Cubist compositions and the highly original "plus-and-minus" renderings of seascapes. The closest one came to a message was in the mediocre emblematic triptych *Evolution*, done around 1911, of symbolic nudes with triangular- and diamond-shaped nipples and navels, which represents Mondrian's immersion in theosophy. His celebrated compositions based on the horizontal, the vertical, and the "unchanging right angle" have not the faintest odor of uplift about them, to say nothing of fumes of the barricades.

If the revolution appears in Mondrian's paintings, it is only in its

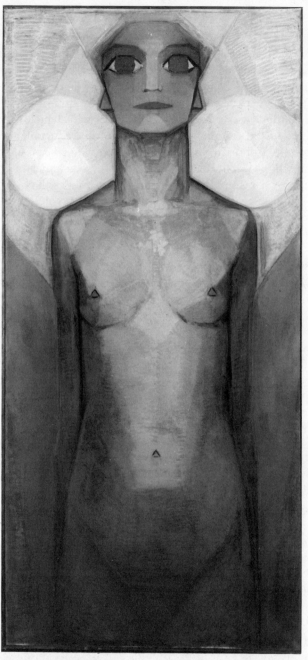

Piet Mondrian, *Evolution* (middle panel of triptych)
1910–11.

inward aspect—the psychic state of the re-maker of history. The out-standing quality of his Neo-Plastic canvases is the feeling of rigorous discipline they convey—a kind of on-guard stance. One entirely unfamiliar with Mondrian's theories and programs could apprehend in the paintings the passionate self-negation with which he complemented his systematic purging of painting and its reduction to a few formal elements. Mondrian's asceticism is not, as has been suggested, that of the monk's cell but that of the laboratory or command post; its tension is that of a manipulation of units of force in which a mistake might lead to disaster. The inner equivalent of the revolution as he conceived it was an impeccable and illuminated rationality, expressed in his clari-fied paint surfaces—an effect now somewhat marred, especially when the canvases are seen close up, by deterioration of the whites and grays and the scuffing of edges.

Mondrian today is the patron saint of formalism, the philosophy that considers each art in terms of its "indispensable" ingredients. Yet in the years immediately following the First World War and the Bolshevik Revolution, when he collaborated with van Doesburg and the De Stijl group, his strictly aesthetic approach did not deprive his paintings of radical social meanings. Criticism of the existing order was in some measure taken for granted in any mode of avant-garde art. The emphasis on form in that period of profound cultural shock—when everything, from moral values to mass housing, seemed to call for reorganization—was essentially different in content from formalism today as a method of painting pictures or analyzing them. Van Does-burg summed up the intellectual overtones of Neo-Plasticism in his 1923 manifesto "Toward Collective Construction." "Today," he said, "one may speak only of those who are building the new life." In that Mondrian's abstractions had, as everyone recognized, carried Cubism to the logical conclusion of absolutely flat and non-representational compositions, they constituted an advancing wedge into the future. They had translated the landscape into the horizontal and the vertical, had compressed the contours of objects into straight lines, and had replaced nuances of nature with strictly quantitative harmonies. Art had never before reached this degree of abstraction except among the Russians in the years around the Revolution—reason enough to expect that an upheaval in form foreshadowed overthrow in all spheres.

Thus social radicalism, though not actually visible in Mondrian's canvases, was reflected in them from the outside, like an image in the blank expanse of a store window. De Kooning says that Frederick

Piet Mondrian, *Composition* 7, 1913, oil on canvas, 41⅞″ x 45″.
THE SOLOMON R. GUGGENHEIM MUSEUM, NEW YORK

Kiesler, looking at some abstract compositions, began softly humming the "Internationale." In the period of its origin, abstract art contained the projected vision of the Marxist revolution in its idealistic, semi-mystical promise of the reconstitution of man and his environment within a totally rational order. Mondrian's de-individualized compositions prefigured in the imagination the communion of the anonymous human units of mass society, the proletariat, reborn through revolution.

With the passage of time and the fading of the Marxist utopia, Mondrian's paintings have lost their political afterimage. History has diminished them to their bars and rectangles; their social and metaphysical meanings have passed out of the paintings and become data of the biography of the artist. Yet without the dimension of thought affixed to it by the artist or his public, an abstract painting cannot exceed decoration—a problem Mondrian acknowledged in reverse when he said that the new painting could be "flat" without being reduced to the merely decorative because flatness made things "appear much more inward." Today, the paintings of Mondrian are in constant need of being filled out with the thought and will of their creator. Neo-Plastic paintings ought to be seen as "events" that belong to their time. To dissociate them from their intellectual origins on the ground that the spectator must confine himself to what is presented to him on the canvas is shallow aestheticism.

In the enterprise of recharging the Mondrians with their meaning, the Guggenheim retrospective was not much help. Its approach was to accompany the abstractions with as many early pictures as possible, on the naïve assumption that the meaning of an artist is evident through the sum total of his work. Nor did the catalogue supply the missing context; far too much of it was devoted to Mondrian's theosophical phase, as if *Evolution* were one of his major accomplishments. Practically nothing was said of his historical outlook, and reminiscences of his personality—his choice of restaurants, his cooking, his stiff way of dancing—were given precedence over his thought as the creator of his paintings. (An interview in the catalogue with Charmion von Wiegand, a friend who watched him paint in New York, did make a contribution to the intellectual features of Mondrian at work.)

Mondrian was aware that in our epoch a division exists between the artist and his creations. The artist conceives a grand vision, such as the salvation of the human race; his painting expresses itself as an arrangement of lines, shapes, and hues. For its meaning, the painting is dependent on the painter, who writes articles and issues statements and manifestos to explain what he has in mind. Not only Mondrian but abstract artists from Malevich and Kandinsky to Reinhardt and Newman have felt obliged to define in words what they were doing on the canvas. Mondrian was deeply committed to the belief that to achieve wholeness the work of art ought to speak for itself. Yet he knew that the intervention of the artist in behalf of his work is brought about by the diffused character of modern culture, which the individual artist can do nothing to cure. For paintings to convey their full meaning through direct sensation, a new phase in human development would have to be reached. "Neo-Plasticism," he wrote, "can appear as a 'style.' In the great epochs of style, the 'person' disappeared: the general thought of the age was the force guiding artistic expression. The same holds true today. More and more, the work will speak for itself: the personality changes its place; that is to say, each work of art becomes a personality instead of the artist. Each work of art becomes a different expression of the *one*."

Mondrian's solution to the division between the artist's intention and the objective meaning of his creations is the recovery of a kind of tribal unity in society. No doubt Mondrian was thinking of some ancient civilization or cult in which—at least to the eyes of outsiders—a single style seems to manifest itself in rituals, myths, and artifacts. In the future, that style was to be supplied by Neo-Plasticism, with its total emphasis on the work as against the subjective impulses of the artist. In a social communion based on "abstract reality," a painting would no longer need to convey a concept or a feeling; it could exist in and for itself, yet its significance would be apprehended immediately. The painting would blend into nature, but a nature transfigured by the common style. Under such circumstances, Neo-Plastic abstractions, in signifying nothing but themselves, would signify the collective vision as a whole, and unite in themselves absolute being with absolute meaning. The conception is, of course, completely theoretical and utopian; in practice, it would result in totalitarianism. But it is an acknowledgment by Mondrian of the rift between his idea and his art, and an acknowledgment that the full realization of the meaning of his work would have to be put off to the future.

In any case, events have decided against Mondrian. The new society has not arrived, and art today is further from a unique style, in Mondrian's sense, than ever before. Nor have the "personalities" of works

Piet Mondrian, *Composition*, 1927, oil on canvas, 17¾″ x 17¾″.
THE SOLOMON R. GUGGENHEIM MUSEUM, NEW YORK

of art replaced the personality of the artist; on the contrary, paintings and sculptures have increasingly become auxiliaries in constructing the image of the artist as a public personage. In regard to Mondrian, the irony is that in our time the meaning of his work lies not in itself, as he wished, but in his ideas, his role, his pathos. He was a collaborator —together with Dada, Surrealism, the primitivism of Klee—in closing out the European past in art. His geometrical abstractions are as alien to Renaissance solidity as are the African shapes introduced by Matisse and Picasso. Not by age but by imagination, he was a figure belonging to the period between the two World Wars, who saw society balanced upon a moment that would be followed by enormous changes. He belonged to the wing of the avant-garde that faced the future with confidence, and his purpose in stripping art to "essentials" was to prepare it for greater feats to come. He embraced the new not as an extension of the past but as representing a complete rupture with it and as a point of beginning. "At each moment of the past," he explained, "all the variations of the old might have been called *new*. But this was never the new as such. For we must not forget that we are at a turning point in the history of culture, at the end of everything *old* in the global sense. The divorce between the old and the new is now absolute, definitive. Plastic art must move not only parallel with human progress, but must advance ahead of it." Apart from the thoughts embodied in them, Mondrian's superb designs are at home in the universe of factories, high-rise, urban layouts, electronic bulletin boards—whatever seems to emanate from the spirit of the machine— and through its influence on the applied crafts his art continues to seek a monopoly for his aesthetics in the creations of the future. In the magazine *Transformations*, edited by his heir, Harry Holtzman, a document by Mondrian predicted the extinction of private life ("home-sweet-home") as well as the street, and the replacement of both by the city as a "unity formed by planes composed in neutralizing opposition that destroys all exclusiveness."

It seems inevitable that Mondrian's career should have ended in the United States, where his angular world had advanced furthest toward realization. Even more than Duchamp, he responded to the "modernism" of New York, to the vast, glittering modules of its skyscraper walls, its Africa-inspired dance rhythms. In New York, the fierce abstractness of his utopianism blended with the abstract constructions and dynamic beat of an actual human habitation. The effect was to relax his style. In some degree, he was won over to "particulars";

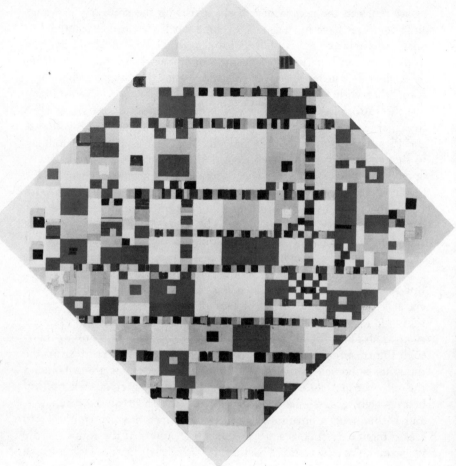

Piet Mondrian, *Victory Boogie Woogie*, 1943–44, oil on canvas with colored paper and tape, 45⅝″ x 49⅝″.

many of his paintings done or completed in New York carry names suggested by places or happenings—*Place de la Concorde, Trafalgar Square, New York, Broadway Boogie-Woogie, Victory Boogie-Woogie*—instead of his customary *Composition*. With his reentry into "nature," stasis gave way to animation, and the black vertical and horizontal bars were transformed into ribbons of red, yellow, and blue, into small, connected blocks of color, and, finally, into dancing motes of pigment on a diamond-shaped canvas. His painting, Mondrian said, had become "homogeneous in intention" with boogie-woogie. Here, as in his conception of the person "disappearing" into the style of the culture, one may catch a glimpse of the witch doctor through the geometrical grid.

4

Newman: Meaning
in Abstract Art II

Neither man nor nation can exist without a sublime idea.
—*Dostoevsky*

The paintings of the late Barnett Newman emerge in triumph out of
twenty years of battle, though not without further critical yapping at
the heels. As is usual in regard to abstract art, the issue is content: are
Newman's areas of color, divided by one or more vertical bands,
able to convey the themes indicated by the titles of his pictures and
by his public statements? Former detractors now concede that the
canvases are attractive and even, to a degree, moving. Paintings such as
Onement I, Abraham, Cathedra, which in the fifties were considered
"nothing but a stripe down the middle," are found to possess depth
and an aura of majesty; in addition, they had inaugurated a new handling of the picture plane. Emily Genauer, hard-crusted foe of expressive abstraction, was plunged by a Newman retrospective at the
Museum of Modern Art into "a sea of vivid, resonant color" by which
she might, she imagined, have been swept away had it not been for the
lifelines provided by Newman's vertical bands. To come close to
drowning at the Museum of Modern Art is a rare ordeal, which probably threatens only those who have lived too long in the driest deserts
of the imagination. And John Canaday, while readying himself for a
new round of insults for Newman, noted that his paintings "looked
better than ever before," and was aware of "responding to them as I

50

had never thought could be possible"—which may have been intended to prove how open-minded and aesthetically susceptible Canaday is even to work he cannot abide.

So much for the augmented impact of Newman's paintings on some nervous systems. Yet, despite the improvement in the reception of Newman's work during the past ten years, his spacious themes and his conception of the metaphysical function of painting have not been welcomed even by those who have become his admirers and followers. The art world has an instinct for what it needs, and it rejects any surplus. Once a work leaves the artist's studio, it is refashioned intellectually to conform to prevailing appetites. It took Newman a long time to convince the art world that he was serious; there is still the problem of what he was serious about. In the fifties, his talk of "awesome feelings" and his evocation of mysteries in the titles of his paintings—*Genesis, Primordial Light, Day One*—were seen as attempts to disguise his derivations from Mondrian and Neo-Plasticism. Later, when the originality of his work became apparent, his philosophy was condescendingly set aside as an irrelevant verbal accompaniment to his formal innovations. Today, his work is honored on the rebound from the fashionable movements—color-field painting, minimal sculpture—founded upon it. But mention of the emotional substance of his paintings can still arouse indignation. The stirrings of approbation by Genauer and Canaday were but preludes to assaults on what Canaday called Newman's "rapturous philosophizing." Had the canvases at the Museum of Modern Art been presented merely as handsomely surfaced expanses of red, yellow, and blue, a reconciliation with his critics might have been effected under the pressure of art history—or, at least, a truce. Not an inch, however, could be yielded to Newman's posthumous insistence that his paintings have to do with such motifs as the creation of man, the division between night and day, the coalescence of order within chaos, the anguish of man's abandonment: in a word—Newman's word—with the sublime. How could all these grandiloquent dramas be seen in the repeated image of a rectangle with stripes? And, anyway, aren't lofty themes out of date? The trend of modernism is toward mixing art with the commonplace, the matter-of-fact. Those who still speak of "high art" see no connection between it and high thoughts or high states. Our age has been taught that elevated sentiments are composites of less elevated ones, or even of desires that are the opposite of elevated. To espouse lofty ideas is something of a scandal. The art world of the 1960s was personified by Andy Warhol and the pace-setting museum curator. In their attack on Newman's *The Stations of the Cross*, both Canaday and Genauer took steps to dissociate themselves from Newman's solemnity. Canaday headed his column "Mike, Elaine, Woody, Mr. Newman, God and Me," and Genauer compared the work to *Jesus Christ Superstar*. First-name intimacy with popular entertainment establishes the critic, one is led to assume, as a regular guy to whom the philosophizing of a *Mister* Newman is an embarrassment.

Newman's behaving as if the sublime had not been dismantled by the modern age was a combination of naïveté and defiance. By naïveté I mean pursuing one's own sense of things regardless of prevailing opinion. It is impossible to identify Newman's philosophy as one can the pantheism of Pollock or Hofmann. Though Newman's art is more abstract than theirs, his thinking seems closer to a world of narratives. Newman looked at the art of the aborigines and at Western masterpieces, he read primitive myths, Greek drama, the Old Testament, the Gospels, mystical apothegms as if they depicted things that were still going on; at any rate, he knew they were going on in him. The predicament was that because the imagination could no longer conceive pictures of such happenings one had to paint *ideas* of them. Nevertheless, he labelled the metaphysical subjects of his canvases and sculptures with the literalism of *Woman in a Red Hat* or *Still-Life with Jar*. He argued that the time had come for painting to replace scenes, images, symbols with abstract figures that had the materiality of things and events. The essential was the idea/object, and, to attain that, any suggestion of appearance and even abstractions derived from nature, such as Mondrian's or Kandinsky's, had to be resolutely purged. In Newman's aesthetics, the Burning Bush might resemble a proposition by Euclid, never a Christmas tree.

Newman's total break with natural imagery led to his innovating emphasis on the physical rudiments of works of art—in painting, the size, shape, and color of areas of the canvas; in sculpture, the importance of the base; in lithography, the problem of the border around the print. In its total quantitative presence, a work is the mystical counterpart of the concept denoted by its title. Embodying an idea in exclusively material quantities (for example, *Cathedra* as a ninety-six-inch-by-seventeen-foot-nine-inch sheet of blue) results, ironically, in an exclusively formal construct (Cathedra as horizontal, rectangular, ultramarine) from which the idea is visually absent. In his pursuit of absolute content, Newman left nothing on the canvas that might pre-

Barnett Newman, *Stations of the Cross*, 1965, acrylic, 78″ x 60″.
ESTATE OF THE ARTIST

vent the spectator from perceiving the marked-off space as the reality indicated by the title. On the other hand, there is nothing to prevent him from considering the painting an organization of colored planes and lines and nothing else. Newman's canvases and sculptures invite the spectator to pass beyond the aesthetic into an act of belief. By implication, they define a work of art as any image or feeling that the spectator (including the artist as spectator) introduces; the difference between a Giotto and a Newman would lie in the degree of control exercised by the image. To render his grand themes, Newman made himself the master of an emotional indeterminacy in painting in which all effects depend on tensions of quantity, of size, and of radiance. No one of his paintings stands for anything definite; it is not a symbol or an emblem, any more than it is pictorial. But, taken all together, the paintings establish an elevated plateau of feeling. Newman was not trying to force Genauer and Canaday to see his fourteen striped white canvases as enactments of *The Stations.* He offered the possibility of sensing, through his whites and blacks, the anguish of the abandoned prophet or artist—his *lama-sabachthani* ("why hast thou forsaken me?") interpretation of *The Stations* affixed to the wall of the Museum. If, instead of responding to the emotional potential of the paintings, the critics sought a visual opera, the paintings left them free to find it.

The catalogue for Newman's retrospective, by Thomas B. Hess, who directed the exhibition, was a heroic attempt to implant Newman's ideas within the substance of his paintings and sculptures, to establish their format and their dimensions and colors as correlatives of exalted experiences. If Hess could succeed in his purpose, Newman's abstractions would communicate as readily as a Pietà or *The Sabines.* Hess studied books on the Talmud and Jewish mysticism that he discovered in Newman's library, and he became convinced that after early immersions in primitive and Greek mythology the artist conceived his creations as equivalents of passages in the Book of Genesis and the Kabbalah. Of *Onement I,* for example, the painting in which Newman settled on his format of the rectangle divided by a vertical stripe, Hess wrote that it "is a complex symbol, in the purest sense, of Genesis itself. It is an act of division, a gesture of separation, as God separated light from darkness, with a line drawn in the void." Hess then interpreted the red-orange stripe in *Onement* as a Kabbalistic metaphor for the fashioning of the first man out of earth, which in turn is represented by the darker red ground that the stripe bisects,

Barnett Newman, *Onement I*, 1948, oil on canvas, 27″ x 16″.

and he goes on to quote the Zohar, the Jewish "Book of Splendor," on the meaning of "one" as the conjoining of the male and the female, and of God and Israel.

Equipped with his Kabbalistic hypothesis, Hess discerned in Newman's compositions a system of "secret symmetry," which introduces squares into the middle of rectangles or divides the canvas into proportions suggested, or confirmed, by Kabbalistic formulas; for instance, there is the frequent recurrence of measurements by eighteen and multiples of eighteen, the number whose equivalents in letters of the Hebrew alphabet spell "life." And in Jewish mystical literature Hess encountered the term *Makom*, which means "place" but is also a Kabbalistic name for God; works by Newman such as the *Here* sculptures and the *Be* paintings seem to evoke this concept, and Newman made explicit reference to *Makom* in his statement about his model for a synagogue. Other Kabbalistic influences include the mysterious notion of *Zim Zum* (the origin of space through God's contracting Himself, which supplies the title of Newman's last sculpture) and reflections on "primordial light," which figure importantly in the rabbinical version of the Creation.

Hess proceeded chronologically through Newman's career, painting by painting, sculpture by sculpture, tacking symbolic meanings to colors ("the man-earth color of cadmium red," "the severe, the grandly formal, the tragic" of black), measuring the placement of the bands (or "zips," as Newman liked to call them) to identify the Kabbalistic proportions, interpreting the works as traditional dramas of spiritual revelation, agony, and salvation. The zips, Hess found, fall into a binary system of symbols: the soft-edged, loosely brushed stripes represent the sensual and the physical; the clean, sharp-edged stripes stand for the intellectual and the transcendental. With a vocabulary of signs distilled from Newman's forms, surfaces, and hues, Hess transmuted *The Stations of the Cross* into a Jewish and humanistic metaphor of the sufferings of mankind, of the artist's own confrontation with death, and of the triumph of life and the act of creation: "Even while committed to the Christian iconography of the Stations of the Cross, he would keep his allusions to the Kabbalah and to its vision of Genesis of the Torah."

Hess's catalogue is an extraordinary document, unique in this genre of writing for its insights, its personal devotion, and its intellectual diligence. It is an essay in poetic criticism, designed to create a crystallization of ideas, feelings, and images in which Newman's paintings are fully reflected. It combines illuminated thinking of the sages with events of Newman's biography, lengthy passages from essays by Newman, incidents of the history of art in New York since the last war, and formalistic analyses of Newman's paintings, sculptures, and prints. Inspired by the works, their titles, the writings, and Newman's personality, Hess conceived a hitherto partly hidden artist, a kind of rabbinical though non-religious New Yorker who reasons in red, yellow, white, and blue and in the carpentry of stretchers about arcane events and trends in the art world, as if divine miracles and the change from oil paint to acrylics were subject to the same logic. With Hess's Newman, metaphysics and art materials have achieved a common lexicon. Such a portrait is bound to contain exaggerations, but—as Plato remarked about one of his myths—though the details may not be accurate, one who sees this picture will not be far from the truth. To think of *Onement I* in terms of Adam, of Adam in terms of *adamah* (earth), to think of the red stripe in the field of red as the first man arising out of the primal ooze, is genuinely to see Newman's painting as a creation, beyond merely looking at it as an object.

In sum, Hess has plunged headfirst into the scandal of Newman's lofty thoughts; he has even been willing to intensify it. To follow him in grasping the content of Newman's paintings and sculptures, spectators would have to become adept in divine emanations. No wonder critics are indignant; in their view, Hess has compounded Newman's crime of polluting painting with words.

I doubt whether the Zohar must become required reading for visitors to the museums. As Hess himself acknowledges, "it is possible that I am pushing the Kabbalist interpretation too far. Certainly Newman never spoke about such a basis for his art." Hess has converted Newman into a Jewish icon-maker, disregarding the fact that icons cannot be Jewish. Newman's philosophy was a private fabrication; in it, the Kabbalistic *Makom* became synonymous with Indian burial mounds in Ohio and the pitcher's mound at Yankee Stadium. Analogies of this sort do not constitute an idea but are an aspect of sensibility, any component of which—for example, Newman's fondness for (to use his favorite phrase) "raising the issue," or his becoming a bird- or weight-watcher—has as much to do with individual paintings as any other. In interpreting specific paintings in terms of Kabbalistic and mystical passages, Hess makes the mistake of isolating them from Newman's intellectual physiognomy. Regardless of their sacred sources, the meaning of Newman's concepts is a secular one and needs to be restated in the pragmatic language of secular and contemporary experience. Newman's concept of the Hebrew God as "one" is less pertinent to his paintings, despite his reflections on the Scriptures and Commentaries, than his passionate continuation of the tradition in modernism—from Emerson to Mondrian—that declares both inward unity and unity of effect to depend upon concentration, reduction, and repetition. When Hess writes that Newman's *Vir Heroicus Sublimis* "refers to a man who, in working to reestablish the unity and harmony of a universe coexistent with God, acts as God in the here and now and aids in the coming of the ultimate reunion," he is presenting Newman's paintings not in the rhetoric of the artist's sensibility but in that of religious philosophy—moreover, in terms that are eroded and vague. I do not believe that *Vir Heroicus* "refers" to any such aims or could have been inspired by any such thoughts. Newman's enthusiasm for Jewish mystics and their sayings was a matter of intellectual delight rather than of religious belief or philosophical programs —a facet of his charming, childlike response to wonders and poetic phrases, whatever their source. As with other modern artists, his readings provided not an organized outlook but a kind of *metaphysical hum* that surround his mental operations. His thinking was truly systematic only when it dealt with achieving the reality of the art object as a "creation out of nothing," which was a common theme in New York art after the last war and the break with the European past. His *Here I* sculpture, which consists of a vertical two-by-four covered with plaster and a white one-by-two, both stuck into mounds of plaster as shapeless as mud pies and mounted on a beat-up wooden box, calls attention exclusively to its own being as a creation extracted from the "chaos" not of primal night but of the inexhaustible junk pile of the present day.

Hess's catalogue expands the range of potentiality of Newman's rigorously restricted format, but it does not settle the problem of what the rectangles and zips mean. For Newman, painting was a way of practicing the sublime, not of communicating it. In the last analysis, all his works are, as he said of *The Stations*, "a single event"—in effect, one painting, though it manifests itself in a surprising sweep of variations, including sculpture. It combines the heroic (*Achilles*), the pathetic (*The Stations*), the metaphysical (the *Be* series), the religious (*The Way*), and the aesthetic (*Who's Afraid of Red, Yellow, and Blue*), which grew dominant in his last years. In its multiple inward shifts, Newman's art must remain partly inaccessible. It belongs to a one-man culture, which as it becomes more integrated becomes more estranged from shared ideas. As Kierkegaard kept repeating, the sublime in our time identifies itself only through "indirect communication."

5

Olitski, Kelly, Hamilton: Dogma and Talent

The 1973–74 art season opened early, and with a massing of major forces. It was as if—like the White House after the suspension of the Senate Watergate hearings—the official art world, shaken by last season's scandals (Metropolitan Museum acquisitions and sell-offs; the Marlborough–Rothko Estate affair) and irrationalities (Japanese go-for-broke bidding), could hardly wait to ascertain whether business as usual could be resumed. Before the fifteenth of September, when commercial galleries had not yet opened or were testing public responses with group shows and newcomers, New York's modern-art museums had already come forward with what were likely to be their chief efforts of the year in contemporary art: retrospectives by Ellsworth Kelly and Jules Olitski, and by the pioneer British Pop artist Richard Hamilton. Each of the exhibitions opened with a ceremonial dinner and/or cocktail reception, and was accompanied by an illustrated catalogue containing the customary untrammelled paean (in the case of Kelly, by a giant illustrated monograph as well). Crowds at the openings were large and animated, and the bars were at capacity, including those at the Whitney Museum, whose new policy of charging for drinks provided the only visible sign of the straitened financial condition of America's cultural institutions. Whatever the situation with painting and sculpture, there was little doubt that the art world, as a segment of society that has crystallized around museums, galleries, and art collecting, is holding its own and perhaps even expanding. It may well be that in any period there is no relation between the quality of art and its social prestige; an evidence of this is that this year Congress increased its appropriation for the National Endowment for the Arts to more than sixty million dollars.

Taken together, the Olitski retrospective at the Whitney, the Kelly at the Museum of Modern Art, and the Hamilton at the Guggenheim evoked the dominant avant-garde styles of the 1960s: Color Abstraction and Pop art. Since the three artists are leaders in these modes, their exhibitions provide a measure of how the sixties movements are making out today. In regard to Pop, it can be stated without hesitation that it has earned an honorable burial, and, to judge by his retrospective, Hamilton, its overseas progenitor, is hardly sorry to see it go; he has been deviating from the characteristic imagery of Pop throughout his career. The status of Color Abstraction is, however, more complex. Statements by Kelly, by John Coplans,* and by E. C. Goossen (in the Kelly catalogue) suggest that a war of attitudes and interpretations has been smoldering under the surface of abstract painting. "My work is difficult," said Kelly to a *Times* interviewer. "It's going to take people a while to get it." In *Ellsworth Kelly*, Coplans speaks of "penetrating some of the confusion that has shrouded Kelly's position" and of "the perplexities the art audience has encountered in fitting his work stylistically into the enveloping dialogue dominating American art." The theme is restated by Goossen, who notes in the catalogue that Kelly is "less dependent on current styles than his colleagues, and less involved in the more obvious 'problem-solving' practiced by many of his contemporaries." The target of this defensive barrage is not hard to spot. What Coplans calls "the enveloping dialogue dominating American art" is not a "dialogue" at all, unless there is such a thing as a dialogue in which only one sound is heard: the ritualistic drumming in the art magazines which for a decade or more has sought to establish that a particular vein in abstract painting is the quintessence of contemporary art. In this propagandistically favored vein, Olitski is today the undisputed chief; for the past three years he has been the most written-about figure in the art press—the artist whose innovations, it is contended, have placed him at the farthest outpost of progress in art. The most meaningful of contemporary creations (hence, it has been argued, also the best), his paintings are the standard by which other one- and two-color canvases, such as Kelly's, are to be appraised, and

* Editor of Ellsworth Kelly's *Ellsworth Kelly* (New York: Harry N. Abrams, Inc., 1973).

it is upon Olitski's achievement that the future of painting is to be constructed. Obviously, if this "dialogue" (a more accurate word would be "chorus") continued to "envelop" Kelly, it could only suffocate him.

From its first words, the catalogue of the Whitney retrospective allows no doubt that in Olitski modern art has found its ultimate master, and that work unrelated to his is irrelevant to art. "Over the past two or three years," writes Kenworth Moffett, curator of contemporary art at the Museum of Fine Arts in Boston, who directed the exhibition, "the painting of Jules Olitski has begun to seem decisive. For a surprising number of younger painters he is like a block, *the* influence that has to be gone through or overcome if any fundamental innovation or breakthrough is to be achieved" (his italics). For confirmation, Moffett cites testimony in *Art Forum* by Walter Darby Bannard that Olitski "has preempted serious new painting. He is for the time being our best painter." Similar judgments have been expressed by Barbara Rose and Thomas B. Hess. The notion that art history is a tunnel barred at the far end by a Cyclops is not a new one: Shakespeare, Mallarmé, Picasso, Mondrian, Pollock, de Kooning—to name but a few—have all been considered, in different periods, to be *"the* influence that has to be gone through or overcome" before new creations could be possible. Should not a critic who undertakes to name the most advanced artist of his time have a fresh sense of things? The irony in Moffett's elevation of Olitski is that he praises him not for opening a new path but for acting as a "block": art history, whose direction has been foretold, reaches an impasse, which makes all present creation invalid, except for the accomplishments of this one master. The painter Dan Christensen's admiringly calling Olitski a "monster" (which Moffett cites as evidence of Olitski's overwhelming preeminence) is an expression of the mood of futility aroused by the use of art history as art criticism. According to Moffett and his ideological colleagues, the "essence" of Olitski's greatness as well as of his novelty lies in his having "developed and revised Jackson Pollock's central innovation, the allover picture, in order to make it serve color." The claim of the Moffetters that art today revolves around a single aesthetic issue, which all artists are ordered to confront, contributes a sense of depression not unlike that aroused in the late thirties by the concentrated political focus of Socialist Realist aesthetics. Abandoned by

Jules Olitski, *First Love*, 1972, acrylic on canvas, 54″ x 78″.
COURTESY ANDRÉ EMMERICH GALLERY, NEW YORK.

philosophy, politics, and sociology, historical determinism continues to hold out in formalist art criticism.

The rhapsodies about the radical originality of Olitski speak of the aptness of his techniques—spraying, saturating, pouring, staining, hard and soft edges, thick impastos and flat surfaces, acrylics, enamels and spackles, brushed framing borders—for dealing with formal problems that presumably lie at the heart of painting in our time. It is by the aesthetics implicit in his handling of materials that his work is glorified as "major," "serious," and "dialectically advanced." Since I do not believe that technical "breakthroughs" and what Baudelaire called "studio jargon" are relevant to art criticism, I have looked to other aspects of his work for Olitski's qualities. The most imaginative notion I can associate with it is his observation, just before his adoption of the spray gun, that he would like to spray color into the air and have it remain there. This desire for a rainbow or a hanging mist of paint provides a poetic perspective toward the paintings done by Olitski after 1964. They are expanses of a single color (one of which is undoubtedly among the largest canvases of our time), in most instances decoratively toned and with a brushed-in narrow edge. Ideally, an Olitski should seem to billow away from the wall, while being held to it by the painted border that has become the artist's trademark. Color detached from the surface to which it is applied could induce a certain psychic state; perhaps it requires that the artist should actually have been in that state. Rothko did manage to achieve suspended color masses in a high proportion of his works; it is with Rothko rather than with Pollock that Olitski's paintings are affiliated—one of the horrors of formalist criticism is its distortion of art history. Since the effect of painted air necessarily occurs in the imagination, each spectator must decide for himself which Olitskis succeed in making it take place. The majority of the paintings at the Whitney were essentially inert, with surfaces disagreeably insensitive, like spotted linoleum or dried milk stains. Lightness is incompatible with being bound to a deterministic ideology. Olitski needs to purge himself of the Moffetts within. Dogmatics aside, his present paintings depend upon the sentimental and the grandiose: the candy-box colors of the smaller canvases, the fever-flushed firmaments of the larger ones. All in all, a second-rate performance.

The aim of every authentic artist is not to conform to the history of art but to release himself from it, in order to replace it with his own history. However the historical pattern is drawn, it will not fit the developing sensibility of the individual, since there is an element in creation that is arbitrary yet cannot be separated from the object produced. It is significant that Ellsworth Kelly, like Olitski a star of Color Abstraction in the sixties, resolutely repudiates the formalist creed cited by Moffett concerning the evolution of American abstract art out of a device by Pollock—the "allover" composition. Kelly appears to believe that historical and ideological pigeonholing have had their day. A painter and sculptor of simple, smooth-textured shapes, mainly geometrical and frequently in primary colors, Kelly insisted in his *Times* interview that he derives his forms from nature and thus stands apart from the typical abstract art of the sixties. An epigraph to his Museum of Modern Art catalogue quotes Leonardo to the effect that "the painter will produce pictures of little merit if he takes the work of others as his standard"—which seems directed against an art whose primary goal is surpassing other art.

Green White, a huge triangular painting consisting of two panels, was inspired by a green-and-white scarf Kelly saw around the neck of a woman in Central Park. "I use reality constantly," he has said. "Only I take a shadow, a fragment from a piece of architecture, someone's legs, or sometimes the space just between things, and make them the subjects of my paintings." Evidences of his interest in nature are the line drawings of plants and fruits he continues to compose. As is true of many other painters, Kelly's "reality" is a reality that bears a resemblance to art. Except for the formalists, the activity of modern artists, whether realist or abstract, centers on establishing linkages between objects in the museum and images in the environment. Despite his response to abstract shapes encountered on the street, Kelly did not come to abstract art through direct experience of things; he found it ready at hand as a mode in which to work. Long before 1949, when he painted his first relief abstraction, *Window, Museum of Art, Paris*, a rectangle divided by horizontal and vertical bars, divided rectangles had been accepted as art. The appreciation of the pure abstraction of Malevich, Gabo, and Mondrian belongs to the period between the wars, and Kelly's discovery of abstract themes in scarves and details of buildings does not differ much from the Soyers' finding Degas ballet dancers in Union Square in the 1930s. Though it is related to Mondrian in form and color, Kelly's work is equally close to Pop Art, in that it is born out of the art phenomena of daily life; Kelly's *Window* and Warhol's Brillo boxes are animated by the same

Ellsworth Kelly, *Running White*, 1959, oil on canvas, 88″ x 68″.
COLLECTION, THE MUSEUM OF MODERN ART, NEW YORK. PURCHASE

kind of aesthetic recognition. The higher reaches of abstract art embody ideas and tensions for which no visible equivalent exists (e.g., Mondrian's *Trafalgar Square*, Newman's *Onement*). Sojourning in France from 1948 to 1954, Kelly missed the far-reaching intellectual exchange of New York abstract artists during those years of discovery. The approach he arrived at with his own resources represents the rudimentary conception of abstract art as paintings of abstract objects and of tasteful divisions of the surface—the conception common among American abstract artists in the 1930s. Kelly found patterns in nature when nature offered patterns—shadows on the page of a book he was reading, the arch of a bridge, fragments of letters on a shop sign. He is the Grandma Moses of abstract art. But he is a naïf who has grown increasingly sophisticated through contact with the variations on abstraction of the past twenty years. (Goossen says that Kelly's return to the United States was stimulated by a review in *Art News* of an exhibition of Ad Reinhardt.) His Museum of Modern Art show contained ingenious redoings of abstract works in many phases, from kissing curves to serial repetitions. *Orange Red Relief* consists of two joined red panels, of the same width but one thicker than the other, so the shadow cast down the center mimics the vertical band of a Newman. For all his absorption of the art around him, however, Kelly retains an original freshness, a naïveté (in the best sense of the word) that have saved him from submitting to a so-called dialectic of "central innovations."

It is Kelly, rather than Olitski, who represents something new in the art of the seventies; that is, the readiness of non-Expressionist abstract art to get along without the support of metaphysics (Kandinsky, Newman) or the "logic of history" (Mondrian, the Constructivists)—that is to say, to be content to be mere decoration. Kelly is the true "minimalist"; with him, abstract art has arrived at irreducible craftsman virtues. He has the feeling of rightness of the first-class designer, a fine sense of proportion, a sensitivity to shape and scale, and satisfying juxtapositions of colors and tones. Add the finesse of his paint surfaces and it is undeniable that he repeatedly deserves an A. The spectator is assured that an excellent job has been done, that the artist's feelings have been neutralized and subsumed in the aesthetic, that irrelevant ambitions and all traces of struggle have been obliterated. It is possible to approve of Kelly's creations yet not be tempted to linger in front of them. They can be noted pleasurably in passing, like a nicely designed building or traffic circle, or admired, like the woodwork in a Rolls-Royce—no less attractive if the car itself has been wrecked. No doubt a great future awaits Kelly in architecture-related projects.

A much more culturally agile artist than his American peers, Richard Hamilton got into Pop and out of it without apparent strain. His show began with drawings for Joyce's *Ulysses* in realistic and Futurist styles done in 1949, proceeded through abstractions that adapt Picabia and figures that echo Duchamp's *Nude Descending a Staircase*, and concluded with experiments using painted photographs and with a parody of Picasso's parody *Las Meninas*. Hamilton's career is one of continual transition; this word itself is the key to one of his complex conceptions—his painting of motion called *Trainsition IIII*, a composition in square format of green dots, stains, and broken lines, the title of which is a pun in the Joycean vein as well as a reference to the name of the Paris magazine in which *Finnegans Wake* was serialized. While the painting by which Hamilton is best known in America is a typical Pop composition of sexy nudes, TV sets, posters, canned ham, vacuum cleaners, and movie marquees entitled *Just What Is It That Makes Today's Homes So Different, So Appealing?*, the bulk of his paintings and reliefs are more firmly allied to Duchamp than to the works of any of Hamilton's contemporaries. AAH!, made up of images of automobile parts, is funny, erotic, and mysterious in the Duchampian mood; it also adapts the Master's wafting, shapeless forms. *Glorious Techniculture*, an abstraction that encompasses bits of recognizable machinery, is produced out of associations of words, shapes, ideas, names, letters of the alphabet which parallel Duchamp's *The Big Glass*: "The three-ring pump agitator of the Frigidaire washing machine," explains Hamilton; "is a motif that I have been trying to place for a long time; it has a strangely architectural quality for me—Chinese pagoda or, upside down, a mixture of Lyons' Corner House and Frank Lloyd Wright. . . . The place that might have been occupied by the cylinders, if they had been there, is given in the picture to a cabin with a bride inside—a bride for no other reason than that the figure was the right scale" (or because she was deposited in Hamilton's head by Duchamp's *The Bride Stripped Bare by Her Bachelors, Even*). Hamilton has discovered his subject in the constant mixing of random language, suggestive shapes, visual and verbal banalities, and critical ideas about art characteristic of the contemporary aesthetic imagination, and his show contained some genuinely surprising images; for

Richard Hamilton, *Towards a Definitive Statement in Men's Wear and Accessories*, 1963, oil and collage, perspex on panel, 48″ x 32″ or 32″ x 48″.

example, those in the series entitled *Towards a Definitive Statement on the Coming Trends in Men's Wear and Accessories*. There is an intellectual coherence in Hamilton's modernism which counts for more than a uniform level of quality. Protruding out of Dada and Pop, he has divined that the only stability for "the 'painter of modern life,' in the Baudelairean sense," as John Russell calls him, is to keep moving. For an artist so oriented, the fading of the vanguard art movements need not be a disaster.

6

Lester Johnson's
Abstract Men

Painting and sculpture today are engaged in finding their way out of abstract art. Artists who haul tons of rock and dirt to construct a "real" work are reacting with typical American literalism against an art of stripes, edges, and geometrical shapes in plastic. In the past, extreme abstract art claimed that geometry provided a language of universal signs which could move people independently of any associations with the images of things. Abstract art also included, however, non-geometrical images that did not match those of the visible world; for example, Duchamp's *Nude* was considered to be "abstract." By the 1960s, abstract art had shed the metaphysical suggestions as well as the expressive content of earlier abstractionists. The hard-line pragmatism of the new American university art departments had changed abstract art into a medium that could speak only of itself and that could tell of itself only its functional problems, like a person whose conversation is restricted to his handicaps. Abstract art as it is conceived at present is a game bequeathed to painting and sculpture by art history. One who accepts its premises must consent to limit his imagination to a depressing casuistry regarding the formal requirements of modernism. As David Antin pointed out in *Art News*, almost all contemporary abstract artists share "a fundamental belief in the 'meaninglessness' of art as an activity or as an outcome." And Antin concludes that "we have come to the end of the line. . . . Formalist art is dead because its formalist aspect is, like chess, a game of no consequence, an image of nothing in which the same ground is gone over

71

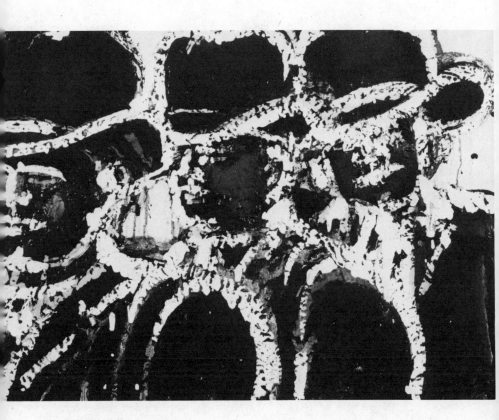

Lester Johnson, *Three Men with Hats*, 1970, oil, 20″ x 28″.
COLLECTION OF MR. AND MRS. HERBERT BURGER, HARRISON, NEW YORK, COURTESY
MARTHA JACKSON GALLERY, NEW YORK

and over in the same way, to the vast indifference of nearly everybody but its dealers."

Lester Johnson is an abstract artist of the pre-formalist variety. Like de Kooning, he has an unmistakable subject—men, as against de Kooning's women. Johnson is abstract in the sense of projecting a content implicit in but not restricted to the marks on the canvas. In this older tradition, abstraction equals metaphor; the painting as visual image has the additional dimension of an external reference that is suggested but not stated by what occurs on the canvas. All the Abstract Expressionists, from Kline to Newman, are abstract artists in this sense, and the formalist abstraction of the 1960s centered on a continual polemical effort to eliminate their metaphorical references and to reconceive abstract art in terms of a grammar of dimensions, edges, and color relations.

Johnson's current paintings are of groups of male figures—an old motif for him, though he has painted single males, too, and women and still-lifes. Indeed, he has for the past dozen years been featured in exhibitions dedicated to the human figure; in thus classifying him with nature-copying artists, such as Philip Pearlstein and Paul Georges, curators have helped to harden public misunderstanding of the abstract-representational issue. Johnson's present males are, like his figures of the past, generalized silhouettes seen full face or in profile. The groups vary in number from three to more than a dozen. All are in motion: some are tensed, as if against the wind; some are letting themselves be carried by a crowd; some are jammed together, as if stuck in a subway entrance; some amble aimlessly; some are advancing, rolling up their sleeves. The real content of the paintings is human energy. Johnson has learned from the Action painters—in particular, from de Kooning and Hofmann—that it is possible to produce equivalents of man and nature by reenacting on the canvas their characteristic forms of vitality.

The men are square-jawed and without expression, like idealized artisans or policemen. Their heads, shoulders, and legs are massive, and they have huge hands drawn with a touch of Pop, as in Guston's *Klan* paintings. The men's hemispherical hats, square faces, and cylindrical arms and thighs supply the formal elements of Johnson's compositions. The image, however, avoids the explicit man-the-machine concept of Léger. Johnson's males have not (not yet) been absorbed into pulleys and pistons. They are generalized men, but not mechanized. Their concreteness survives in their physical solidity. Johnson models his

Lester Johnson, *Four Walking Figures*, 1970, oil on canvas, 22″ x 24″.
COLLECTION OF SY AND THEO PORTNOY, COURTESY MARTHA JACKSON GALLERY,
NEW YORK

figures in depth and flirts with the space of Renaissance painting. Yet he does not hesitate to draw the outline of a face on top of a three-dimensional head. He makes use of the ambiguity of depth and flatness in painting to comment on the ambiguous condition of man in our time: that, abstract as he is, he has not yet been reduced to a figure in a pattern. In *Emerging Crowd*, arms and shoulders are modelled in accordionlike folds, as though the artist imagined that human limbs might be able to extend themselves much farther than they do. Johnson's vision comprehends both losses and possibilities.

These are anonymous men, their features consisting of cartoon clichés or else half hidden and indistinct; the humanity of Johnson's figures is restricted to their motions and gestures. They pass in profile, come forward in a row, are pressed together in tightly packed crowds. The figures of *Fourteen Men Passing* are jammed into the foreground, seemingly pushed from behind. It is notable that though the groups are in motion, they are not doing anything, in the sense of carrying out a task. In one of the largest canvases, the nine-foot-wide diptych *Approaching Men*, a mob of figures is striding forward, their big hats pulled down over their eyes—some almost at a run, with their hands in front of them, as if ready to attack. Yet these men are not menacing; they are, rather, presenting themselves in their potential for action. Being able to do but without doing is the human situation presented by these paintings.

Johnson's canvases carry no social message. His men are, however, vaguely proletarian, with their big slouch hats and derbies, their old-fashioned curved-front jackets, their broad, round pants. *Three Men with Caps* is like an old news photograph of a group of rigidly posed Bolshevik leaders. Perhaps in our time the proletariat has become an object of nostalgia, as has perhaps, too, the old-time capitalist with his pearl-gray derby, the gold chain on his vest, his spats. Johnson's men wear no gold chains, and when they smoke it is cigarettes, not cigars; his preference is not for the rich. In an earlier phase, he did drawings of men on the Bowery, their hats over their eyes, their hands in their pockets, trudging through the rain. Working in the Action-painting manner—that is, not from a subject but with forms that might evoke a subject—Johnson now invites these figures of memory to transform themselves into the shapes being fashioned by his brush. As they emerge through his action on the canvas, the personifications of the human situation are grim and prosaic.

The machine-proletarian atmosphere is realized through color and paint quality rather than through "scenes." I was reminded by one painting of a sculptured group in iron, or some other gray-black metal, set up in Washington in honor of early trade-union leaders. Johnson commonly works in dark browns, and at times in blue and black, and his pigment is thick and greasy; one reviewer joked that his paintings are made of tar. In certain lights the surface shine renders the picture invisible. Johnson galvanizes the heavy, resistant substance of his paintings through the rhythm and occasionally the color of his contours. Lines that mark the curve of a hat brim, the borders of a coat or sleeve flow through the composition like channels of vitality. Added energy charges are imparted by varying the outlining edges in width, the consistency of the pigment, and the color—from black or brown to white or blue. In *Four Men with Hats*, the forms are drawn in pink, chalklike lines on overlapping planes of gray, and the motif all but vanishes into the linear animation. The figures of *Three Men with Hats* and of the diptych *Passing Crowd* are half obliterated by the rhythmic outlines of hats and shoulders, so the pictures appear to be abstractions unless they are viewed from very close. Johnson's blue paintings often take on a jewellike radiance from the surface shimmer and the incandescence of the contours.

The dynamism of Johnson's compositions lies in the artist's concept of the relation between the individual and the group. The spatial organization of the paintings is determined by combining the figures or by separating them into "private" spaces—Johnson's way of stating the feeling of a particular human occasion in plastic terms. His theme of the individual and the crowd is not dissimilar from that of Giacometti in his walking-figure sculptures. In Paris, the issue of occupying isolated space versus marching together was construed, Giacometti told me a long time ago, to have an anti-Communist connotation. Johnson's groupings encompass both the self-segregated stroller and the purposeful corps, but he also explores other relations. *Crowd in Profile* consists of men marching in file. In extreme contrast, each figure in *Emerging Crowd* occupies his own space, though all are packed tightly against the others, and in *Four Walking Figures* there is a similar diffusion of direction—including a pair of feet that is going its own way at the top of the canvas. The male on the left in *Early Arrival* is leaning backward as if pulling a taut rope. Neither marchers nor self-detached individualists, the three magnified bodies of *Park Scene* are locked together in sleep, or perhaps a dance, while the orange-contoured

Lester Johnson, *Nine Men*, 1971, cray/o/p, 30″ x 80″.
COURTESY MARTHA JACKSON GALLERY, NEW YORK

homunculi of *Nine Men* seem caught in a trance of motion, like science-fiction dummies shot from a rocket gun.

Disposed in an expressive order, Johnson's hats, heads, shoulders, and flanks have the double purpose of building, on the one hand, a compositional machine equivalent to a structure of rectangles, circles, cylinders, and cones, and, on the other, of conveying his theme of man's place in the world. Over the years Johnson has broadened his repertory of shapes—earlier shows were dominated by frontal silhouettes—and expanded the range of his emotional statement. His reflections on the human situation have, it seems to me, inspired him to invent more spontaneously, to be less controlled by the object or by preconceived forms. But this increased spontaneity has caused no relaxation of his aesthetic rigor, which is based on the principle of formal self-limitation. Though his golemlike figures, with their domed heads, no longer divide the canvas into vertical sections, they introduce problems of balance of which each painting must take account. "Croppings" of the top and sides of the canvas create effects of compression and letting-go that reflect physical sensations of crowding and dispersion. Accident has been reduced; drips and blots, which were at times out of key with Johnson's firmly established forms now appear in only two or three canvases. Yet the sensitively handled contours remain, as the means for speeding the eye along linear intervals. The innovation of the paintings consists, however, in their interchange between formal and substantive concepts of a controlled disorder, in which a person or a thing can be anywhere by an independent act of decision.

Out of his twenty-five years of painting, Lester Johnson has drawn a mysterious, unpredictable, and moving image. One could not have arrived at this image either through analyzing society or through analyzing painting. It was brought into being by the act of painting itself, and it could emerge only in painting (not, for example, in film)—justification enough for this art, if justification is needed. Formalist abstraction is very likely finished. But Johnson's generalized man can hardly be included with it as "meaningless." It is an image that derives from the simultaneity of the artist's consciousness of art and his feeling about the state of man. It presupposes the appropriation of experience by a sensibility synthesized through the practice of painting. The survival of abstract art depends on such inner syntheses.

7

Joan Mitchell: Artist Against Background

In the hullabaloo of innovations that have replaced the academic tradition, the artist's problem of switching from one style to another is probably the most crucial in the practical life of art. Picasso's abandonment of Cubism remains a source of wonder, as does Ernst's and Miró's firm clinging to Surrealism. Decisions of this order carry overtones of morality and even of politics—which may explain the apparent reluctance to discuss them in writings on art and artists. To relinquish a style is a repudiation of colleagues, and to adopt a new style is, since modern art is a continuing war of tendencies, tantamount to going over to the enemy. It is undeniable that defections weaken an art movement and foreshadow the time when it will no longer be represented by any of the living but will exist, if at all, only in history. Yet unshakable adherence to a mode or format also has serious drawbacks. To go on being a Dadaist or an Abstract Expressionist or a Conceptualist when the interest of the art world has turned elsewhere implies ideological rigidity, the introverted belief that one's own revolution was destined to be the last. No art movement can continue to represent the new forever, so to hang on to a style is to repudiate the principle of innovation that brings modern styles into being. On the other hand, to forsake what may be the most valid approach of one's time because it has ceased to be fashionable, or because the young are too benighted to live up to it, is to fall into shallow opportunism and to sacrifice the possibility of establishing an aesthetic identity. To change or not to change—the issue cannot be resolved on objective grounds. Fortunately, there are no treason trials in the art world, and no orders of merit for loyalty.

It used to be said that the style is the man. This significant-sounding maxim gives rise to complex questions when it is applied to the modern situation, in which styles are often put on and taken off as if they were costumes. Does a change of style dissolve the artist and put another in his place? It would seem so in extreme instances, as in the difference between the early, theosophical Mondrian and the late, Neo-Plastic one, between early and late Rothkos. In our epoch, it is rare to find an artist who has not undergone metamorphosis. Is the second self as authentic as the first? Or is the new man an impostor contrived out of usable elements in his cultural environment—for example, a Mondrian who came into being because of Paris and Cubism? On the contrary, the usurping identity may owe its existence to the divesting of a false self and the painful evolution of the embryo of an original style. It would be difficult to demonstrate that either the first self or a later one deserves an absolute precedence. In the grammar of modern existence, any fragment of a man is equal to the whole. Each stylistic portion of an artist's total time span constitutes a separate sum of artifacts, and this is recognized by the art market in the values it places upon certain "periods" of an artist's work in contrast to others. The magic of Picasso lay in his ability to stretch over into separated styles—"blue" and "pink," Cubist, classical, Surrealist periods—without self-fragmentation. Other artists who partake of two or three lives in this manner lose themselves, as if their fingerprints had faded. At any rate, for an artist to be one or more than one appears to be a matter of choice. Freedom is the privilege of surrendering what one is. Matisse was impressed by the report that "Japanese artists of the great period changed their names several times during their lives. This pleases me; they wanted to protect their freedom." Still, if abandoning a self has only the aim of locking oneself into a new one, the effort seems frivolous, a game of masquerade. Should not the aim be to develop a style of freedom? of continuous divesting of self? Of course it, too, would tend to produce restrictive mannerisms.

Joan Mitchell's newest paintings, recently shown at the Whitney Museum, are the creations of an Action painter who has chosen to retain the aesthetic identity in which she began her career more than twenty years ago. Her compositions revel in the liberationist draftsmanship and paint handling developed by postwar American abstract art. In the presence of her energetic canvases, one feels that Kline, Hans Hofmann, de Kooning, Guston are functioning in the neighborhood. Secure in the validity of its premises, Mitchell has disdained to dissociate her work from the smearings and splashings of the latecomers of the fifties who brought the style into disrepute. Dripping paint masses—orange, red, blue—settle against loosely brushed areas in giant canvases splattered and stained like the abused walls of a slum. The disintegrated rectangles and messy surfaces of mammoth diptychs and triptychs such as *Wet Orange, Close, Closed Territory, Plowed Field* confidently assert themselves in opposition to art-world fashions and the critical chatter of the past decade and a half. Mitchell's work comes as close as any by an American to belonging to a tradition. Her exhibition shows that this can be a tremendous advantage.

Mitchell has absorbed the physicality of Action painting—the element of dance in it. Her stance, in the photograph in the Whitney catalogue, suggests, like the momentary stance of Pollock in numerous well-known photographs, a pause in a rhythmic movement; it is this movement that realizes itself in the paintings through the laying on of pigment and the balancing of forms. Moods or states of mind expressed in impulses of the body, as they change and build up in the activity of the painting, provide the subject matter of these restless compositions. Mitchell's giant triptych *Clearing* is a thrice-repeated tightening and relaxation: the dark, heavy squares in the upper part of each section, like the gathering of storm clouds, diffuse ("clearing") into blue, airy circular forms below. Composing by means of tensions and relaxation, Mitchell carries on the principle, common to Hofmann, Pollock, de Kooning, and other founders of the Action movement, that painting is an extension of the artist's inner life in its highest intensity. "Painting is what allows me to survive," she has said, confessing to the attitude that came to be denounced, by those who wished art to be practiced as a normal profession, as the "desperation" of Action painting. Endowed with the original meaning of the style in which she works, Mitchell differs drastically from contemporary heavy-pigment painters—Olitski, Poons, Bannard—who, having circled back to the Action mode by way of formalist theories, attempt to animate the canvas without a corresponding animation within the artist; regardless of their techniques of applying paint, their surfaces remain inert.

As with de Kooning and Kline, the raw, slapdash texture of Mitchell's paintings, with its effect of letting go, is a partial camouflage for precisely intuited harmonies. To see her paintings fully is to see

Joan Mitchell. *Clearing* (triptych; *left to right*: left panel, center panel, right panel), 1973, oil on canvas, 110¼" x 236".

through them. Their subsurface order ought not, however, to be mistaken for a rationally conceived structure executed according to plan, then defaced for effect. Mitchell's order is an order of feeling modulated by her veteran practice in the origination and deployment of forms. There are various levels of spontaneity: they range from the total automatism of the sleepwalker to the instantaneous riposte of the master fencer; in each, a different degree of form results from the interplay of movements in the action itself. The notion that an Action painter plunges into the canvas and activates it, so to speak, in the dark is a myth derived from Surrealist games. At the extreme of his "contact" with (immersion in) the canvas, Pollock was conscious of where his ribbons of pigment were falling. Mitchell repudiates automatism; "I don't close my eyes and hope for the best," she is quoted as saying. But though she studies her painting while she is creating it, the essence of her pictures is that they come into being through unanticipated responses to what is taking place on the canvas. The activity she has instigated provides the clue and the motivation for her next move. This is another way of saying that, like Action painters generally, she plays the middle registers of spontaneity. The title *They Never Appeared with the White*, a diptych featuring a vaguely bluish circular form in each panel and three vertical strokes of color in the right-hand panel, is suggestive of both her aim and her method: it expresses delight at having been taken by surprise.

Mitchell's paintings of the sixties were strongly influenced by Philip Guston's. *Sans Neige II* (1969), the earliest painting in the Whitney exhibition, retains this influence: short, nervous lines nudge through pats of dense pigment toward a concentration in the top central portion of the canvas. *Blueberry* (1969–70) is a similar clustering formation, but without the linear dartings. In her paintings of the seventies, Mitchell has moved closer to Hans Hofmann, particularly to the late paintings in which inlays of slabs of color hold the composition in place. Perhaps Mitchell meant to indicate her move by the title *La Ligne de la Rupture*, done in 1970–71, a powerful Hofmannesque canvas that approaches the Master himself in variety and lyricism. *Close* (1973), the title of which may refer to the closely scaled values of its colored oblongs, reminds me of one of Hofmann's walls built of yellow and red blocks. Mitchell's color masses differ, however, from Hofmann's in that they do not consist of flat, clean-cut plates of pure color but decompose at the edges and on the surface like cakes of colored ice under a beam of torrid light. Differing also from Rothko's soft but evenly bevelled rectangles, Mitchell's eroded oblongs take on a variety of tones and even of hues, and become elements of an original art of shifting volumes. Line has disappeared, except as decorative drips and as a means for establishing a vertical movement to counter the lateral drift of the diptychs and triptychs. The four-panelled "The Fields II" has the pronounced sidewise animation of a seascape with ships.

Action paintings tend to become landscapes that are metaphors for feelings. Pollock's *Blue Poles* and *Lavender Mist*, Kline's ramplike paint structures, de Kooning's *Gotham News* and East Hampton beach motifs are instances of scenes evoked from moods. These inner countrysides are different from those of the dream in that they take form under the pressure of conscious purpose. The landscape is the emanation of the artist, and it has his emotional physiognomy rather than the atmosphere of a place. On the other hand, the artist's environment inhabits him in its totality as a tone of his being; it is not an external scene to be abstracted into observed details. Hofmann was predominantly a creator of landscapes seen for the first time when they manifested themselves on the canvas. Instead of copying nature, he saturated himself with it; each evening he ritualistically attended the setting of the sun from a high point among the dunes of Provincetown. "I bring the landscape home in me" was his way of describing his approach. It was through subjectivizing their surroundings that American artists of the postwar years were enabled to overcome the separation between sensibility and object which had made art in this country dependent on European models.

Mitchell's paintings have been firmly rooted in this tradition, and in the recent show the landscape theme was more pervasive than ever. Denying that she is an Expressionist (that is, an artist whose work is an emanation of the ego), she insists that the subject of her canvases is "the feeling that comes from landscape." In a formula almost identical with Hofmann's, she declares, "I carry my landscapes around with me." It is worth noting, however, that her titles refer almost as frequently to people (*Salut Sally, Bonjour Julie, Iva*) and to abstract ideas (*Close, Chasse Interdite, Clearing*) as to concepts of place (none are names of particular places). Apparently, landscape is one among several categories of subject that to her stand for feelings.

It is unfortunate that Marcia Tucker, curator of the Whitney, who organized the show, strives, in her eagerness to establish Mitchell's originality (or perhaps her independence of males), to segregate her

Joan Mitchell, *Sans Neige II*, 1969, oil on canvas, 64″ x 51″.
COLLECTION OF MR. AND MRS. LEON A. ARKUS, PITTSBURGH, PENNSYLVANIA

from the Action painters and Abstract Expressionists among whom she developed. As the epigraph of her introduction to the catalogue, Tucker has found a quotation from Cézanne: "The landscape thinks itself in me." Granted that this represents a subjectivization of the outer world, the Cartesian self-meditation conceived by Cézanne is quite remote from Mitchell's "carrying landscapes around." (One wonders if Cézanne's landscape in its introspection discovered itself to resemble a Poussin.) Having intimated an ancestry for Mitchell broader than Action painting, Tucker argues that by virtue of her subject she "stands somewhat apart from other Abstract Expressionists"; and in her obsession about proving Mitchell's self-origination she attributes the huge dimensions of her canvases not to the example of Pollock or Kline but to the fact that she wore glasses when she was a child and still finds it easier to see big things than little ones. The natural bigness of stretches of countryside is also brought in as explanation—or, as Tucker puts it, the scale of Mitchell's paintings "is analogous to the scale of the subject matter." Luckily, it did not occur to her to paint the Atlantic Ocean.

Possibly, Mitchell abetted Tucker in denying the historical roots of her paintings in order to present her as isolated and self-invented. What could seem less advantageous in the present-day art world than identification with a movement that petered out in the 1950s and, as some art historians have it, never existed in the first place? Besides, who doesn't want to be considered unique? More interesting, however, than Mitchell's ocular peculiarities is the coherence that her work has derived from her being a member of the first generation of artists in American history to find a native innovative style in which to begin. Grounded in the insights of postwar abstraction, her work during the past twenty years has achieved constant renewal and freshness. Her presence as a leading "second generation" Action painter has made her a kind of companion figure to de Kooning in the diptych of younger and elder continuators of this mode. Like de Kooning, she grows freer —in the assured elaboration of a style whose substance is the heightened life of the artist.

8
Dubuffet: Shockers and Fairy Tales

Of the many paintings and sculptures by Jean Dubuffet in the United States, his *Four Trees* sculpture, at the Chase Manhattan Plaza, in the downtown financial district, ranks among his best. Made of epoxy and fiberglass, and decorated with the eccentric linear edgings and patterns characteristic of this artist's *Hourloupe* series, it is composed of irregular horizontal shapes that appear to float above deliberately clumsy bases—the "trunks" of the trees. The scale of the work in its setting of skyscrapers is exactly right—large enough to assert its presence, yet maintaining a human dimension that softens the surrounding cliffs of stone and glass. Its cool colors and pleasantly textured surface are physically relaxing. The total image, resembling that of giant mushrooms, evokes associations with illustrations of fairy tales. In summer it should serve as a shady arbor and have fountains of iced drinks flowing out of it. On school holidays it might be festooned with ropes of licorice and rows of old-time candy buttons on narrow strips of paper. The Thirty Years' War declared by Dubuffet against culture has culminated in a midsummer night's dream cradled in the embrace of one of the world's largest banks.

As has been customary with Dubuffet, the unveiling of *Four Trees* was accompanied by an exposition by the artist of the significance of his sculpture and how to appreciate it. (Dubuffet is one of those artists who make things easy for reporters and reviewers by giving them inside information into the aims of the work.) In the case of *Four Trees*, his statement is in essence a reconciliation. In it the ideologue

Jean Dubuffet, *Four Trees*, 1972.

of Art Brut and the author of "Anticultural Positions" and "Asphyxiating Culture," whose declared ambition has been to replace Western art with that of the jungle, the lavatory, and the mental institution, reveals the harmony of his creation with "the high-intensity activities" and "I would even say, poetry" of Wall Street. "I could not have hoped for a place better suited to this monument. . . . Indeed, this plaza, and the prodigious buildings which rise above and surround it, are the dramatic illustration of an extraordinary celebration of reason, logic, and calculation."

Dubuffet's newly proclaimed enthusiasm for the rationality and practicality of banking places his work, it seems to me, in clearer perspective than does his normal attitude of cultural insurrection. For the past ten years, Dubuffet has been engaged in the series to which he gave the name *L'Hourloupe,* the sounds of which suggest to him "some wonderland or grotesque object or creature, while at the same time they evoke something rumbling and threatening with tragic overtones." The *Hourloupe* fantasies, he says in connection with the Chase Manhattan Plaza opus, constitute a "parallel world" to that of the everyday rational reality. In brief, Dubuffet conceives art to be a kind of Disneyland—a notion that is, of course, in no sense subversive but is, on the contrary, the traditional middle-class view of art as a relaxation from the serious business of life and the rigors of competitive enterprise.

Dubuffet's "Remarks on the Unveiling of the Group of Four Trees" was printed, in French and in English, in the catalogue of his retrospective at the Guggenheim Museum. Despite this unambiguous document, however, the Museum doggedly refused to relinquish the myth of Dubuffet's radicalism. In the introduction to the catalogue, Thomas Messer, director of the Museum, invoked the "anguished outcries from the world of institutional culture" that resounded like pistol shots throughout the Dubuffet story, and he concluded that the artist is still laying waste the foundations of Western forms and that his "lifework is of one piece." Consistent with this view, Margit Rowell, the Guggenheim curator who organized the show, began her presentation of Dubuffet's "art on the margins of culture" by testifying that "over the span of his thirty-year career, Jean Dubuffet has refused to be . . . coöpted by the culture which in 1943 he set out to undermine." Rowell took note of the oddity that this sworn foe of art was being honored by retrospectives in New York and Paris, but she argued that he had somehow forced himself on the civilization he hates and that "he remains nonetheless a thorn in twentieth-century culture's side."

Since no "anguished outcries" emanated from the Guggenheim (on the contrary, the Dubuffet retrospective, according to Messer, "had been sought by the Museum for a long time" and the show was the largest ever assembled there), it must be assumed that the Guggenheim is not part of "institutional culture." Nor, by the same measure, are the National Endowment for the Arts and the Association Française d'Action Artistique, both of which provided grants to make the retrospective possible. Considering that the Museum of Modern Art, the Art Institute of Chicago, the Los Angeles County Museum, the Walker Art Center, the Musée des Arts Décoratifs, the Tate Gallery, the Stedelijk Museum, and the Museum of Fine Arts in Montreal have, beginning as far back as 1960, presented retrospectives of Dubuffet (in some cases, two), one wonders in which portion of the anatomy of culture that Dubuffet thorn is lodged. No artist since World War II has had a quicker rise to fame: within two years after he began to paint seriously —in the mid-forties, at the age of forty-two—he had an exhibition at a leading Paris gallery, and three years later he made his début in New York at the Pierre Matisse. No one has received more consistent support from the international chain of official art agencies, and he has done equally well with the collectors who form part of the same cultural framework; at any rate, no owners of Dubuffets known to me have rings in their noses. What, then, can be the explanation for these pretended shrieks of pain, especially since indignant attacks on art have not been in vogue since the war? This question is interesting apart from the actual qualities of Dubuffet's art—qualities that become visible only when his work has been lifted out of its nest of propaganda.

Apparently, institutions of contemporary culture find a need to sponsor activities that will make them seem opposed to themselves. Modernism is a revolutionary movement, and if this revolution is no longer being continued in fact, it must be continued in fiction. To create the illusion of an adversary force, everything that has been overthrown must be overthrown again and again. Dubuffet is at one with his museum directors and curators in boldly challenging the *nineteenth* century. To appreciate his work, one must keep in mind that art as Dubuffet found it when he entered the art world had already made all the moves on which his reputation rests. It is precisely in appropriating the fruits of old revolts that he represents revolt in the museum. The aesthetic subversion that ended with World War II lives on in Dubuffet as revolutionary pantomime.

In the past, culture consisted of impulses toward a center of inherited values—religious, moral, political, aesthetic. It was this concept of culture that T. S. Eliot had in mind when he called for an organic culture that would be on guard against including "too many" freethinking foreigners. In the twentieth century, however, culture has moved in the opposite direction—toward the frontiers where the familiar and accepted touch upon the alien. Today, the mark of cultivation is a capacity for penetrating previously dark areas (geographical, social, and psychological), for assimilating forms regardless of when or where they originated. The limit of modernist culture is man himself. The days of anguished outcries at the sight of strange creations are long past. Our institutions are upset not by new forms but by confrontation with facts, as in connection with the deaccessioning procedures of the Metropolitan or, to come closer to our topic, the rancorous cancellation of the exhibition of Hans Haacke by the Guggenheim a couple of years ago because it called attention to slum tenements and publicly named their owners. To be, like Dubuffet, a sworn enemy of cultural institutions is, it appears, not at all disturbing to the representatives of those institutions, though to expose aspects of the actual character of the culture is an act on the verge of high treason.

For all his anticulturism, Dubuffet's art exists entirely within the matrix of established modernist forms and ideas. His work is the exact antithesis of that of the naïve or untrained artist, and of the individual who creates in the grip of an obsession. Miró, for instance, imitated the mental state of psychotics, Dubuffet only their compositions. Art Brut, with which Dubuffet has identified himself, is the product of an attempt to render what is seen or felt with whatever means are at hand. Dubuffet mimics this in his crude scrawls and his assemblages of waste. His art, however, is completely motivated by artistic objectives; it has no concern with reality, visual or subjective. Nothing in his variety of modes is based on observation, except the observation of recent styles in art. His aesthetic is a shrewd, self-conscious compendium of methods of composition that have been liberated from all external demands. His successive formats, modes, and mediums—the Guggenheim catalogue listed twenty-four separate phases—have this in common: all expedited immediate production of art works, like the music schools that promise you can play a tune the first day. For subtleties

of the hand or originality of conception, Dubuffet has substituted
formulas for fabricating objects authenticated by modernist aesthetics
—for instance, paintings based on the accidental behavior of their
materials, or assemblages featuring textures produced by combining
leaves, banana skins, and bits of bark. The "brutal" artist concentrates
on one work at a time, in which he finds absolute meaning or satisfaction. Dubuffet, on the other hand, sets in motion processes capable
of yielding undetermined quantities of products in one medium or
another.

The outstanding impression induced by the Guggenheim retrospective, which presented some three hundred samples of the artist's thou-
sands of paintings, drawings, sculptures, prints, illustrated books, models for monuments, stage properties, and animated personages of the
Coucou Bazar, was that Dubuffet's output comes as close as possible to
having been created by a crowd. The non-stop improvisations of the
Hourloupe decorations of the past ten years—initiated, we are told,
by doodlings with red and blue ball-point pens—bear a significant
resemblance to the miles of calligraphy with which youngsters cover
New York subway trains. For any one of the categories of works in
the master list of Dubuffet's products, an equivalent could have been
substituted without altering the artist's total statement.

In principle, Dubuffet has been an advocate of anonymity in art—a
principle he has advanced with maximum personal publicity. He made
his reputation by allying himself with a body of creations without
signatures—the art of the mentally ill, whose "authors" he has celebrated as "obscure individuals, alien to the milieu of professional artists." For his own part, Dubuffet as an artist has never been either
obscure or alienated. As champion of art by anybody, he has directed
his fire against art by somebody; that is to say, the figure of the artist.
His stated hostility to Western culture is, ultimately, hostility to the
human product of that culture—the autonomous individual and his
unique sensibility. "I feed on the banal," he has written. "In my paintings I wish to recover the vision of an average and ordinary man."
Though this is totally inconsistent with his interest in the art of psychotics, it is a way of reiterating his repudiation of artistic intelligence
as a force in the ongoing cultural transformation. Dubuffet's exalta-
tion of ordinariness, and sub-ordinariness, fits him—as it does Warhol,
who has also expressed the ideal of being like everybody else—into

Jean Dubuffet, *Coucou Bazar*, 1972–73.

Jean Dubuffet, *Landscape with Flag*, 1958, epoxy, 39" x 67" x 47¼".
COLLECTION OF RUDOLF ZWIRNER, GALERIE ZWIRNER, GERMANY, COURTESY THE
SOLOMON R. GUGGENHEIM MUSEUM, NEW YORK

the pseudo-radical philosophies of anti-élitism which have been bringing art into accord with the aesthetics of big business and the mass media.

The descending spiral of the Guggenheim Museum is the ideal site for a comprehensive overlook of Dubuffet's contribution. The works are most satisfactorily seen as groupings of images and objects by the spectator in motion, instead of being scrutinized individually. Dubuffet produced them in sequences, like frames of a film, and the movement of the spectator in drifting down the ramp is the next-best thing to animation of the images. Observed while passing, the retrospective, through which there echoed in one's imagination Dubuffet's uninterrupted anti-cultural monologue—"My operation is to erase all categories and regress toward an undifferentiated continuum"; "I am convinced that art has much to do with madness and aberrations"; art "is a duet between the artist and his medium"; and so on—could be seen as a twentieth-century parody of Kenneth Clark's celebrated film survey of the treasures of civilization. One began at the top level of the ramp with the most agreeable of Dubuffet's creations—the sophisticated three-dimensional painted shapes of his most mature period, the *Hourloupe* abstractions, domestic objects (tables, chairs, telephones, water glasses, teaspoons, candelabras), kites, landscapes, plants (including the maquette for *Four Trees*), personages made of polyester resin or epoxy and covered with random tattooings of contours and colored stripes, like the face paintings of savages. The *Hourloupe* red, blue, and black doodles are a version of Pollock's dribbles of paint, but their indentations, curvatures, convexities represent the high point of Dubuffet's originality to date. Some of the *Hourloupe* sculptures are genuinely elegant and inspired by a childlike gracefulness; *Landscape with Flag, Candelabra Tree, Biplane Tree, Monument to the Phantom* are reminiscent of the best of early Arp. In these works Dubuffet lets himself go lyrically, instead of yielding to sadistic impulses, as in the squatting nudes of 1950. But the earlier compositions were also a species of doodling; Messer was right in seeing Dubuffet as all of a piece. The descending ramp is a travelogue showing his adventures in automatism and whimsey: paintings of cows and beards, blank expanses of earth, imprintings of botanical materials, blottings, scribbles, caricatures, figures scratched or molded in thick pastes, boards enamelled with pigment containing odd junk, figures made of pasted-together scraps of newsprint and butterfly wings. One cannot avoid

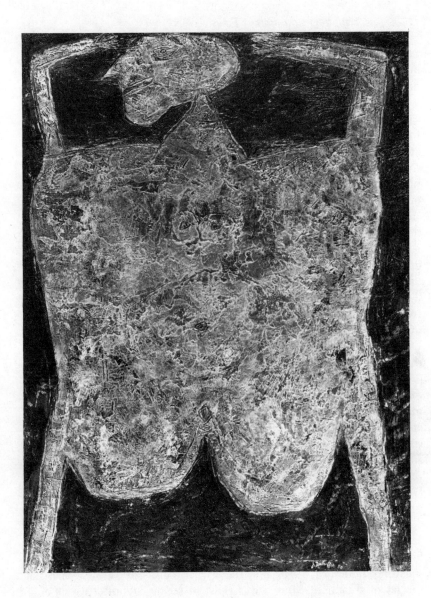

Jean Dubuffet, *Triumph and Glory (Corps de Dames)*, 1950, oil on canvas, 51″ x 38½″.

being impressed by Dubuffet's tirelessness and the variety of his improvisations. But the variety is in the modes of making and occurs on the surface of the things made. There is nothing in Dubuffet's approach to create a resistance to any suggestion that presents itself. The individual works lack tension; their charm, where it exists, seems a matter of luck. Even the violent imagery of the *Corps de Dames* series.results simply in a gallery of ghastly pinups. Dubuffet invents; he does not explore. He sets down his pictorial ideas; he does not develop them into persuasiveness. Perhaps this accounts for the endless verbal voice-over that has accompanied his inventories of objects.

9
Warhol: Art's Other Self

The innovation of Andy Warhol consists not in his paintings but in his version of the comedy of the artist as a public figure. "Andy" (the first name was one of his means of establishing himself as a household word) has carried the ongoing de-definition of art to the point at which nothing is left of art but the fiction of the artist. "Why is *The Chelsea Girls* art?" he inquired, referring to one of his movies. "Well, first of all, it was made by an artist, and, second, that would come out as art." To this, one is given the choice of replying either "Amen!" or "Oh, yeah?" Though Warhol's retrospective, at the Whitney, was loaded with some two hundred and forty items, many of them huge, he had succeeded in approximating the performance of the painter who does not paint. Twenty years ago, the late Barnett Newman said to Rauschenberg that if the artist's aim is to produce empty canvases he ought to do it with pigment. Warhol lives up to this injunction, but with modifications. His Campbell's Soup cans, Brillo boxes, portraits of public figures, tabloid horror photographs, and flowers are for the most part images silk-screened on canvas in numerous replicas. A capsule biography in *Art in America* records, under 1961–62, when he was emerging as an artist out of commercial design, that "Warhol rejects hand-painting canvases." His performance goes beyond that of Marcel Duchamp, who for almost half a century was a dominant presence in the art world without publicly producing a work. Warhol does produce, and in profusion; even after his "retirement" he was represented at the Los Angeles County Museum exhibition of "Art and Technology" by an "environment" of "hundreds of three-dimensional daisy images, made by Cowles Communications' Xography process, seen through fluctuating sheets of sparkling artificial rain." Warhol is not an anti-artist, since to be one implies acknowledgment of the presence of art. He blandly takes his fertility for granted, but depletes his creations of any quality that might separate them from products of the conveyor belt or the machine. Within a year after his début, he set up his studio as the Factory, from which his imprinted Brillo boxes, Marilyn Monroes, and electric chairs streamed in required quantities. Instead of the no-works of Duchamp, Warhol supplied near-non-works—Andythings. He has shown the drawings of flowers and butterflies, the gold-paper shoes, the greeting cards, and the souvenirs he did in the thirteen years before he declared himself an artist. These exhibits are art *ex post facto*—objects elevated retroactively into the realm of aesthetic significance. Or, if one prefers, Warhol's pre-art products of whim and drudgery blend with his art-world output in that all are extensions, or relics, of the Warhol-figure; he could, if he chose, include his old sneakers or his mother's recipes.

By underwriting as art objects available in hardware stores, Duchamp demonstrated that art lay in the artist, not in the art object. The Action painters repudiated picture-making in favor of acts of discovery and self-transformation. Warhol interprets literally the overshadowing of the artwork by the artist; that is, he sees it strictly in terms of the art market. His mass production of paintings and his dramatization of himself are a radical reflection of the values that came to the fore in the art world toward the end of the 1950s. The new, expanded art public—and its representatives among dealers, collectors, and curators—had little taste for the enigmas and the exhausting bouts with the experience of creation of Gorky, Pollock, de Kooning, Guston. It preferred images taken in at a glance and "glamorous" colors translatable into dress patterns. Above all, it admired reputations. Warhol not only understood this public but had the wit to draw practical conclusions from his encounter with it. "We fixed it like this," he said to Grace Glueck, of the *Times*, about his Whitney exhibition, "so people could catch the show in a minute and leave." Warhol was aware that whether or not visitors actually left in a minute (that might depend on the presence of free drinks) they would devote only a minute to the paintings. For the great majority of the avant-garde audience, art was not something to look at; it had become, in the newly popular phrase, an "environment." It was not necessary to scrutinize

Andy, "the Kids," and the Cows.
FROM THE SOLOMON R. GUGGENHEIM MUSEUM WARHOL RETROSPECTIVE, 1969.
PHOTO BY BETSY JONES

an exhibition; one needed only to know that it was there; one apprehended it with one's back. Warhol put his painting where the spectator wanted it—behind him. I once asked Leo Castelli, Warhol's dealer, about an exhibition of silk-screened flowers that was to open at his gallery. "No need to see it," said Castelli. "The pictures are the same as the announcement I sent you." Warhol had something for everyone: for gallery-goers easy art, for collectors a signature.

Warhol's practice constitutes an extremist appraisal of the status of art in present-day America; by comparison, any political or sociological pronouncement he might have made would have been superficial. A painting is a picture, *any* picture (since any can be reproduced), with a respected signature. Art is a cliché given renown by a name; this applies to the *Mona Lisa* as well as to a Rauschenberg, and to Warhol's silk-screenings of the *Mona Lisa* and of a photograph of Rauschenberg. Art history, which determines what shall be identified as art, devotes itself to authenticating attributions and to supplying signatures when they are missing. Greatness in an artist consists in his high worth as a label; early on, Warhol declared to a friend that he wanted "to be Matisse," but there is no evidence that he was ever interested in Matisse's paintings. Duchamp's bottle rack and bicycle wheel are in museums, but they got there through fortuitous and unpredictable developments. With Duchamp for a precedent, and with the example of Duchamp's emulators of the 1950s, such as Rauschenberg and Johns, Warhol could avoid the difficulties both of painting, on the one hand, and of overcoming the anonymity of found objects, on the other. By mechanical duplication, he could adjust supply to demand without being subjected to the hardships and uncertainties of creation; his duplications would even arouse critical admiration as a contribution to "serial imagery." At one swoop—his first New York exhibition, at the Stable Gallery, in 1962, of painted and silk-screened soup cans, "celebrities," and do-it-yourself pictures—Warhol demonstrated that art-world evaluation of the objects presented to it could be programmed by mustering attention around the artist. The power to make one's signature count is acquired through a fiction launched upon the public; no less than the President of the United States, the artist gains his authority through marketing an alter ego. The bottle rack of Duchamp, the bronzed flashlight of Johns possess formal resemblances to treasures of the museum; Warhol swept aside these academic subtleties. His undistinguished art needed only the support of a distinctive Warhol.

It was in conceiving the creator of his works that Warhol proved genuinely creative, and penetrating to the point of subversion. The archetype of the modern artist has been the Dandy, Baudelaire's detached and intellectually tormented "hero of modern life." This figure survived in a variety of versions to the threshold of the sixties. Duchamp, in his refusal of art, was a resurrection of the lone Dandy in his discipline of pride and estrangement. The "accursed" artist was emulated by Gorky with du Maurier exaggeration, refurbished by Pollock as a cowboy riproarer, reenacted by de Kooning in dungarees and workman's jacket, and, recently, by Rauschenberg as a Leatherstocking. Despite cosmetic modifications, the elegant stranger engaged in a mysterious and probably hopeless mission, equally resigned to failure and success, persisted as the model of the artist in our time.

Warhol buried the Dandy under an avalanche of soup cans. His sensibility distinguishes him not only from artists of the fifties but from other Pop artists as well. With Oldenburg, Segal, Wesselmann, Lichtenstein, America's visual banalities are suspended at the edge of the imagination; in different degrees, the 7-Up bottles and the gasoline pumps seem about to change into something else. In contrast, Warhol purged art-making of every residue of subjectivity. He externalized himself and his creations into an identity as devoid of individual references as a rubber stamp. "If you want to know all about Andy Warhol," he declared, "just look at the surface of my paintings and films and me, and there I am. There's nothing behind it." Of course, this façade—or billboard—personality is a fiction. The all-surface poker face is derived from the gunfighter of the Westerns; before Warhol moved upstage, the long, flat countenance of Jasper Johns recalled that of William S. Hart. The deadpan of the prairies and the mining-town card table is secretly in love with his horse—or with money. Something similar is true of Warhol. And although he hasn't shot anyone, he has been shot. Warhol's mask is a bit too awry to be a face. The interesting question is why the art world has been so eager to be taken in by it. The answer is that for the new collectors, critics, and curators *art* has "nothing behind it." Warhol has been the personification of their experience of art, with a fidelity that has earned him the title of St. Andy—though his self-negation is less that of saintliness than of capital accumulation.

As the fabricator of silk-screened clichés in enamel makeup, Warhol

Andy Warhol, *Flowers*, 1970, silkscreen, 36¹⁄₁₆″ x 36¹⁄₁₆″.

Andy Warhol, *Portrait of Robert Rauschenberg* (with his family), 1963.

presented himself as the made-up artist. His philosophy might be summed up as "I am recognized, therefore I am." For him, the artist is eliminated from the art object except as the supplier of a trademark. In the year of his initial success, he adopted a costume of black leather jacket and silver-sprayed hair and a mask of bewildered non-commitment; the ensemble gave him a faint resemblance to the silver-topped de Kooning, then the Champ of American art. This effigy and the Factory are the initiators of Warhol items, and Warhol united the two by lining his studio with silver foil in reiteration of the emblem of his hair. The creative efforts unexpended on his painting were invested in making the public aware of their source. By 1966, he was in a position to trumpet his triumph and the limitlessness of his art-making capacity by advertising in a newspaper that he would sign anything brought to him, including (without being guilty of megalomania) currency, the value of which he now had the power to increase.

Warhol replaced the Dandy with the non-person, the demiurge of the Factory. As the originator of his all-surface non-works, he has meticulously constructed the figure of the artist as nobody, though a nobody with a resounding signature. His performance has featured an elusiveness of identity centered on the nucleus of his name. "I'd prefer to remain a mystery," he explained in an interview. "I never give my background, and anyway, I make it all up different every time I'm asked." In keeping with this principle of self-substitution is his origination of the artist's stand-in—friends sent to impersonate him at openings and at lectures. Testing whether he will be recognized is an aspect of his passion for fame and perhaps of a genuine doubt about who he is. Part organization man (he is president of Andy Warhol Films, Inc.), part cult-gang leader, he moves surrounded by a company that participates in the execution of his works. He boasts that his taste is that of the man in the street: "The artificial fascinates me, the bright and shiny." This is as good an explanation as any of his fondness for lavenders, oranges, greens, and pinks in his paintings. He might have added that horrors fascinate him—criminals, "celebrities," and erotica. Like other tabloid readers, he has snapped up images ranging from bleeding demonstrators to weekend supermarket specials in a single gulp, and he has marketed them with the color devices of product packaging without altering their psychic blankness.

In demonstrating that art today is a commodity of the art market, comparable to commodities of other specialized markets, Warhol has liquidated the century-old tension between the serious artist and the majority culture. His art is, essentially, an art for the masses—a fact not altered by its "élitist" price tag. By way of the popular media, he has reawakened the 1930s idea of the artist as mass man, though "mass boy" would be more accurate in regard to his style, which is related to motorcycle bands and acid-rock crowds.. His patrons have been mass men with money who, in a momentous development, have overcome the traditional American deference before the culture of Europe and its masterpieces. Warhol marks the point in Western culture after which art is destined to contend for its survival against the flux of the popular media.

Another significant Warhol innovation is the artist who has a limited engagement with art. He has not abandoned painting, but from the start he has manifested a readiness to depart. Though Duchamp publicly repudiated creation, he remained permanently attached to the art world as the normal habitat of the man of imagination. In contrast, Warhol sees no privilege in art as an activity, and, as we have learned, for him the artist is devoid of individual attributes. After five years, he terminated his career in the art galleries and transferred himself and his "apparatus" to the milieu of the discothèque and the movies. The Whitney Museum retrospective took its form from Warhol's refusal to present a continuity related to the inner continuity of an individual. At his insistence, the exhibition was limited to five themes, repeated as on sheets of postage stamps: soup cans, Brillo boxes, portraits, tabloid catastrophes, and flowers.

A retrospective is a résumé of an artist's development. Instead of development, which both he and his work lack, Warhol presented a career of five separate "acts," any one of which could have been the last. This amounts to an assertion that for the contemporary artist art lacks necessity and is dispensable; art today is what one can make of it. It possesses no intrinsic qualities that invite devotion. For de Kooning, art has been "a way of living"; for Warhol, it is part of one's self-projection or something to do for gain. By the force of his indifference, Warhol strips painting and sculpture of any shreds of transcendence left over from their religious and metaphysical past. He is the prophet of the Minimalist art of the sixties that sought to allude to nothing beyond itself. But he gives dramatic clarification to Minimalism by minimalizing the artist, too, and the world he inhabits. The thoroughness of his anti-illusionism, his systematic "I-am-what-I-seem," make Warhol the hero of art of the period that followed Abstract Expressionism.

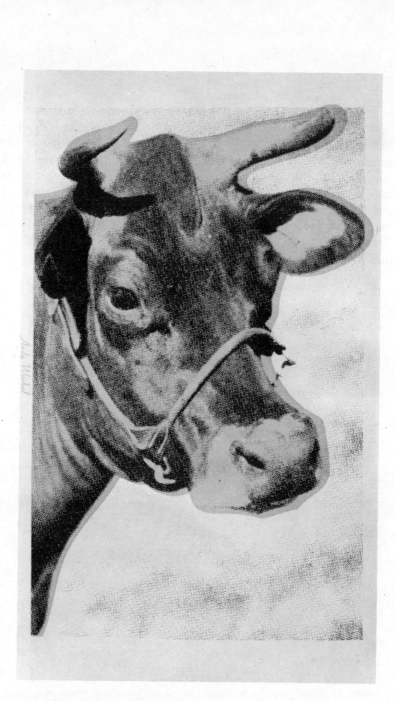

Andy Warhol, *Cow Poster*, 1966, silkscreen.
DAVID WHITNEY COLLECTION, COURTESY LEO CASTELLI GALLERY, NEW YORK

Since the war, the American artist has been emerging from behind imported disguises. The artist as Dandy, the self-proclaimed aristocrat of feeling and sensibility, had grown seedy and somewhat ridiculous, like the Devil in *The Brothers Karamazov*. Art today needs a new protagonist, and Warhol's detached art-supplier with Hollywood-style ambitions has the virtue of grounding himself in the realities of the current art situation. His weakness is that he expresses no desire to change that situation and suggests nothing capable of doing so. In the Warhol perspective, the dissolution of painting into the mass media has already taken place. But the drama of art today lies in the possibility that it still has the vigor to produce its own type of creator.

10

Steinberg: Self and Style

When I look at a scene in the country, I see a signature in the lower right-hand corner.
—*Saul Steinberg*

An expectation of irony hovers over an exhibition of works by Saul Steinberg—it creates an intellectual tension even when the irony itself is absent. For example, *Country Still Life*, in Steinberg's recent show at the Sidney Janis Gallery, is a lyrical drawing in colored pencil with flowers and a view through the glass doors of Steinberg's living room in eastern Long Island. It is a picture of things Steinberg cherishes, and it makes no demands on the spectator. The exhibition, however, was made up largely of strange, multi-sectioned landscapes stamped with circular seals like random moons and of assemblages on boards of pens, pencils, paintbrushes, and drawing tablets that were not pens, pencils, paintbrushes, and drawing tablets but simulations carved out of wood. Flanked by these ambiguous creations, the still-life was scrutinized for what its ostensible innocence might be hiding. Detailed examination was needed to ascertain that this particular cigar was not going to explode.

Over the years, Steinberg has frequently made drawings and paintings for the sheer pleasure of doing them, and without the surprises of his cartoons—but even they have tended to end up with ulterior purposes. For instance, his half-comical counterfeiting of modern masters

Saul Steinberg, *Collection*, 1971, mixed media on wood.
COURTESY NATIONAL COLLECTION OF FINE ARTS, SMITHSONIAN INSTITUTION, WASH-
INGTON, D. C.

—Mondrian, van Gogh—came in handy for his ingenious takeoff of an art show in his exhibition at the Betty Parsons Gallery which ran concurrently with the one at the Janis: a mimic picture gallery was presented in perspective by means of a row of painted vertical slats that became narrower and shorter toward the center. Steinberg is a craftsman whose skill drifts into ideas—as when his hand whips out at full speed a bit of his complex calligraphy, and he then applies it to a wooden cutout of a comic-strip "balloon" and uses it as an element in his collages. (At the Janis, a six-foot-long official-looking scroll, *Dogma,* carried Steinberg's penmanship to new heights of monumental illegibility, and suggested that he should have been commissioned to execute the document of the Vietnam cease-fire.)

Technique is Steinberg's apparatus for arriving at philosophical insights. Through drawings, paintings, and assembled images, he investigates the process by which art and reality are interchanged. He has discovered, for example, that a picture, no matter how farfetched, will be given credence as readily as an object seen on the street. Hence images in different aesthetic modes can be juxtaposed in the same setting, as in *Waiting Room,* in which two male heads are shaped like daggers, exclamation points, or figures by Giacometti, and two children have the heads of cartoon animals. Conversely, an actual thing will be seen as a picture, especially if one paints a bit of shadow alongside it, as Steinberg has done with wooden boxes in some of the collages Like the trompe-l'oeil painters, Steinberg revels in deception; but he goes beyond the simple magic of pictures mistaken for objects to show how devices by which the spectator is fooled can be repeated and inverted—as when the fake box is a real box that has been made to look fake—and that *there is no point at which the "real object" is finally unveiled.* Appearances in nature can be duplicated, but it is no longer necessary to duplicate them in order to achieve credibility. With the immense accumulation of styles in all categories of image-making, from paintings by naïves to computerized nudes, almost any mark on a surface can be viable as the sign of something—in *Five Women and Two Landscapes,* each of the seven units belongs to a different manner of handling, including primitive, Impressionist, comic-strip, naturalistic, and geometrical, and the cutouts are in aluminum, canvas, wood, and cardboard.

Style, with its power of creating assent (and thus deception), is Steinberg's ultimate subject matter. Each mode in art is in its beginnings the realization of a mood or sentiment—for example, the Barbizon mood in contrast to that of Art Nouveau. This characteristic mood remains locked in the images done in the given style, whether in its masterpieces, in its imitations, or in its mass reproductions. As the style keeps reappearing, however, in works of diminishing quality, its emotional content is coarsened and reduced to a reflex of its most easily recognized features, as in the piled-on paint of late Abstract Expressionism. Thus, styles survive as masks, or as masquerades, of the original feeling embodied in them. Steinberg has grasped the history of art as a form language of ready-made sentiments, at once self-evident and spurious, like the beard of Santa Claus or the red heart of a valentine. Available styles, including styles abandoned by art, provide the substance by which the popular arts are welded to the masterworks of the past. Steinberg accepts all art present in the contemporary consciousness as charged visual matter out of which he can mold moods to which he need not commit himself. They are the ideal vocabulary for a pictorial autobiography that can be exhibited without giving oneself away.

The exhibitions at the Janis and Parsons galleries consisted, in the main, of two groups of works: oil-on-paper landscapes that recalled places visited in the past two years, and drawing-table assemblages related to inner events of the same period. In both groups, touches of stylistic anachronism conveyed overtones of nostalgia and, occasionally, loneliness, but in externalized and impersonal terms. In Steinberg's art, estrangement itself is estranged through being projected into other times; critics who fail to penetrate this method of universalization of feeling disparage Steinberg as excessively cool and remote. In several of the landscapes, low-lying foregrounds and immense empty skies, with a pinkish-yellow glow at the horizon, mimic the solitary shoreline panoramas of American scene paintings of a century ago. An oddity of the landscapes is their division into two or more separate scenes, as if snapshots taken in the same general locality had been fastened together on a page. In the prim literalness of their handling, they might be colored illustrations accompanying an old report of a surveying expedition or an oil-drilling operation. Where these activities occurred, however, and what happened cannot be determined from the pictures. Titles such as *Kunming* and *Ottumwa*, which sound Asian and African (Ottumwa is actually in Iowa), convey a sense of distant places, and in some of the landscapes there are queer-looking machines and barely perceptible figures whose costumes suggest that they are natives or adventuring Westerners; they confront the spectator full face, as if get-

Saul Steinberg, *Five Women and Two Landscapes.*
PRIVATE COLLECTION. PHOTO BY GEOFFREY CLEMENTS

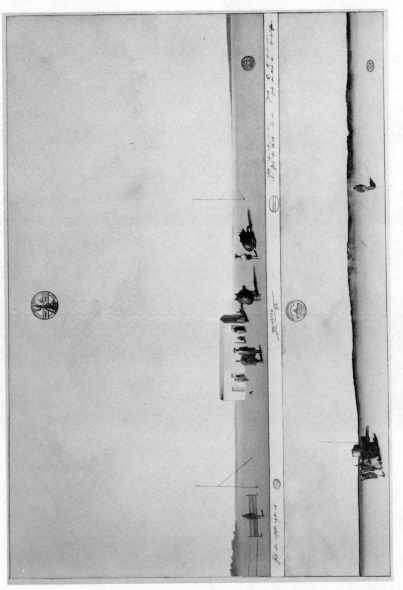

Saul Steinberg, *Kunming*, 1972, oil on paper, 29″ x 40″.
HARRY N. ABRAMS FAMILY COLLECTION, NEW YORK, COURTESY SIDNEY JANIS GAL-
LERY, NEW YORK. PHOTO BY GEOFFREY CLEMENTS

ting their pictures taken, or stand with their backs to him, waiting in what might be a desert. At the Betty Parsons, many of the landscapes identified themselves as Egyptian by pyramids towering in the background. In contrast, a few of the place-names were of Long Island villages—Sag Harbor, Wainscott—near Steinberg's country residence.

Steinberg refers to these paintings of places as "postcards," perhaps because they are souvenirs of travel and are done in a deliberately debased style reminiscent of mass-produced beauty. They are, too, conventionalized messages available to anyone; and they can be reproduced as postcards (copies of works of art that copied postcards), as has actually been done with a Steinberg landscape of an earlier series. They are "postcards" also because Steinberg thinks of painting them as a "non-intellectual" pleasure, compared to the conception of his cartoons, drawings, and collages.

Here and there, the landscapes bear rubber-stamped insignia, which may signify that they were stamped on their way through Steinberg's metaphysical post office or were certified as authentic by the authorities that rule his made-up world. The seals also appear on the assemblages called *Tables*. Apparently, they serve a purpose similar to that of the fingerprints in Steinberg's drawings of several years ago—the purpose of identification. They are the artist's mark, and they declare that the subject of these creations is his own self. But, of course, the seals are not fingerprints, as the fingerprints of the past were not fingerprints but reproductions of fingerprints. They are signs produced by rubber stamps ("inked," incidentally, with oil paint rather than the ink pad, hence not even conventional rubber stamps), and they are not a unique identifying mark but a prefabricated cliché, a trademark imprinted on a professionally made and distributed commodity. Thus Steinberg straddles the contradictory functions that constitute the reality of art in our time: on the one hand, the use of art by the artist to affirm his identity in his work; on the other, his use of it as an object for the art market and the museum. Steinberg's subjective autobiography consists of creations in which these conflicting motives have been symbolically synthesized. It is the ironic biography of an abstract personage whose practice encompasses the dramatic polarities of contemporary creation.

Steinberg began the *Tables* by idly whittling wooden copies of pencils, pens, paintbrushes, rulers, notebooks, and drawing pads, and painting them to resemble the real things; an added item was carved versions of the balloons that carry dialogue in comic strips. Unlike

Cubist or Dada collage, nothing in the *Tables* is a found object, though their entire contents are commonplace and, with the exception of the balloons, could be obtained in art-supply stores. The paraphernalia of the studio which constitute the *Tables* are objects of a special sort: they belong to the realm of material things, yet they are extensions of the artist's self; they are the connection between him and his creations, thus objects transformed into subject.

Steinberg underscores the subjectivity of the pencils and paintbrushes by the fact that they are not taken from the external world but are made by the artist. In putting together these whittlings, Steinberg assembled bits of himself—his organs, so to speak. The *Tables* are mementos of decisions to confront the public with the results of a gratuitous playing with the forms of things grown intimate through daily use. Enclosed in Plexiglas, they are a parody of objects in the display cases of a museum. The satire includes the bitter point that in making himself visible the artist by the same means submits to being entombed. Representing buried creation, the *Tables* are, in mood, miniatures of the worktable at which an architectural draftsman (*T Square*) or an eccentric bookkeeper (*Colored Pencils*) dissipates his span of life in the monotony of a Bartleby. Arranged in symmetrical groupings, as if by a neat head clerk, they have an atmosphere that is technological but is not of contemporary technology—they convey the nostalgia of worn wooden penholders, chewed pencil stubs, imported-bonbon boxes now used to hold paperclips.

Like the landscapes, the *Tables* give an account of the artist's life in terms that are generalized and betray no secrets. For the artist, the implements he uses in his art are the objects of his deepest feelings—his "erotica," Steinberg calls them—and the model of what he experiences as indubitably personal. In the assemblage called *Portrait*, Steinberg put his past, his art, and his affections on the same level: a plaque labelled "Milano, 1935" commemorates the city where Steinberg began his career; a balloon inscribed with illegible handwriting represents a floating statement without a speaker; a pen, a pencil, brushes, and a ledger are relics of the artist at work; and an open page of a trompe-l'oeil drawing pad shows a pencil portrait of the young woman who is the artist's friend.

On television, P.O.W.'s returning from Hanoi were shown passing the time by watching P.O.W.s returning from Hanoi on television. A man

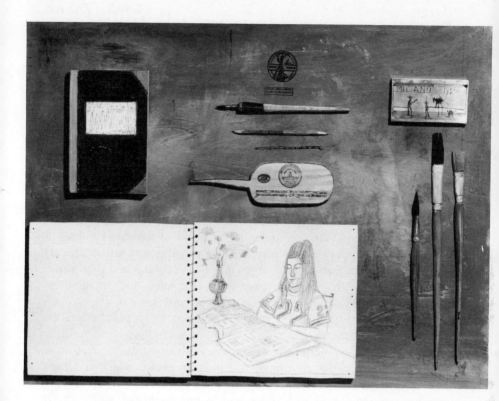

Saul Steinberg, *Portrait*, 1971, polychrome wood, 23″ x 31″.
COLLECTION, ZAIRA MIS, BRUSSELS, COURTESY SIDNEY JANIS GALLERY, NEW YORK.
PHOTO BY GEOFFREY CLEMENTS

rows across Main Street to buy a newspaper reporting his town is flooded. We have entered an epoch in which nothing is real until it has been reproduced. With events and their copies standing in for each other, like twins in Elizabethan comedy, the objective form of modern culture has become the farce of mistaken identity. Facts no longer enjoy any privilege over various renderings of them. The victory of objective farce was proclaimed at the time of the Hitler-Stalin Pact in the statement of Molotov that facts are nothing but propaganda. It was in exactly this period that the art of Steinberg began its development in Milan. Fugitive from fascism in the years that followed, immigrant to the Western Hemisphere, O.S.S. operative in China during the war, Steinberg is the inspired medium of mid-twentieth-century "information" culture, including its flashes of loneliness and sentimentality. Enacting the interplay between actuality and artifice, his art is a species of realism with a unique claim to accuracy and pertinence. Long before Pop Art, his drawings exemplified the merging of museum art with the popular media, and the conversion of art, through consciousness of its own history, into an aspect of popular education and entertainment.

But though Steinberg's art lies at the center of the debate on the relation between the art object and non-art nature which has been preoccupying the art world, he remains an outsider. He is the only major artist in the United States who is not associated with any art movement or style, past or present. Nor has art history found a place for Steinberg, perhaps for the reason that he has swallowed its subject matter—the evolution of styles—and regurgitated it as a mass of expressive leftovers. Cubism, for example, which in the vision of the American art historian is the core of twentieth-century formal development, is to Steinberg merely another figure in the pattern of contemporary moods. In thus dissolving art history into its original imaginative components, Steinberg stands at the outermost edge of the current art situation—a Duchamp who has transcended anti-art by exposing the power of form within every level of human expression, from children's drawings to the shape of letters in the alphabet. In theory, Steinberg is today's avant-garde, except that, by definition, a single person cannot be an avant-garde. Thus, Steinberg's role automatically disguises itself, and his performance continues to prompt people to ask, "But is he really an artist?"—the question by which each legitimate avant-garde has been greeted. Other avant-gardists—Pollock, Warhol, Newman, conceptualists, earth artists—succeeded in raising this question for varying intervals, then were naturalized into the museum world. The genius of Steinberg is to have kept the question alive about himself for thirty years.

11

Giacometti: Reality at Cockcrow

As a legend, Giacometti is a match for Duchamp, though of an opposite order: against the celebrated impresario of non-works ("ready-mades"), he represents the absolute worthwhileness of engaging in the processes of creating sculptures and paintings. His elongated thin figures, axe-blade heads, and portraits in oil and pencil have aroused more notions about their meanings than have the works of any other artist of his generation. Giacometti turns the human body and physiognomy into a metaphysical substance. Picasso, who regarded him as his sole competitor in fame, said that he had conceived "a new spirit in sculpture." Breton, Genet, and Sartre—names outside those that usually swell the bibliographies of museum catalogues—have written of him as one who enlarged their points of view. He was close to Beckett, and is said to have realized the theory of perception of Merleau-Ponty, the Sisyphean vision of Camus, and the narrative reductionism of the *nouveau roman*. In the introduction to the catalogue of the large retrospective at the Guggenheim Museum. Reinhold Hohl, also the author of the exhaustive *Alberto Giacometti*, found himself obliged to deny that the thinness of Giacometti's personages (who include an emaciated cat and dog) has to do with war, famine, or concentration camps, "as has often been proposed." Nor, in Hohl's opinion, does a work such as *The Cage*, in which a bodiless male head on a long, stringy neck confronts an erect, pencil-thin mummy of the same height, stand for "existential solitude." Yet, for all his objections to inflated interpretations, Hohl identified Giacometti's women with "the myth of Life"—a myth that culminated in the monumental group that was planned for the Chase Manhattan Plaza but never executed—and he concluded that "Giacometti belongs among the artists who set a milestone not only for their own century but for a millennium."

Hohl's conception of Giacometti as a thousand-year artist is in line with the overtones of fable of Giacometti's art itself. His sculptures and paintings are overlaid with intimations of antique mysteries: Egyptian tomb deities, sentinels in the desert, darkening caverns. Giacometti's imagination is anthropological. His giant buried up to the shoulders at the feet of an array of entranced vestals (*Composition with Seven Figures and a Head* [*The Forest*]); his erect nudes with bodies and faces eroded by time (*Large Figure*), and others with tiny heads but features starkly detailed, as in a dream (*Woman of Venice II*); his male heads poised piteously on stakes, like victims of a jungle massacre (*Head of a Man on a Rod*)—all these are evocative less of the art of the past than of its rituals, celebrants, and talismans. Giacometti "museumizes" his subjects; in *The Cage* and *Figure Between Two Houses* the figures appear in display cases, and his completer portraits are built into frames drawn on the canvas—often a succession of frames, one inside another, receding into the distance. His sitters, including his brother and his wife, who modelled for him continually, as well as passersby on the street, are taken out of time and transformed into exhibits. Yet the museum into which they have entered is not an art museum but a museum of man, of ways of life alien to Western idealizations.

Extending into fable, Giacometti's theatre without words reaches at the same time into contemporary fact. The rigid, hieratic women, arms pinioned to their sides, suggest temporal remoteness. But they are also women of our day, seen according to certain spatial hypotheses, and the sitters for his portraits, for all their odd staring and removed location, wear sweaters and business suits and pose in the artist's messy studio. Basic to Giacometti's vision is the phenomenon of distance, in actual space and in the psychology of seeing. Observed from afar, a standing figure appears to be fused into a narrow, compact monolith, armless and with legs grown together into a tree trunk, while a walking figure is surprisingly slender and long-legged, as are Giacometti's reedlike men. In his art, stick figures of the kind incised on the walls of caves become pedestrians in chance combinations on busy street corners. The celebrated wedge-shaped heads of his brother, Diego, with their uncanny likeness, are demonstrations of Giacometti's notion

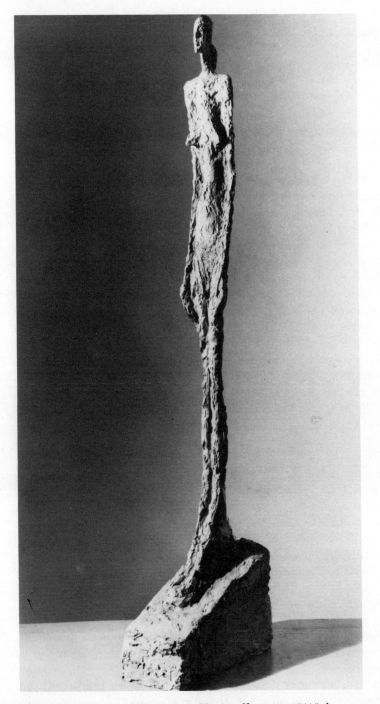

Alberto Giacometti, *Woman of Venice II*, 1956, 47½″ h.,
painted bronze.

that where the gazes of the right eye and the left intersect, the width of objects diminishes toward zero and a head consists of a wafer of two profiles, a ketchup bottle of a vertical red line. Narrowing and elongation, accompanied by a strange fixity and transparency, occur, too, in faces seen reflected in a bottle or a convex mirror.

With Giacometti, one may also speak of metaphysical distance—the space by which the dead are separated and in which they are enveloped, and the space of apparitions. Throughout his life the artist recalled two decisive experiences when he was about twenty, during a trip to Italy; each resulted in a radical transformation of his apprehension of size and distance. One was the sudden death of a travelling companion, who thought he would be better the next day but of whom Giacometti recalled that "by late afternoon I had the feeling his nose was growing longer." Then his friend was dead, "had turned into an object," and things "started to fall apart." The dead are smaller and less material than the living; they weigh less. Giacometti's sense of the separation and motionlessness of objects, of space as a void in which all physical contact has foundered, was what impressed Sartre. Giacometti himself described in rather melodramatic terms ("I looked at my room in terror," "cold sweat ran down my back") the way he saw the furniture in his studio become weightless and immobile, the legs of the table not resting on the floor but barely touching it. Later, it occurred to him that weightlessness was the explanation of why his sculptured figures were so thin. He also associated this impression with the absence of weight of people who pass one on the street—a way of saying that the flowing crowd is a throng of ghosts, as in Eliot's *The Waste Land*. "All living things," said Giacometti, "were dead, and this vision often recurred, in the Métro, on the street, in restaurants."

The other experience that changed Giacometti's apprehension of things came while he was walking through the streets of Padua, painfully trying to resolve conflicting feelings aroused by the impact of Giotto on his admiration for Tintoretto. "These contradictory feelings shrank to nothing when I saw two or three young girls walking in front of me. They appeared immense to me, all out of proportion to normal size. . . . I stared at them like a madman, fear shot through me. It was like a fissure in reality. . . . The connections between things had changed." For Giacometti, the "two or three" oversized girls (it is notable that he is vague about the number but absolutely positive about the total impression) became the representation of "reality"—a reality that stood against art, even at its highest (Giotto), and nulli-

Alberto Giacometti, *Head of a Man on a Rod*, 1947, bronze,
21¾″ h.

fied it. The vision of the girls and the vision of the companion alive one moment and turned into an object the next had in common the suddenness and unexpectedness of the metamorphosis. Reality became defined for Giacometti as a flash struck from dead space by an ecstatic apprehension of particulars. This dual theme of death as an impassable distance and of reality as a transcendental glimpse recurs in each phase of his career, accompanied by episodes of shock and illumination. One day he leaves a movie house and sees the Boulevard Montparnasse "as I had never seen it before. . . . Everything appeared different to me and completely new." Twenty years later, James Lord, after numerous sittings for his portrait, observed that "if Giacometti cannot feel that something exists truly for the first time, then it will not really exist for him at all." The identifying mark of the newborn reality, painfully sought in the portraits through repeatedly painting out likenesses, is an evanescent presence; he had hold of it, he told Lord, but "stopped five minutes too late." Giacometti's formal devices consist of his otherworld stagings of his subjects, as in the live-wire highlighting of the blackened faces of his portraits and in their backgrounds that sink into nowhere, or the amazed staring of his busts of Annette, as if she had been transported to some non-terrestrial realm, or the truncated and incomplete bodies on which his heads are mounted. In his search for their final image, Giacometti portrays his sisters in the process of being lost, and barely prevented from disappearing like ghosts at cockcrow.

Giacometti's moods, his rhetoric of fear and despair, his symbolism of death and isolation associate him with the Existentialists. In addition, his major style—the elongated sculptured figures—belongs to the period of Existentialist prominence, the years immediately following the last great war, although he had been a well-known Surrealist in the thirties and his *Palace at 4 A.M.* is an outstanding Surrealist masterpiece. In the journalism of art, all new creations of 1945–55 are "Existentialist." (The label has been applied also to the American Abstract Expressionists, and with much less justification.) Actually, however, there is no such thing as Existentialist painting and sculpture. Existentialism, a tendency in philosophy and literature, never developed a style in the plastic arts. "People talk so much . . . about Existential anxiety," Giacometti remarked, "as if it were something new! Everyone at every period in history felt it. You only have to read the Greek and Latin authors!" He broke with Surrealism in 1935, but his practice as an artist owes more to Surrealism than to Sartre, Camus, or Merleau-Ponty. The glorifying of surprise in his seeing and as an aim in his work was basic to Surrealism, too; like his Padua girls, Breton's Nadja identified herself as a super-reality by the suddenness of her presence. Mystery, dissociated images, primitive signs, exaggerated and distorted perspectives, chance meetings, fabulous coincidences belong to the Surrealist prescriptions for circumventing the everyday. "The state of expectation," wrote Breton in 1934, "is wonderful, no matter whether the expected arrives or not. That was the subject of a long chat I had with my friend Alberto Giacometti."

Giacometti parted with the Surrealists on the issue of "reality," but his conception of how to attain that reality drew upon the heritage of Surrealist conjurations. His new style emerged through a species of automatism: "I wanted to make her [the model] about eighty centimetres [thirty-one and a half inches] high. To make a long story short: she got so small that I couldn't put any more details on the figure. It was a mystery to me. All my figures stubbornly shrank to one centimetre high." Later, his figures reversed themselves, and, with the same autonomy, became tall and thin. In his application of Surrealist processes to non-Surrealist ends, Giacometti is a post-Surrealist—or, preferably, since he extended Surrealism by contradicting it, an anti-Surrealist. More important in regard to his work than the ideology of Existentialism is the fact that his art *carries the psychic revolution of Surrealism into new regions of experience*. The postwar American abstractionists had a parallel relation to Surrealism, but they developed their styles on a narrower theoretical basis.

Surrealist aesthetics presupposes a dual world—that of the ordinary and that of the mythic. For Breton, actuality could be taken for granted: its reproduction had been successfully assumed by the camera. Relieved (or deprived) of his old function of looking, the artist had become a "seer," according to Rimbaud's prophetic vision. Giacometti's defection from Surrealism came with his return to nature, to the study of the model. To Breton, this could mean nothing but abandonment of the imagination and a surrender to the conventional view of things. "A head," he protested, "everybody knows what a head is!" It was precisely the Surrealist notion of a reality exhausted by common knowledge which Giacometti had resolved to challenge. Everybody knows what a head is at first glance—but that glance has grasped only an abstraction. A head looked at for a long time becomes increasingly strange and inaccessible. What is more "arbitrary" than a nose—and the way it is attached to the face? Or that human faces are wrapped in skin, a cat's face in fur? Giacometti had discovered the "fissure in reality," the change in the connections of things, that made ordinary subjects more imaginatively prolific than the dream.

There is a hiatus of seven years in Giacometti's accomplishment after 1935; apparently his break with Surrealism reached very deep. When I met him in Paris in 1951, his new style in sculpture had become famous, yet he was still replying mentally to Breton. Reality, he assured me, had by no means been commandeered by the camera; there was an absolute difference between people on a movie screen and people in the street. His ambition was to paint a café or a taxi just as it was. "*I* can be boring. Reality never!" was his rejoinder to Breton's fear of the banal. His sculptured groups of pedestrians possessed, in his view, a political content distinct from both Surrealism and Marxism: in them the individual appeared neither as the isolated ego of the dreamer nor as the regimented marcher of totalitarian politics but as a participant in the ever-shifting relations of actual existence. This concept is visually confirmed by a sculpture such as *City Square*, whose five figures create the illusion of constantly changing places.

In Surrealist paintings and collages, art images mingle with impressions of daily life, as they do in the Freudian analysis of dreams—for example, Ernst's gentlemen in dinner jackets but with the heads of Egyptian bird deities. For Giacometti, with his goal of "reality," art was the obstacle that stood in the way of truth. "The more I studied the model, the thicker the veil between its reality and me became. At first one sees the person posing, but little by little all the sculptures one can imagine interpose themselves." Thus, in each work the artist begins his task by putting himself in the condition of one totally lacking in the technical means for carrying it out. In his anti-Surrealist mode, Giacometti sought to impose upon himself the limitations of the primitive or naïve artist. Like a self-educated painter, he placed himself at the mercy of his subject. His assumption of naïveté in his day-to-day drama of incapacity and failure is the subject of James Lord's remarkable notes on posing for the artist over a period of almost three weeks.* Lord questioned Giacometti about his "technique" for translating his "vision into something which is visible to others."

* James Lord, *A Giacometti Portrait* (New York: Museum of Modern Art, 1965).

"That's the whole drama," Giacometti replied. "I don't have such a technique." He then said that despite his excellent training he had never been able to paint what he saw. "So I had to start all over again from scratch . . . and things have been going from bad to worse."

The struggle for perceived reality is a struggle against inherited styles—an extreme reversal of values introduced by modern art. (In the past art took its departure from imitation of styles.) The effort to realize images independent of known art forms has long been a feature of American painting, as part of the aim of depicting the New Land; this experience may account for the emergence of American artists after the war as leaders in the final phase of modernism. Giacometti was ideally qualified for the modernist role of divesting himself of his training and talent in order "to see a landscape instead of seeing a Pissarro." An exhibition at the Guggenheim running concurrently with the Giacometti retrospective—*Three Swiss Painters*—of canvases by Giovanni Giacometti, Alberto's father, by Cuno Amiet, his god-father, and by Augusto Giacometti, his father's second cousin, showed the skill, sensitivity, and sophistication of the artists among whom Giacometti was brought up. Augusto in particular stands at the aesthetic peak of his time, with an individual Art Nouveau style and pioneering excursions into abstract art; *Summer Night* is a lyrical anticipation of Hans Hofmann. Giacometti was literally born into an avant-garde academy; he had only to go forward under the influence that surrounded his cradle. Before he was fourteen, he was able to draw so well from nature that he was convinced he could "copy absolutely anything" At sixty, he could only repeat, "It's impossible to reproduce what one sees. . . . I've been wasting my time for thirty years. The root of the nose is more than I can hope to manage."

It is Giacometti's practice of art as ignorance in the Socratic sense that has endeared him to philosophers and poets. He had found the means for attaining to the springtime of direct intuition, the vision of "the first man." Sartre spoke of him as placing himself "at the beginning of the world," a contemporary of the cave painters of Altamira. Painting and sculpting are transformed into a process of knowing and self-knowing; "whether an art work is a failure or a success," Giacometti said, "is, in the end, of secondary importance." The repudiation of aesthetic objectives makes finishing a painting impossible, since reality has no formal goal. The artist is "only working for the sake of

Alberto Giacometti, *Annette*, 1961, oil on canvas, 21⅝" x 18⅛".
THE HIRSCHHORN MUSEUM AND SCULPTURE GARDEN, SMITHSONIAN INSTITUTION,
WASHINGTON, D. C.

the experience that I feel when working," and he could keep busy forever on a single canvas, producing a rubble of feelings, sensations, perceptions, all passé, like those in a stack of rejected photographs or the chaos discovered at the end of Balzac's *The Unknown Master-piece*. Giacometti brought work on Lord's portrait to a finish when he was given a deadline for shipping it to an exhibition. Basically, the artist paints the struggle between himself and his subject. In the Lord portrait, the struggle is represented in the circling lines, the darkening tones, the background masses, the white neon highlighting. There are intervals in this transaction in which the painting comes to life. The reality of James Lord keeps appearing and slipping away. Yet each act of return is a further separation from the mere appearance of the sitter. Liberating himself from the habits of the eye and the preconceptions of the hand, the artist attains an automatism that is the opposite of letting go.

An artist who interprets his own creations rarely lacks collaborators. Giacometti's legend focuses on his inability to attain the real, a legend consistent with the literature of Existentialism. With or without Existentialist editorializing, his striving to circumvent existing forms continues the tradition of self-estrangement from nature and society that is inherent in advanced art. That there was nothing in art that he could not do lent significance to his complaints that he could do nothing—for this consummate craftsman to exclaim, "If one could only paint a tree!" was to raise bottomless questions as to what painting a tree means; it calls to mind Magritte's Surrealist painting of a pipe with the legend *This Is Not a Pipe*. Like Duchamp, Giacometti was aware of the impression he was creating, and he kept recounting the chief episodes of his history and revising them. In their sum, they achieve a greater unity and coherence than are possible in autobiography. "Giacometti," writes Hohl, "corrects 'yesterday's facts' with 'today's truths.' " For an artist to whom past art is no longer available as a standard of reference, mythmaking and myth management are essential in order to shape the aesthetic identity that gives meaning to his creations.

The exhibition at the Guggenheim of more than two hundred sculptures, paintings, drawings, prints, and other items covered the entire career of Giacometti and, through the accompanying *Three Swiss Painters* show, extended into early-twentieth-century styles that he absorbed and surpassed. The Guggenheim ramp, which prevents the

sculptures from being seen from behind, was favorable to the frontal-
ity intended by the artist. But the spiral ramp and the Museum's open
center were totally destructive of the aura of an enclosed silence
which Giacometti's hieratic figures generate. The show emphasized
the degree to which the Guggenheim Museum was designed to display
artwares for people moved along by the descending curve, and its
imperviousness, by no means accidental, to any atmosphere but that
emanating from the aesthetics of Frank Lloyd Wright. The ramp
assembles works in a linear order like the glass-covered bins of the
Automat, with which Wright's work is contemporaneous. Giacometti's sculptures call for an environment of a different order—one in
which space is taken out of circulation. Related in their mysteries to
semblances once glimpsed in shrines and sacred groves, they require
four walls or a raised platform.

II. REFLECTIONS

12

Criticism and Its Premises

The first requirement of art criticism is that it shall be relevant to the art under consideration; how correct are its evaluations of specific art objects is of lesser importance. The accuracy of a critic's judgments cannot be determined by his contemporaries, in any case. But the inflection given by art criticism to the general thinking about art affects not only the responses of appreciators of art but the creative attitudes of artists as well. When this thinking is trivial or beside the point, painting and sculpture become the specialty of feature writers, decorators, dealers, and speculators in masterpieces.

In order to be relevant, art criticism today must maintain a continuing sensitivity to major characteristics peculiar to the modern epoch which affect the situation of art, including the outlook, rituals, and objectives of those who create it. A mind blind to the radical material, social and intellectual innovations of the twentieth century, and the influence of these innovations upon contemporary modes of creation can only respond to significant modern works with confusion and/or bitterness. For such a mind, criticism has one purpose: to provide a defensive barrier against new work and new ideas by applying "values" presumably drawn from the great achievements of the past. Criticism so oriented leads neither to intelligent perusal of individual works nor to genuine debate concerning the cultural losses and gains of modernism. It merely drops a curtain of polemics between the critic and the artist and contributes to the estrangement of the public from all art, past as well as present, since only through apprehending, by means of present-day creations, how art is created, can the creations of other periods be genuinely appreciated.

The following are propositions which in my opinion ought to be more or less explicitly recognized by contemporary critical thinking as creating new problems for art and for art criticism.

PROPOSITION 1: That creation of art in the twentieth century is an activity within the politico-cultural drama of a world in the process of remaking itself.

Modern art is saturated with issues and ideologies that reflect the technological, political, social, and cultural revolutions of the past one hundred years. Regardless of the degree to which the individual artist is conscious of these issues, he in fact responds to them in choosing among aesthetic and technical alternatives. By choosing a certain mode of handling line, form, and color he will have affiliated himself with an aesthetic grounded on the obligation of art to communicate judgments of the artist's environment, while a different choice will have identified him with the concept that for art reality is that which comes into being through the act of painting. *Thus, choices having to do with method in art become in practice attitudes regarding the future of man.* Hence, art in our time cannot escape having a political content and moral implications. Criticism that is unaware of this is fatally poverty-stricken.

In the changed relation between art and history, the automatism involved in the application of craft skills has been replaced by acts of the mind occurring *at the very beginning of the making of a work.* Whether these acts be acts of the artist or of the teacher, their effect is to remove art from the realm of habit, manual dexterity, and traditional taste into that of philosophy. In the new situation, art emerges from theory. We shall return to this subject—the new dependence of art upon ideas—in Proposition 3.

The consciousness of standing in the midst of developing events lends urgency to the painter's meditations on possible courses to follow. In the past a single tradition, rather than a selection among possible futures, determined stylistic affiliation. Modern art tends toward separate concentrations of energy and conflicts of will rather than toward homogeneity of style and meaning. The historical consciousness also pervades the art museum, the art gallery, and the private collection in the form of attempts to forecast which trends and personalities in art will survive. Art today shares in the general awareness that tomorrow is being shaped by a relentless weeding out of short-lived impulses. On its profounder levels, modern art is acutely aware of itself as a participant in the contest to affect the future, as one of the powers engaged in giving form to the unknown.

PROPOSITION 2: That the politico-cultural drama has in our century assumed global dimensions and that the artist now works in an environment unbounded by time and place.

Under the unrelaxing pressure of political, social, and intellectual development since World War I, local, regional, and national traditions have been steadily dissolving and are being absorbed into worldwide systems. The individual artist, whether in Tokyo, New York, or São Paulo, is confronted by the activity of art everywhere, without the mediation of an inherited outlook or style. He is confronted, too, by the constant unveiling, through anthropological and archaeological research, of the totality of human thought, belief, and accomplishment.

The almost simultaneous transmission of works and styles throughout the world by means of film and print has brought into being a universal pictorial vocabulary. This communication, however, is restricted to surface approximations. Lacking the scale and texture of the originals, to say nothing of their physical and cultural settings, the reproductions fall short of conveying the experience that gave rise to the artworks themselves. Art in the global interchange tends to appear as consisting of various categories of decoration. The constantly augmented mass of art studied in the form of emotionally vacant images facilitates the rise of new academicism based on abstractions drawn from art history. Contemporary art, especially, is dealt with as if it consisted of designs the emotional and social content of which may be ignored. Also, the description and classification of art as artifacts contributes to the formation of a worldwide bureaucracy with scholarly pretensions concerning the goals of creation.

Thus the internationalization of art becomes a factor contributing to the estrangement of art from the artist. The sum of works of all times and places stands against him as an entity with objectives and values of its own. In turn, since becoming aware of the organized body of artworks as the obstacle to his own aesthetic self-affirmation, the artist is pushed toward anti-intellectualism and willful dismissal of the art of the past.

PROPOSITION 3: That with the weakening of traditional attitudes, assumptions, techniques, and subjects, styles now originate in abstract ideas and idea-based art movements.

Aesthetic programs have replaced regional masterpieces as authority and as inspiration. "Every modern activity," said Paul Valéry, "is dominated and governed by *myths* in the form of *ideologies*" (his italics). The roots of contemporary creation lie not in observations of nature nor in earlier works of art but in theoretical interpretations of these. The new relation of art and ideas has imposed upon art the necessity for a self-consciousness that has rendered skillful copying obsolete. The theoretical content of modern art imposes new demands upon criticism, primarily for clear differentiation between what may be analyzed in a painting or sculpture and what must be left to the intuition of the spectator as unique and inaccessible to language.

PROPOSITION 4: That with change established as the norm of present-day life, the capacity for innovation and for recasting old art into new forms has become a primary virtue in art.

The centrality of art in our civilization depends upon its role as the testing ground of the conditions and possibilities of creation. Imitation of the art of earlier centuries, as that done by Picasso or Modigliani, is carried on not in order to perpetuate ancient values but to demonstrate that new aesthetic orders now prevail. In our era, art that ceases to seek the new becomes at once intellectually insignificant, a species of homecraft. The nature of originality is open to debate—in fact, needs desperately to be debated. But no disagreement exists regarding the value of the new in art. On the other hand, the dedication of art to novelty complicates the problem of values and exposes art to sensationalism and the influence of fashion and publicity.

PROPOSITION 5: That the break between the present and the past makes the future opaque and plunges art into a permanent state of uncertainty.

"No one can say what will be dead or alive tomorrow in literature, philosophy, aesthetics: no one yet knows what ideas and modes of expression will be inscribed on the casualty list, what novelties will be proclaimed."—Valéry

That condition in which the future cannot be depended upon to resemble the past constitutes a state of crisis. Or, if one prefers, a state of permanent expectancy. Under such circumstances art takes as its point of departure the effort *to arrive at or create values* rather than to accommodate itself to existing criteria.

Criticism, too, must seek its values through particular instances—works, artists, art movements—rather than through the application of rules formulated by criticism in advance of the works. The modern mind is tempted to end its suspense by affirming systems of value, including aesthetic systems. Thus, in totalitarian countries the future course of events is charted and the duty is imposed upon art to serve in realizing that future. Means that promise to make art most effective as propaganda—e.g., the idealization of facial expressions and bodily postures—are translated into aesthetic values. The result has been the ruin of art by political dictation. Comparable results have followed attempts in the West to reduce the risks of the unknown through calculating the future direction of art. The following observation of Valéry might be adopted as a critical axiom: "Since, henceforth, we must deal with the *new* of the irreducible type, our future is endowed with *essential unpredictability*."

PROPOSITION 6: That vast shiftings of population, both geographically (through migrations, exiles, displacements) and vertically (through revolutions, mass education, equalization of opportunity), have destroyed the stabilized social character of individuals and brought the problem of identity, personal and collective, into prominence as a theme of contemporary cultural forms.

Art movements in the twentieth century have tended to swing back and forth between extremes of individual self-searching (Surrealism, Abstract Expressionism), self-identification with groups (Regionalism, Social Realism), and technological objectivity (Bauhaus, Optical Art). The rhythms of self-affirmation and self-negation arising from the dialectics of identity stimulate the formation of new modes of art through opposition, overlapping, and merger, as in the rise of Pop Art as a depersonalized counterstatement to Action painting. Impulses toward and away from identity should be recognized by criticism as providing an essential content of modern art, figurative as well as abstract.

PROPOSITION 7: That ours is an epoch of excavations—archaeological, psychoanalytical, philological—which keep emptying into contemporary culture the tombs of all the ages of man.

Absorbing the flood of past art, art in our time continually reconstitutes itself as a theater of revivals. Styles of earlier periods, far and near, from the funerary carvings of the Aztecs to the realism of Courbet, are reawakened as experiences and as slogans by contemporary painting and sculpture.

Modern art is at one with radical politics and with psychotherapy in its fascination with the abyss of lost forms and powers. Like other significant modes of present-day action and research, its explorations periodically lead it to the verge of changing into something else. Thus modern art often crosses over into non-art and adopts anti-art attitudes. Besides augmenting consciousness, this negative strain acts as a lightning rod to divert from society and individuals more perilous temptations to self-surrender—totalitarian politics, drugs, mysticism. The reawakening of forms seems to have a profound function in a culture of change.

No doubt other propositions regarding the groundwork of contemporary art might be added to the seven I have sketched. My purpose, however, is not to be exhaustive but to give examples of the kind of phenomena which criticism must absorb into its consciousness and its vocabulary if it is to grasp the dynamics of current art production. These are matters which artists think about and feel, as do philosophers and men on the street. Unless critical discussion achieves the intellectual scale of our revolutionary epoch, it cannot be taken seriously. In practical fact, current writing on art consists largely of opportunistic sponsorship of trivial novelties and of assertions of personal taste for which support is sought in pedantic references to art history. Mere technical recipes—e.g., shaping of canvases, ways of handling the "edge" of forms—are heralded as if they were goals dreamed of by Giotto and Rembrandt but unattainable by them. As a result, art criticism today is looked down upon by other forms of critical thinking as an unintelligible jargon immersed in an insignificant aestheticism. Of course, specialization has overtaken all learned pursuits in our society; if art and art criticism have become ingrown, so have literature, music, philosophy, sociology, history. Thus each feels justified in attacking the others for being excessively engrossed in their own techniques. Beyond sharing in this common narrowness, however, art criticism consists for the most part of an indescribable compost of promotional copy, theoretical air bubbles, history without perspective, readings of symbols based on gossip and farfetched associations of ideas, visual analyses which the eye refuses to confirm, exhibitionistic metaphor mongering, set phrases manipulated to supply copy for indifferent editors, human-interest coddling of Sunday art-page audiences, in-group name-dropping, ritually repeated nonsense. Given this sum of amateurishness, lack of talent, and willful absurdity, the value of values for art criticism must be the effort to reintroduce art into the framework of humanly serious concerns.

The following is my response to "Charges to the Art Critic" presented to me by the directors of "A Seminar in Art Education for Research and Curriculum Development" held at the Pennsylvania State University in 1965, for which this paper on criticism was commissioned. I take no responsibility for the terminology in which the "charges" were formulated or for the preconceptions underlying them.

Charge #1, first item: *Identify the range of values and/or categories appropriate to making critical judgments of works of art.*

It follows from our premises that the work of art should be evaluated, first of all, as an act performed by a contemporary. It embodies energy and skill directed toward appropriation of what is still alive in art or what is susceptible to resurrection. A genuine work has the effect of demolishing styles and images that have turned into visual conventions; in this destructive activity lies its critical and revolutionary role. By displacing works from which vitality has departed, each new painting helps to define the effective content of current aesthetic culture. It is also an act of unique and original perception; thus it is an event in the self-development of the artist. To its public it reveals connections with other works of art and contributes to an expansion of individual and collective sensibility.

Hence all categories of experience, past and present, from fetishism to laboratory discipline, are potentially relevant in making critical evaluations. The critic's primary act of judgment consists of choosing the modes of insight—aesthetic, psychological, social, metaphysical—which he regards as significant in the particular instance. For instance, in writing about the paintings of Barnett Newman I found it necessary to dwell upon the quality of his taste, his counterstatement to the abstract art from which he derived, the rigor of his logic, his humor, his metaphysics of the sublime. In connection with Gorky and de Kooning the question of the sublime did not arise, nor did the question of taste seem to merit much discussion. In regard to Jasper Johns, my major emphasis was on his technique and his motifs as responses to Abstract Expressionism and to the presence of the new Vanguard Audience in the United States. I also noted the changed mood manifested in his later canvases as bearing upon Johns's aesthetics and as being a clue to his possible development.

The elements to be taken into account by criticism will vary from artist to artist and from one critic to another. So, too, will the stress placed on those elements and the way all are balanced. Each valid piece of critical writing represents a synthesizing act that presents the artist in his simultaneous elaboration of form and content. The medium of the critic's synthesis, like that of the artist, is style. The critic demonstrates his competence by his effectiveness in handling his materials, which consist of words and concepts. A critic who writes badly may have deep insights into painting, but for all his connoisseurship, he is not a critic.

Charge #1, second item: *What steps might be taken to overcome barriers and confusions in critical language?*

In dealing with modern art, criticism is confronted by a flood of new forms, new motives, experimental attitudes. To react intelligently to these, criticism must test itself and develop new forms of insight and expression (e.g., multiple perspectives, a rhetoric hospitable to the ambiguities and paradoxes of art itself).

Reduction of confusion in critical language and of the barriers between criticism and the art to which it is applied should begin in eliminating abstract universals, such as "quality" or "expressive form," which presumably provide a handle for artworks of every time and place. These residues of old systems of essences should be replaced by concrete analyses in a terminology of action, conflict, intention, creative hypothesis.

Charge #2: *Within each system or category, identify the specific concepts and methodologies that make possible critical discourse about works of art.*

The art critic is the collaborator of the artist in developing the culture of visual works as a resource of human sensibility. His basic function is to extend the artist's act into the realm of meaningful discourse. Art in our time is itself criticism. Each painting embodies a choice in regard to available styles and works, including the previous work of its creator, and to the possibilities arising from them. Into this dialogue in pigments the critic interjects a vocabulary of words. Having thus put himself into the act (not, he needs to remind himself, at the invitation of the other performers), he assumes the role of responding with a trained rhetoric to the pantomime of the artists.

Can the critic be anything more than the intruder that artists have traditionally considered him to be? If he is the representative of a social interest, as, for example, a reviewer who coordinates his opinions with the cultural program of a newspaper or propaganda institution, he functions as a kind of policeman on the lookout for misdemeanors. He will not interpret the motives of the artist; he will endeavor to keep art in line. His criticism will consist of reporting delinquencies—the virtues he discovers in paintings will be of the sort that are held up as examples to the wicked. Such a critic has forced himself on art, and he continues in it as a squatter only because there is no way of gettting rid of him.

The critic who is to be the intellectual collaborator of the artist, not his truant officer, must possess, above all, a mind that shares the realities of the painter or sculptor. Besides knowing art, he must be conscious of those processes by which art and life are being transformed. He must have a point of view to affirm; it is this point of view that determines which trends, personages, ideas he will support or combat. An interest in painting may be the result of chance or temperament. The impulse to criticize is inherent in every energetic response to the existing human situation. It is the development and verbal clarification of this impulse that leads to the calling of critic. Knowledge of art is not enough to make one a critic, any more than knowledge of art is enough to make one an artist. The student who turns to art in order to avoid reflecting upon his condition may become a specialist, a scholar, a connoisseur, but not a critic. For the latter exists through curiosity, indignation, and the widest practice of intellectual freedom.

The art critic is the outpost of the art educator. He has made his way into the wilderness of values in which art originates. If he is to be of use, it will be by opening a route into the collectivity of artists and to their creations, present and past.

Each critic tends to return to certain attitudes and phrases. For example, I have, perhaps too emphatically, been insisting that reference to certain features of twentieth-century culture are indispensable to discourse about works of art. I should not, however, like to see those features translated into concepts and organized into a methodology. No systematic approach is viable in art criticism. Nor in my opinion is it desirable for criticism to mimic the techniques or objectives of science. Let the readers of the criticism *find* the "systems" in it, if there be any. The critic who resorts to formulas does so out of laziness, haste, or uneasiness about making himself understood.

Since the past no longer enlightens us about the future, values cannot be abstracted from earlier masterpieces and applied as a measure to current art. By the same token, values cannot be abstracted from current work and held in readiness to classify the art of tomorrow. *In our time values must be created alongside the art which they propose to evaluate.* The intellectual center of gravity of criticism must be capable of shifting with the emphasis of new art. Dealing with creation, criticism must maintain its openness to innovation.

This does not mean that criticism is forced to abdicate before each manifestation of the unfamiliar. Continuity is inherent in events, including events of creation. It is this objective continuity that makes discourse possible. It provides the ground for acts of judgment which can cohere into a living nucleus of values augmented and made more firm by each new encounter with the unfamiliar. The weakness of methodology is that it tends to circumscribe this process of creating value by neutralizing areas of the imagination which cannot be readily absorbed into the conceptual system. The effect is to pulverize criticism into neatly spaced piles of rhetorical powder; for examples one has only to look to the products of our "methodologized" literary criticism.

Charge #3: *Can we assume a continuum of maturity and sophistication in critical insights? If so, what are the elements of such a continuum?*

There are no grounds for assuming that any particular intellectual premises will continue to prevail in criticism, any more than in art itself. Forms, terms, concepts are susceptible to an inner erosion that empties them of meaning or changes their meanings, perhaps even into their opposites. Criticism is in constant danger of losing touch with its object, the work of art, or with its own purpose, enlightenment. It can be significant only through the unforeseeable practice of it by interesting minds and by the appearance of writings addressed to real things. Besides experience, intelligence, and talent, criticism demands also courage and independence—and these, too, cannot be counted upon to answer a roll call.

Today, the outstanding menace to critical consciousness is that in place of an intensification of insights and a deeper awareness of problems there is being substituted a structure of bureaucratic assents. Everyone is in agreement, for instance, that van Gogh is a forerunner of Expressionism, that his heritage is subjectivism, "distortion," and thick paint, and that the value of his paintings is to be found in the fierce efflux of something called "personality." Everyone agrees, too, that Jackson Pollock represents violence and self-abandonment and is thus descended from van Gogh. On the other hand, there is, we are told, an art achieved through rigorous analytical reason, as by Seurat, Mondrian, Albers. Such a collection of received ideas may represent a continuity of sorts; perhaps it is even "mature" and "sophisticated." Its advantage is that it can be handed on to each incoming group of students and that it makes the meanings of works of art as easy to memorize as a deck of cards. But a credo is the opposite of a critical consciousness—and incidentally, not one of the opinions mentioned holds up under analysis: for instance, van Gogh's passion to seize the reality of the object has nothing in common with the fantasizing of German Expressionists with whom he is customarily grouped.

Along with the replacement of criticism by bureaucratically supported articles of faith, there comes into being a bureaucratically supported art with its own vocabulary of mystification and double-talk. In recent years artists have appeared, to say nothing of dealers and reviewers, who study the advance schedules of leading New York museums as leads to the kind of art with which to identify themselves.

Critical continuity depends on an ever-deepening comprehension and clarification of the tradition of the new. There is, for instance, important research to be done in bringing to consciousness attitudes taken for granted in the modern practice of art but ignored or denied in art's public relations; these bear on the issue of the so-called revolutionary or nihilistic nature of twentieth-century painting and sculpture. The tradition of the new in art is a tradition precisely because it transmits desires, ideas, myths of which the receiver is unaware and which he takes for granted as fact. Within this tradition there exists a continuing strain of revolt—against society, against art, against the orders of the mind, against all existing conditions of life and work. This strain, though often submerged, is so fundamental to the integrity of art in our time that when it disappears, as in the Soviet Union, creation ceases. For criticism to extend itself into the future as a coherent energy requires not only intellectual apprehension of the elements that make up the tradition of the new but an unillusioned responsiveness to its rebellious spirit.

Charge #4: *What relationship exists (or should exist) between art criticism and art historical knowledge; between art criticism and art theory; between art criticism and statements of intent or biography of the artists?*

Art criticism today *is* art history, though not necessarily the art history of the art historian. In discussing a painting the critic reports on an act that relates to previous acts of the painter and to events in art. The painter's act could not have taken place without preceding acts of creation by himself and others; and in estimating the value of the work, the critic considers what it has brought to the history of art, as well as to the experiences communicated by art. It is a truism that all art derives from art. To know what has been derived from whom and in what manner and degree sheds light on the artist's processes of creation, his motives, and the shape of his imagination—not least illuminating is what he chose not to derive from the works that influenced him.

The critic must, then, be familiar with the art of the past; above all, he must have reflected upon it. But art-historical knowledge has for the critic a different function than it has for the art historian. The critic is not primarily concerned with tracing the evolution of styles and arranging works within them. He approaches the work not as the product of a past time set in its niche. He sees it rather as an act that has taken shape through the painter's battle with uncertainties, counter-forces, temptations. One might say that the critic unrolls the creation of the picture as an intellectual drama, while keeping his eye on it as a visual object. In this, his approach corresponds to that of a painter who looks at a painting by another artist; he sees it as a complex of situations met, resources employed, leaps executed. Without being aware of it, the painter as spectator imagines himself as a performer; he becomes automatically the original artist. The critic stands in the same line of vision as the painter, but he stands farther back. For him, not only is the painting "to be done again" in his mind; the painter is also something to be "done"—that is, to be intellectually constituted as an artist acting, feeling, and choosing within his medium and his culture.

It is to this end, and only to this end, that he may resort to the biography of the artist, to his ideas, and to his statements of intent. The critic reads the artist's words and interprets events in his life solely in relation to his acts on the canvas. Like the painting itself, they are data from which he constructs the fiction that is the author of the work and the key to its meaning. Statements by artists, though frequently of great value to criticism, are to be regarded with suspicion and never taken as the last word as to fact or attitude. Jealous of their originality, artists are prone to deceit and self-deceit; for instance, American artists, especially, tend to deny their indebtedness to other artists and to art movements that have determined their work. For criticism, this denial is not merely a way of claiming undue credit; it has the effect of disguising the circulation of thought within the community of artists and in the culture of the period.

The critic sees art history backwards, from the painting he is studying to works that anteceded it. (On another plane, there is for the critic no earlier and no later.) In any case, he will refuse to believe that a work of art was produced through the operation of impersonal forces. The scandal of art history is its ability and in many instances its willingness to dispense with artists, a problem that is for historians themselves to deal with.

One cannot, however, avoid saying a few words about individuals who lay down the law to art in the name of art history. Art criticism today is beset by art historians turned inside out to function as prophets of so-called inevitable trends. A determinism similar to that projected into the evolution of past styles is clamped upon art in the making. In this parody of art history, value judgments are deduced from a presumed logic of development, and an ultimatum is issued to artists either to accommodate themselves to these values or be banned from the art of the future. An aesthetician founded on art history wields a club of dogma similar to moralistic criticism in the nineteenth century or political criticism in the Soviet Union.

A practical problem exists in properly defining the uses of art history, in view of the fact that an academic degree in this subject has become the accepted means of accrediting people for careers in art, including that of art critic. The study of art history develops in people the professional habit of tracing the forms and imagery of a work to their influences and sources; also the habit of taking it for granted that doing so establishes the value of the work. Uncovering sources is an accomplishment of which the historian is justly proud, and it is not unnatural that he should project the value of what he himself has been doing into the painting. It is not unusual to hear a painting praised as if its merit lay in working out a successful campaign for capturing the qualities of earlier works and transferring them into the present.

Perhaps ways can be found to direct art history toward scholarship, and to develop appropriate curricula for other specialties, including that non-specialized specialty, criticism. Both art criticism and art history need to scan more thoroughly their philosophical substructures. Both ought to consider, for instance, the difference between the intellectual origins of art in our time and in earlier periods. Art history no longer comes into being in the same way that it did in earlier eras. Art used to wander on its way, responding to the cues given to it by tradition and chance, until the historian pounced upon it and set it into the order of its time. In the twentieth century, art has lost its innocence. Its naïveté in regard to its own history had been replaced by a complex sophistication in manipulating that history. Today the art historian is dealing with an art that is conscious of itself as engaged in making art history and that in order to impress the art historian (especially the art historian turned critic) deliberately takes his prejudices into account. The historian is no longer telling a story of raw events; he is repeating a story told to him in the form of ideas and happenings with which he is implicated. The first requirement in such a situation is to know that he is implicated and to what extent. Both the art historian and the art critic must be wary of responding to a mirror held up to them by the artist for the purpose of arousing their admiration for the image of their own outlook. History in our time—and not only art history—is history that is being deliberately tampered with by the object of the historian's study, the history-makers.

In art, the prime history-makers are painters and sculptors. As indicated earlier, there are writers and cultural commissars who wish to appropriate this privilege of the artist and to use him as an instrument for their own art-history-making. The result is a new kind of conflict —between the artist and the professional representatives of his public. This conflict is an aspect of the conflict of ideas which has characterized the creation of art for more than a century. The style is the man, but modern man becomes himself—that is, acquires style—in a wrestle with ideas and even ideologies. In our time, art arises out of a dialectical tension between individual temperaments and art movements founded on various theories. The work itself is neither personality nor idea. But to equip the future artist, art critic, or art appreciator to understand what has been created, art education must familiarize him not only with works of art but with the alternatives over which the campaigns of modern art have been fought. For example, art as the instrument of the state or of business and art as individual discovery or creation.

Statements of intent by artists illuminate their work only when interpreted in the context of the continuing struggle of ideas in art itself. Read in isolation from the artist's concrete intellectual situation, they often appear in reverse and lead criticism up blind alleys. For instance, the painter Malevich once pointed out that in the work of a famous medieval icon painter the hairs of God's beard were exactly the same as the hairs on the Devil's tail. This was intended to prove that what counted for the artist was not the *what* but the *how*: the painter cares neither for God nor the Devil but only about painting. All content is a mere pretext for the exercise of skill and the solution of aesthetic problems. Following this logic—and Malevich did, of course, follow it —subject matter can be eliminated entirely, and everything valid in the art of the present or the past can be translated into space, line, color, design. We arrive at what is called "pure" painting.

By the same type of reasoning we arrive also at "puristic" criticism or formalism—that is, criticism that evaluates paintings exclusively in terms of their formal elements and by formal standards.

Yet a formal conception of art by an artist and the same theory in the hands of a critic have widely different results. The purist objectives of Malevich, or of Mondrian or Albers, have brought into being paintings that vibrate with vigor and sensibility, in a word, with emotional and psychic content. In his act of painting the artist lives inside his idea, and the more he has narrowed it to exclude all but essentials the greater the psychic pressure to which it subjects him. This subjective pressure is not, however, comprehended in his formalist scheme. The absolutist thinking of the artist gives him direction and assurance rather than supplying an inventory of everything that goes into his work. Also, the artist's ideas are polemical: he wants the art of painting to have a certain character, and he attempts to realize this wish through what he does himself rather than through affecting others.

In contrast, the critic who allows himself to be circumscribed by statements of painters runs the risk of missing the totality of experience embodied in their own paintings. The point is underscored by the inadequacy of formalist criticism in dealing with formalist art, i.e., precisely with the art with whose principles it is in full accord. Taking literally the notion that art aims solely at art, the critic participates in the painter's idea—but he misses the qualities brought into being by the act of painting. These qualities arise not from the theory that instigated the painting and determined its mode but from the positive or negative drive of the artist in regard to himself and the art by which he is confronted. The Neo-Plasticism of Mondrian reacting to Cubism and World War I produces a result quite different from that of a hard-edge painter of the sixties reacting to Abstract Expressionism and the apolitical art world of New York. Granted that the formalist painter paints neither for love of God nor from fear of the Devil; that he paints for the sake of painting, perhaps in order to carry art to its next step; that for him art is the absolute and he lives only in order to serve it; that he takes orders from it (not from nature or his own feelings) as to how he shall serve it and what he shall bring to its altar; that painting has for him a life, a mind, and a will of its own; that the chief impulse of this living independent entity is to purge itself of anything not itself and to reduce itself more and more to its own essence— granted all these motives and beliefs, the painter will not succeed in making himself into nothing but a painter, nor his painting into a crystal reflection of relations immanent among the elements of art. As a painter he is in the painting—he is, so to speak, its flaw. Purist painting is work within a value system, most often the system of the ascetic. It is from the will to order, to purgation, to (one adds automatically) salvation that it derives its passion for neatness, for hygiene, for shapes such as the square and the rectangle (presumably immune to emotional associations), and its practice of banning tones and restricting itself to hues cleansed of atmosphere. In the end, painting for the purist is God (without a beard). At its most intense, pure painting is religious painting. As such it is as "expressionistic" as the most agitated figurative art. When art in this mode is not caught in a religious trance it is mere interior decoration. And what measures whether it is one or the other is the desperation, self-denial, and transcendence communicated by the tensions of its vacant shapes and fields of color. Recently I received a message from Albers by way of a student from California. "Tell Rosenberg," it said, "that angst is dead." What message could be more anxious?

Charge #5: *What definition of style provides the most useful structure for art critical study? On what bases may be established the limits or extent of a style?*

The concept of style must be related to the function assumed by certain modes of handling within the experience of the artist and the history of art. Visual similarities are not sufficient to define the features of a style or its limit—that is to say, the eye is not sufficient. The emotional and intellectual ends to which the visual means are put are intrinsic to the definition. For example, the stylistic similarities between a Mondrian and a Newman are obvious. But the Neo-Plastic style has with the latter assumed a new function, resulting in a deflection from Neo-Plasticism and in moods and purposes in opposition to it. Out of the new use of the style come new stylistic possibilities, and these tend to develop in directions visually unrelated to the original mode; in the example just given, "pure" abstraction develops into an aspect of Abstract Expressionism. The shifting and transformation of modern styles center on the fact that style in our time originates in ideologies and is cultivated by theory—thus it is constantly affected by changes of meaning and may even undergo a total erosion of meaning. As de Kooning put it several years ago: "We are all working on the basis of ideas in which we no longer believe."

This brings me to an additional proposition concerning art in our time that ought to be added to the seven with which this paper began. From this Proposition 8, I shall draw a few concluding remarks about criticism.

PROPOSITION 8: That the ubiquitous presence of the visual mass media, from advertising posters to industrial design, has introduced into painting and sculpture a new factor which art criticism must reckon with—and that to do so, the critic must clarify his position toward contemporary society as a basis for evaluating its art and non-art.

Art in the twentieth century, *including the art that has come to us from the past*, is affected by the mass media both directly (e.g., the use of the *Mona Lisa* in an advertisement) and through their impact upon modern culture generally. Especially in the United States, creation in art is accompanied at every step by the gigantic shadow of the commercial art output which mimics and adapts every new style in painting and sculpture, extending it into a totally different context of meaning, feeling, and purpose. Thus Pollock inspires the design of dress fabrics, Calder a beer advertisement.

The utilization of art for the objectives of the market causes styles to become widely familiar without there being any comprehension of their meanings. Popular museum programs contribute to the same end; the exhibition of the *Mona Lisa* under the auspices of public relations is intellectually equivalent to its reproduction in an ad. The result is that art in America, both new and old, is subjected to a constant process of alienation. The vast pool of skills directed toward specific economic, political, and educational ends challenges art to define its own function and to differentiate its products, if any real difference exists, from those whose efficiency is measurable. A mystification of values causes all novelties to seem of equal significance and breeds the widespread belief that the ultimate function of the fine arts is to contribute visual devices to utilitarian design—e.g., the justification of Mondrian by linoleum patterns or by Sixth Avenue skyscrapers. Raised in this belief, young artists have been bringing painting and sculpture steadily closer to utilitarian ideals. The shift in art training from bohemian studios to university art departments threatens to accelerate and deepen the trend toward the kind of art whose uses are foreseeable.

What but criticism can tell us what we are doing and if it is what we want to do? What but criticism can indicate other ends, explain what makes those other ends essential, and indicate what must be done to serve them?

III. SITUATIONS

13
Art and the Crowd

At the Salon des Refusés, the huge Paris exhibition of 1863 in which modernist art began its open contest with the academic tradition, the outstanding response of the spectators was hilarity. In *The Shock of the New*,* Ian Dunlop quotes first-hand accounts of the irresistible laughter provoked by the exhibits. Word would get around that in this or that gallery there was a funny picture, and, as Zola reported in his novel *L'Œuvre*, "people came stampeding from every other room in the exhibition, and gangs of sightseers, afraid of missing something, came pushing their way in shouting 'Where?'—'Over there!'—'Oh, I say! Did you ever?' And shafts of wit fell thicker here than anywhere else." Zola's "here" refers to the most memorable item of the show— Manet's *Le Déjeuner sur l'Herbe*, which was also the chief target of the giggles, guffaws, and wisecracks. Today, *Le Déjeuner* is a national treasure of France and a revered icon of modernism, and so no one, of course, any longer laughs at it. This does not prevent it from still being a ridiculous picture—a realistically painted scene that consists of a completely naked woman sitting on the grass with two fully dressed young men near the remains of a picnic, while in the background another girl in a pink chemise is gracefully picking something off the ground. That only the female has taken off her clothes apparently brought an explosion of comment similar to that evoked by the one-sided undressing in *Last Tango*; after disparaging the *Le Déjeuner*

* Ian Dunlop, *The Shock of the New* (New York: American Heritage Press).

nude's figure, a prominent critic complained that the fellow beside her hadn't thought to remove his "horrid padded cap." What made Manet's contemporaries laugh was the literalism of the picture; it led to their comparing *Le Déjeuner* not with other paintings but with a scene that might have taken place at a private party in an upstairs room of a restaurant.

Had the painting been hung in an official Salon, the spectators might have been reluctant to regale themselves with such illicit associations. The fact is that nakedness as silly or perverse as that of *Le Déjeuner* was abundant in the Salon of 1863—from the fleshy Venuses washed up on beaches of Cabanel and Baudry to Puvis de Chavannes's allegorical *Work*, which centers on the highlighted buttocks of an athlete with a sledge hammer—but while there was criticism of Salon entries, it is not recorded that anyone died laughing. Piety toward art embodied in the Salon and its august jury inhibited the jocularity of crowds faced with erotic or unfamiliar subjects, and induced what a contemporary critic called "that serious state of mind which is necessary to a fair comparison of works of art." The Salon of the Rejected placed no such restrictions upon the spectators' behavior. Rejected art exists on the metaphysical level of ordinary objects, if not on a lower one. It gives the spectator the license to react as he is.

But is not the absence of piety manifested at the Salon des Refusés exactly the condition to which modernism in art aspires? To strip art of its sheath of transcendence—religious, political, moral, aesthetic—has been a continuing motif of the modernist revolution. For the vanguard sensibility it is a matter of principle that nakedness should provide sensuous enjoyment and not be a means of summoning the mind to ideal realms. But when transcendence is cast out, everything that in the past made art art is cast out, too. Wherefore, confronted by the representatives of instituted values, such as the nineteenth-century Salon or the museum of today, vanguard art must be synonymous with *rejected* art—not because advanced art desires to fail but for the deeper reason that only art officially cast aside can arouse in the spectator authentic feelings uncoerced by vested authority. The advanced artist has preferred to run the gauntlet of derision of an audience "on leave" from values instead of seeking acceptance by the high priests of acknowledged art. Thus a complicity automatically takes shape between the vanguard and that part of the public which has escaped the "serious state" of the pious art lover. The radicalism of *Le Déjeuner* lay in providing a channel through which the ribal-

Edouard Manet, *Le Déjeuner sur l'Herbe*, 1863.
COLLECTION JEU DE PAUME, THE LOUVRE, PARIS.

dries of the crowd at the Refusés could be transmitted to earlier masterworks whose status was beyond question—for example, to Giorgione's *Concert Champêtre*, which *Le Déjeuner* had parodied in part. Through the Salon of the Rejected, all art became susceptible to the taint of rejection, and thus potentially avant-garde. A chain of aesthetic subversion was set up, accompanied by the reiterated demand that works of art be treated on a par with phenomena of daily life. Over *Le Déjeuner* at the Refusés hovered the phantom of Mona Lisa with a mustache.

"Let art no longer depend on 'serious states' " echoes through the aesthetic insurrections of the hundred and ten years since the Salon des Refusés. The man responsible for inaugurating the epoch of upheavals was that mysterious adventurer Louis Bonaparte, stigmatized by Marx as the Prince of La Bohème, who "divested the whole state of its halo." According to Marx's analysis in *The Eighteenth Brumaire of Louis Bonaparte*, Louis, the enemy of all classes, was the personification of the farcical reversal of values which had overtaken bourgeois society in the middle of the nineteenth century. The Salon des Refusés was the epitome of Bonaparte's cultural classlessness. Having learned of complaints of widespread exclusions from the Salon of 1863, the emperor suddenly ordered an exhibition of rejected art to be set up alongside the official Salon in the Palais de l'Industrie, in order "to let the public judge the legitimacy of these complaints." To put on trial before a "people's court" the academic authority he himself had appointed was nothing less than a democratic revolution against the cultural pretensions of middle-class society, its experts, and its arbiters of taste and high seriousness. The Salon des Refusés was the first of the great uprisings against the establishment and established values which have marked the history of art in our epoch. Crowds came to the Palais to jeer at the rejected art, yet attendance at the Refusés seems to have outstripped that at the official Salon. But the important social innovation was the discovery by the populace that it could, if it chose, treat art disrespectfully. After 1863, art became the object of a polemical struggle that has never been without its political dimension.

Dunlop's *The Shock of the New* covers seven historic confrontations between advanced art and a public wider than the usual art audience; from the Salon des Refusés to the Nazi "Degenerate Art" exhibition of 1937, these confrontations constituted the pitched battles of cultural change. Dunlop is not a professional art historian, and his account of the emergence of new styles and key innovators in terms of dramatic Big Shows has the advantage of keeping in the foreground the social and psychological tensions that accompany alterations in the forms of art. The Impressionists, the Fauves, the Post-Impressionists were each introduced to the public through the kind of aesthetic flea market represented by the Salon des Refusés—and to the accompaniment of philistine malice, defensive rhetoric, and mounting popular excitement. To what extent, and in what manner, anyone was "shocked" by the Big Shows is difficult to say, unless "shock" is something that makes people turn out in droves and enjoy themselves. Moreover, the desire to *épater le bourgeois* is less in evidence in Dunlop's narrative than is the will of new talents to bring their creations into the light. In effect, the exhibitions were semi-illicit festivals in which spectators felt free, often for the first time, to express themselves on matters toward which they had previously maintained a posture of empty reverence: the Post-Impressionist show, says an author quoted by Dunlop, "stirred people who are not particularly interested in art." The "New" of Dunlop's title is particularly inapposite in regard to the last two shows it deals with: the International Surrealist Exhibition in Paris in 1938, and the "Degenerate Art" show in Munich in 1937, were not exhibitions of new art; in fact, the purpose of the Nazi display was to arouse contempt for a modernism that had become a tradition.

The pattern visible in Dunlop's seven Big Shows is that, though they begin by baffling and upsetting the aesthetically unsophisticated, their circus atmosphere tends to undermine the position of the educated: the Big Show incarnates the primitivist streak in modern art. Roger Fry, who organized the Post-Impressionist Exhibition in London in 1910, identified the cultivated, "who had hitherto been my most eager listeners," as "the most inveterate and exasperated enemies of the new movement," and announced that this hostility had its basis in social class. To appreciate traditional art required erudition and was thus a mark of status, while "to admire a Matisse required only a certain sensibility. One could feel fairly sure that one's maid could not rival one in the former case, but might by a mere haphazard gift of Providence surpass one in the second." Fry's notion that advanced art is accessible without intellectual preparation is hard to reconcile with early popular reactions to *Le Déjeuner*, to Cézanne's *A Modern Olympia*, to Matisse's *Woman with a Hat*, to Duchamp's *Nude Descending a Staircase*. But even if "a certain sensibility" cannot be found ready to hand in one's maid, the repeated reversal of feelings in the history of modernism suggests that both ridicule and rejection are phases of appreciation.

As part of their program of inverse revolution, the Nazis in 1937 presented an anti-exhibition of advanced art under the title of "Entartete Kunst," or "Degenerate Art." The object of the show was to stir up the antagonism of the masses to advanced art: the former *refusés*, who now occupied places of honor in leading museums, were to be re-refused, or rejected again. Like the original Salon des Refusés, the "Degenerate" show was paralleled by an exhibition of officially accepted paintings and sculptures. Though the Nazis echoed Louis Bonaparte in calling upon the people to judge, they were unwilling to trust to the spontaneous derision of the public, and they surrounded the "Degenerate" exhibits with scurrilous inscriptions regarding the pathology of the artists, their charlatanry, their "Jewish" outlook. In addition, according to Dunlop, pressure was put on the spectator by the museum guards, who were instructed to watch whether he laughed loudly enough or appeared sufficiently shocked. The issue of the reaction of the crowd to modern art was raised once more, but in a distorted way and with a direct assertion by the organizers of the show of the political significance of modernism. *The Shock of the New* does not tell us how the visitors to the "Degenerate" show actually responded; very likely the information is not available. But even if most of the spectators laughed sufficiently to appease the guards, "Entartete Kunst" demonstrated—as did the Big Shows in Paris, London, and New York—the attraction that work in modern modes exerted, in that it was, according to Dunlop's data, "the most popular of all the exhibitions covered by this book," with an attendance far exceeding the rival exhibition of art favored by the Führer.

The Big Show of the type examined in *The Shock of the New* can no longer take place. After the solemn responses to Henry Geldzahler's "New York Painting and Sculpture: 1940–1970" exhibition at the Metropolitan Museum, some recent Whitney Annuals, and the Documenta 5 show in Kassel, it is inconceivable that any exhibition can be mounted that would cause people to guffaw or howl. What has vanished is not advanced art, as the Nazis planned, but the independent and unruly spectator—the inexpert citizen who laughs when a picture (as of two dressed-up men conducting a debate with a naked lady on the grass beside them) strikes him as funny and who is irritated when works are boring. The outstanding fact about art in the past fifteen years is the restoration of public piety toward works under official auspices; it extends to anything, from pre-Columbian potsherds to big-edition prints, that has entered the precincts of art history. While avant-garde art was pulling down the pillars of the Salon, art theory was already toiling to restore them. Roger Fry's maid equipped by sensibility to appreciate Matisse has been replaced (*was* replaced, immediately after Fry discovered her) by the new intellectual aristocrats trained in aesthetics by Fry or successor critics and historians; in an introduction to a collection of Fry's lectures, Sir Kenneth Clark gave credit to Fry's theories, rather than to "a mere haphazard gift of Providence," for the popular acceptance of the French Post-Impressionists in Britain. Indoctrinated with awe toward art, the new "eager listeners" never scoff at what is placed before them, nor are they shocked. The aesthetic religiosity of the academic Salon has been restored on a worldwide basis, and is sustained by a voluntary oath of devoutness that overrides critical differences. As was the case at the Salon of 1863, to enter the door of the contemporary art world is to be possessed by "that serious state of mind which is necessary to a fair comparison of works of art" (and to refuse to compare them with things that are not art). Until there appear influxes of aesthetic outsiders capable, like the crowds of the Big Shows of the modernist century, of giving vent to their outsiderness, absurdity and mediocrity in art will remain secure against the grin.

14

The Cubist Epoch

Modern art doesn't begin at any identifiable point, but the modern situation of art undoubtedly begins with Cubism. Among its other innovations, Cubism changed the relation of art to the public, and, in so doing, changed the nature of the art public itself. It excluded those who merely responded to pictures and replaced them with spectators who knew what made pictures important. The howls of indignation that greeted Cubist contributions to the Armory Show in New York in 1913 resound through the history of twentieth-century art as evidence that a genuine cultural revolution had taken place. The educated middle class had been challenged by a new power: the band of art professionals armed with advanced intellectual weapons. In Russia ten years later, a similar uprising of modernism was repulsed as a serious threat to the party's control of taste and judgment.

Cubism ended the reign in art of what Gertrude Stein called "nature as everybody sees it"—that is to say, of common sense. Thenceforward, every art movement would propound its own conception of reality, and within the movement every artist would insist on his own uniqueness. A new public, open to doctrinal persuasion, would stand ready to welcome each effort toward expanded consciousness, while the majority could be counted on to reproduce what might be called the Khrushchev syndrome (or, recalling Theodore Roosevelt's reaction to Cubism at the Armory, the Roosevelt-Khrushchev syndrome) of violent denunciation. Instead of depicting things, or even fantasies or distortions of things like the Nabis and Symbolists, the Cubists made art esoteric by projecting into the mind of the spectator the secrets and problems of the studio.

Douglas Cooper, author of *The Cubist Epoch*,* a comprehensive survey of Cubist painting and sculpture, confirms that the problems of the artist constitute the content of Cubist paintings when he declares that Braque and Picasso, co-founders of the new style, "thought more about forging the language of Cubism than about the aesthetic value of their subject-matter." A painting in a language-in-progress could not be understood simply by looking at it, and if it was not understood it could not be appreciated. Thus, Cubism launched the transformation of painting into an intellectual specialization, a compendium of old and new technical discoveries, methods, assumptions, errors to be corrected. The spectator was called upon to acquire this lore or to be guided by the knowledge of professionals. No more amateur gazing at pictures. Every manifestation of art since Cubism has depended for its reception on a phalanx of spectators governed by the opinions of intellectual leaders. The quarrel between Gertrude Stein and her brother Leo as to whether to go on with Picasso after *Les Demoiselles d'Avignon* represents the archetypal drama of twentieth-century art appreciation. Everyone must stop somewhere—the *Demoiselles* shocked even Braque—but there's always someone else to advance farther. With Cubism, the issue of the avant-garde in art was no longer a matter of responding to a new sensibility, as with Impressionism or Fauvism; Cubism built avant-gardist ideas into the body of art as the principle of constant experimentation by which the aims and functions of art would be redefined.

The paintings in *The Cubist Epoch* actually consisted in large part of challenges to Cubism (by Futurism, for example) and of deviations from it through insufficient comprehension (as by the Czech Cubists) or in the name of logically more advanced concepts (as by Mondrian). Cubism, says Cooper, was "a new pictorial language," but apparently only the "true" Cubists—Picasso, Braque, Gris and, for a short while, Léger—could speak it; everyone else received it in mistranslation or proceeded to adulterate its meaning.

The esoteric nature of Cubism gave rise to the modern art audience, composed of experts, intermediaries (or explainers), and a mass conditioned through publicity and art education to react to whatever is presented to it as art. Thus, Cubism inaugurated the enfolding of art

* Douglas Cooper, *The Cubist Epoch* (New York: Phaidon Publishers, 1971).

Robert Delaunay, *City of Paris.*

creation within increasingly numerous layers of auxiliary professions, from showman-curators to art-movie makers—a process accelerated to the point of near suffocation by recent museum and foundation programs. The core of the new-epoch art audience, however, has consisted of individuals who have gained direct understanding of the innovating ideas through personal intimacy with the artists; Cooper himself is characterized in material issued in connection with *The Cubist Epoch* as "a close personal friend" of many of the Cubist painters, and this factor has no doubt contributed to his success in tracing the changing attitudes responsible for different phases of Cubism. In its campaign against naturalistic art that tricks the eye, Cubism consolidated the position of modern painting as creation based on ideology and directed toward concentric circles of insiders able to prefer art that, as Picasso said of Negro sculpture, "is not visually but conceptually true." The axiom that pictures cannot be checked against the visual world carries the corollary that art is for experts only. In the early days of Cubism, Cooper reports, Braque and Picasso kept largely apart even from other painters—in the last analysis, any spectator was an intruder.

The strength of Cubism lay in its bypassing of "false traditionalism" (as Braque put it) in order to express the modern world. Cooper is convinced, as Gertrude Stein was, that Cubism, despite appearances to the contrary, is a species of realism; its original ancestor, he contends, was Courbet. Cooper is a strict constructionist. Adherence to "solid tangible reality" is the criterion by which he distinguishes true Cubists from painters who merely "cubify" for decorative effect or who paint according to systems. Of Delaunay's *The City of Paris* Cooper says that it "is anti-Cubist by virtue of the unreality of its conception," and of Gleizes that "while using certain Cubist procedures," he "came more and more to disregard visual reality and evolved a predominantly decorative, formalized style of painting which was virtually abstract." The enigma of Cubism, which has baffled observers since its first appearance, is that while it seems to have originated abstract art and at times lacks an identifiable subject, so that to its foes it has been a "Navajo-rug" pattern of lines, shapes, and colors, it is essentially antipathetic to the nonrepresentational modes that evolved out of it.

In making the issue of reality central to his evaluation of Cubist creation, Cooper enters into direct conflict with the present-day school of formalist criticism, for which the meaning of Cubism consists in its handling of space, line, and color, and which applies Cubist-derived

formulas as the measure of artists as different from one another as
Ernst and Duchamp, Miró and Mondrian, Pollock and Frank Stella.
This approach, diametrically opposed to Cooper's, was illustrated by a
"Fact Sheet" distributed by the Metropolitan Museum in connection
with its recent Cubist exhibition. "Its lasting significance," this document declared of Cubism, "lies in its role as the origin and key to all
subsequent styles of twentieth-century painting." Cubism is given a
monopoly on formal innovations at the cost of being stripped of its
contribution to the consciousness of our time. For Cooper, in contrast,
the flattened pictorial space of Cubist paintings and the dissociation of
pictorial elements, such as shapes and planes of color, were conceived
not for their own sake but to attain a new grasp of reality, to provide
"a viable alternative to naturalism." In Cooper's view, once this mission, begun in 1906, had been accomplished, the Cubist epoch was at
an end; after 1920 its spirit survived only in the work of those artists
who had been involved in its creation, and by about 1940 it had been
"supplanted by artistic conceptions of a wholly opposite order."

The formalist view of Cubism as the mother of all twentieth-century styles is a simplification that has been accepted largely because of
its usefulness in the audience-building processes of modern art—what
could be more reassuring than a single "key," as the "Fact Sheet" calls
it, to the art of the past fifty years? Yet Cooper's interpretation of
Cubism as "concerned with the solid tangible reality of things" also
presents difficulties. Isn't it odd that a realistic art engaged in investigating twentieth-century phenomena should have been compounded
of Egyptian drawings, Iberian sculpture, and African figurines? Also,
that Picasso, inventor of this advanced mode of apprehending reality,
should in his late Cubist paintings have diluted it with naturalistic
(commonly recognizable) ingredients and should finally have abandoned it entirely? A method for apprehending reality is rarely discarded until a more efficient method appears.

That Cubism provided a new pictorial language superbly suited to
dealing with modern experience ought by this time to be apparent
beyond question. In destroying the illusionism of painted apples and
bodies, it exposed the illusory nature of actual apples and bodies.
Through collage, it blended images with objects and made objects
seem images. Collage is this century's outstanding contribution to mystification—it holds the seeds of events fabricated for the purpose of
being described in the mass media, and of political personages reshaped
by professionals to capture votes through matching other people's

Pablo Picasso, *Absinthe Glass, Bottle, Pipe and Musical Instruments on a Piano*, 1910–11, oil, 19¾" x 51¼".

Georges Braque, *Still Life with Dice and Pipe*, 1911, oil 31½″ x 23″.
PRIVATE COLLECTION. COURTESY LOS ANGELES COUNTY MUSEUM OF ART

faces and temperaments. The decentralized composition of Cubist painting and the derivation of its forms from geometry and from random objects—for example, Picasso's *Absinthe Glass, Bottle, Pipe, and Musical Instruments on a Piano*—resulted in the "democratization" of data and asserted that the identity of things lies not in the things themselves but in their placement and function. Cubist paintings and collages could contain anything—matchbooks, menus, wine bottles, contents of the artist's pocket—and this caused the everyday world to feel at home in art. Cubist disintegration of the object emphasizes that an apple in a painting may in actuality be the result of a hundred acts of looking and applying paint. In addition to the solution it offered to the problem of transposing objects from deep space to a flat surface, Cubism's replacement of linear perspective by two-dimensionality provided a metaphor of the psychic condition of modern man. Twentieth-century philosophers talk of the "flattening out" of the individual, and aspects of Cubism have reappeared in literature—Joyce, Pound, Eliot, Marianne Moore make use of collage, parody, and verbal "faceting"—and in music and the theatre. In sum, there *is* a Cubist epoch, and it is impossible to grasp the full dimensions of present-day experience without the Cubist reformulation of the sensibility, just as it is impossible to hear sounds in extremely high and low ranges without electronic equipment.

But though Cubism has illuminated the modern world, and is not a mere episode in the history of aesthetics, I cannot detect what in Cubist paintings makes them represent "the solid tangible reality of things." In regard to objects, it seems to me that Cubist painting was involved in a contradiction: it wished to dissolve objects into directly apprehended forms—the stem and the bowl of a pipe glimpsed separately— yet it wished to preserve the objects themselves as presences. Cooper describes how the "high" Cubist paintings of Picasso and Braque came to teeter on the edge of total abstraction, and he resorts to the rather silly suggestion that these paintings, elements of which were "primarily dictated by spatial considerations and pictorial necessity"—that is to say, by motives of abstract art, not by concern for tangible reality —can be recaptured for realism by finding the hint of a nose here, a watch chain there. (Perhaps it was to mock the notion that in a Cubist painting a rectangle is a cone is a nose that Gertrude Stein delivered her grand affirmation regarding the rose.) Guided by the belief that a painting must represent objects, or perhaps out of instinct or habit, people still peruse a painting such as Picasso's *Clarinet Player* or

Braque's *Still-Life with Dice and Pipe* in search of the clarinet or the dice, as if they were hunting for clues in a detective story or trying to find the cat in the tree in one of those puzzle pictures that used to appear in Sunday papers. The only merit, if any, in this type of scrutiny is that it repeats the activity of the Cubist painter in painting his picture. In Cubist painting, the object is grasped in tiny spurts of perception. It is a pile of clues submitted to an intuitive sense of order. Strictly speaking, the picture is never complete (another Cubist attitude passed on to later art modes) and it never reveals a "tangible reality."

Cooper's postulate of a re-created reality works very well for the detection of mixtures of naturalism and mannerism posing as Cubist paintings, as in Metzinger's *Cubist Landscape*. Cooper fails to consider, however, that the "true" Cubist painting achieves not the reality of the object—why the reality of a pipe, in any case?—but an aesthetic generalization of it in terms of its appearance and its surroundings. In effect, the Cubist painting is a mask covering the model or still-life—though a mask composed of the model's own visual substance, as was the case with the mask-portrait of Gertrude Stein from which Picasso moved on to Cubism. Picasso himself, in a famous remark, noted that Cubist paintings were an anticipation of the camouflaged war machines he saw passing through the streets of Paris in 1914. Masked objects represent the essential image of Cubist art. In the most literal sense, every Cubist painting and, even more obviously, sculpture is a masked entity. Cubism manipulates the physiognomies of things (and for it, all sides are frontal) in order to dissipate the secrecy of Being into an organization of unprivileged facts; the "object art" and "thingish" novel of the sixties are resurrections of the Cubist spirit. With Picasso, the mask is an explicit theme, from the portrait of Gertrude Stein and the "high" Cubist *Portrait of D. H. Kahnweiler* to his late Cubist *Harlequin* and, of course, the celebrated *Three Masked Musicians*, with which he closed his Cubist development, in 1921. Gris was also inclined to the harlequinade (the motif that connects Cubism with Picasso's Blue Period), while Braque suggests what might be called the masked still-life—in his 1912 oval *Guitar*, a recognizable section of the instrument is repeated with vertical markings that transport it behind a series of columns and dissolve it under the lettering ETUDE. In Cubism, the object is hidden behind shutters of forms that open and close at the will of the artist.

Despite any ambitions to capture reality, the ultimate aim of Cub-

Pablo Picasso, *Daniel-Henry Kahnweiler*, 1910, oil on canvas, 39⅝″
x 28⅝″.

ism, as of all effective art movements, was not reality but art. (Later, Dada and Surrealism, despite their radical anti-art manifestos, also defected to art.) One might say that Cubism asserted the independent reality of painting in its relation to things, people, and landscapes. If, as Cooper says, the founders of Cubism clung to intuited reality, it was not for the sake of reality but for the sake of their painting. Indeed, a fundamental intimation of Cubism is that the art object is the only real object—nothing is anything until it has been reconstituted by the artist. It followed that, liberated by Cubism from the restraints of things "as everybody sees them," artists less dialectically subtle than Picasso and Braque were bound to believe that objects of the studio or the street—in fact, the entire objective world—could be dispensed with if the objects stood in the way of art. Logically, Cubism implies abstract, nonrepresentational art, and art history since 1920 has again and again taken the path of this logic. In reducing painting to its elements, Cubism made it possible to separate each element from the others and deal with it as sufficient for painting.

Not the least of the innovations of the Cubist epoch was its instigation of the crisis of the object in art, both as external reference (the finding of noses) and in regard to the work itself (as a product of craft); Duchamp's "readymades," which dispensed with the making of art objects, were already implied in collage. Cubism proper remained dedicated to making art objects; through paintings composed of colored papers it strengthened the idea of the *"tableau-objet."* Yet the ideal of Cubism was not the individual picture but a method of painting that could interpenetrate with the art of any time, place, or culture. In the years of World War I, artists saw Cubism as the culmination of the era of picture-making, and postwar art movements from Dada to the Bauhaus were anti-Cubist in spirit, however much they took for granted the formal innovations of Cubism. The Cubist epoch consciously brought to an end the old European aesthetic culture. It brought itself to an end as the last period in which artists would engage themselves in reconstituting pictorially the reality of fruit bowls, pipes, and guitars. Since the close of Cubism, the crisis of the art object has been mounting from art movement to art movement.

15

Collage: Philosophy of Put-Togethers

Collage is a way of making art, but it is not a specific art form, nor is it a style. Cutting and pasting have been practiced in the kindergarten, by housewives making their own home decorations, by Matisse at the culmination of his powers. In itself, collage has no aesthetic or intellectual character: it has been employed for centuries to compose craft objects, such as arrangements of artificial fruits and flowers and colored papers, or to arouse surprise by sewing real buttons on a painted garment or inserting an actual clock in the tower of a landscape. In our century, however, collage has become more than a technique or genre for folk artists and amateurs. It has entered into painting and sculpture as an intrinsic part of their history. The incorporation of scraps of paper, cloth, printed matter, coins into compositions of painted forms was hailed by the Dadaist Tristan Tzara as "the most poetic, the most revolutionary moment in the evolution of painting." Considering the many different things that are now done with collage, this revolution is not easy to define. An elegant composition of colored papers by Esteban Vicente seems to have little in common with a box of forks and spoons by Arman. Both were included in the "Assemblage" exhibition at the Museum of Modern Art a dozen years ago, but that show was organized on the how-to-do-it concept of collage, and it was a chaos, intellectually and aesthetically.

Presumably, the components added to the canvas or sculpture contribute qualities to a collage that paint or plaster cannot achieve. But the significance of these additions varies importantly in works belonging to different categories—for instance, in the paintings of Adja Yunkers with their rigorous strategy of superimposed bands, as compared to the torn, rugged automobile parts of John Chamberlain's sculptures. For Yunkers, strips of painted paper provide a restrained variation of the surface that could not quite be matched by built-up strands of pigment; that is to say, he uses collage to obtain a formal low-relief figure on a flat ground. In contrast, Chamberlain's chunks of crushed, rusted, enamelled metal convey a sensation of physically menacing edges and fears associated with wrecked cars; when his work gained attention, artists took to noticing junk piles. Critics who consider Chamberlain's assemblages to be merely a translation into three dimensions of the forms of de Kooning and Kline (which are especially apparent as influences in Chamberlain's *paintings*) dismiss the aura of highway, crackup, and obsolescence clinging to Chamberlain's material. So, too, do those who, defending his originality, praise his progress from his junk works to the ones executed in new metals, foam rubber, and plastics. Chamberlain's recourse to the wreckers' lot was his primary creative act; his work in other mediums has to win interest on new grounds (which in my opinion it has failed to do). A similar instance of diminution of quality with a change of materials occurred when the Italian Alberto Burri renounced the stained and patched burlap sacks with which, in the 1950s, he made his début in the United States. In collage, the introduction of an emotionally expressive physical component can enable a work to surmount its formal background as well as the inventive limitations of the artist.

For Tzara, the revolution of collage consisted in its incorporating "a piece of everyday reality which enters into relationship with every other reality that the spirit has created." This idea of collage as a mixture of realities belonging to different orders identifies modern assembled art with a metaphysical principle beyond mere technique. Collage opens art to the common stuff of daily life, to Rimbaud's "poetic junk" of the city streets, in order to fix in time and place the abstractions of form. The collage révolution brings to an end the age-old separation between the realm of art and the realm of things. With collage, art no longer copies nature or seeks equivalents to it; an expression of the advanced industrial age, it appropriates the external world on the basis that it is already partly changed into art. Painting and sculpture encompass tangible entities that have origins and functions of their own. The newspaper cuttings in *Man with a Hat*, at the Museum of Modern Art, not only supply compositional and color elements but refer to tuberculosis and dental care, and, according to a note in a catalogue by William Rubin, were snipped from the December 3, 1912, issue of *Le Journal.*

The unity of collage lies in the metaphysics of mixing formal and material realities through introducing the concreteness of the paste-in. As art, collage lacks an independent history. Herta Wescher's *Collage,** is actually a history of art movements since Cubism, retold in terms of pasting and assembling. A monumental accumulation of data, it is receptive to works in every mode of modern art in which a shuffling of materials or images has been employed—from a photomontage of a pair of hands with wide-open eyes in their palms to an abstract composition of rope, leaves, and rags. Wescher calls the roll of Cubists, Futurists, Dadaists, and so on, gives brief biographical accounts of their careers in collage, and quotes their views on the advantages of using non-art substances. Albers "urged the students [at the Bauhaus] to make use of rubbish for the simple reason that he found it too expensive to provide fresh materials for their class exercises," and artists working in different places, periods, and styles also stressed the economical aspect of collage in legitimizing substitutes for art supplies, especially during crises of war and depression. In contrast, for Johannes Itten, like Albers a Bauhaus master, the attraction of waste lay in its tactile variety: his students were instructed "to keep our eyes open, while out walking, for rubbish heaps, refuse dumps, garbage buckets, and scrap deposits as sources of material by means of which to make images (sculptures) which would bring out unequivocally the essential and the antagonistic properties of individual materials."

Several artists cited by Wescher reiterate the thought expressed by Tzara regarding the bringing of everyday reality into painting and sculpture, but there is no discussion of what this radical adulteration means, and the problem is submerged in the encyclopedic survey. *Collage* mentions large numbers of craftsmen, including architects, photographers, and members of art-related professions, who have made collages after the models of leading Dadaists and Constructivists. But a précis of, say, the career of Ladislav Sutnar in Prague or the contribution of H. H. Stuckenschmidt to the Berlin Dada Fair is not a satisfactory substitute for analysis of why collage became so pervasive in twentieth-century creation. The net effect of Wescher's volume is to present collage as a technique for producing avant-garde

* Herta Wescher, *Collage* (New York: Harry N. Abrams, Inc., 1971).

paintings and sculptures by other means. Photographs of collages are often indistinguishable from photographs of paintings and reliefs, since the inserted elements tend to blend with the painted forms: even when newspaper clippings supply a clue, there is the possibility that the artist has reproduced them on the canvas. In any case, the visual effect of the paper-covered area is similar to that of a painted one. The dangers of relying on reproductions in presenting developments in art are serious enough in painting and sculpture, but they are immensely heightened in dealing with collage. Wescher has grouped her illustrations from Cubist through Abstract Expressionist, and this facilitates the presentation of collage as a technical variation within the history of modern styles.

Collage is part of art history, but it also represents a decisive upheaval in that history; Tzara, among others, was justified in using the word "revolutionary." Collage changed the relation between painting and the world outside painting. The combining of formal qualities with crude fact in Cubist collage contained the seeds of anti-art that have flourished in the half century that followed; to arrive at found objects, readymades, conceptual art, information art, anti-form heaps, or earth art it is necessary only to discard Picasso's compositional objectives in *Man with a Hat* and to elaborate upon his pasted-in news items and aging paper (process art). From collage it is logical to move outside the picture to the aesthetic appropriation of bottle racks and ticker tape; in *Guitar* Picasso cancels the picture frame as an enclosure by painting it on the canvas.

Collage is the form assumed by the ambiguities that have matured in our time concerning both art and the realities it has purported to represent. Collage manifests itself in modern art modes as a kind of adversary within the mode itself. No sooner is a new manner established in painting or sculpture than it is duplicated in alien materials that seem to make painting and sculpture superfluous: one of the earliest assaults on Action painting was the "combine paintings" of Rauschenberg, begun in 1953 and described by Wescher as follows: "Into paintings with the techniques of American Action painting he inserts wildly disparate objects which he integrates by dashing paint over them. Whatever he can lay hands on is serviceable: pieces of cloth, underclothing, frames and wood panels of earlier days, objects useful and useless. Empty fields of color are filled with letters and words. News photos of current events are slapped down side by side with irrelevant drawings." There is an inherent element of mockery in collage: the

Pablo Picasso, *Man with a Hat*, 1912, charcoal, ink, pasted paper, 24½″ x 18⅝″.

put-together is like a painting, but without the effort of painting or the need to know how to paint. Its materials, besides being inexpensive, have the air of having been picked up by chance, so the collage seems to say to the spectator, "See how easy it is to make a work of art." In Picasso's *Guitar* the sheet of paper representing the guitar is fastened to the canvas with pins, though it seems to be held down by a nail, which is actually a paper cutout with painted trompe-l'oeil shadows. Parody upon parody upon parody—but the use of pins has the effect of a method even more casual than pasting, and Picasso's easy-does-it attitude dramatizes itself unmistakably in *Baboon and Young* with its head of toy automobiles and its tail of a length of spring. The undermining of refinement in art through masterworks of old nailed boards and chicken wire, broken bottles, and soiled wrappings is in keeping with the spirit of derision that collage brings into painting and sculpture.

The mingling of object and image in collage, of given fact and conscious artifice, corresponds to the illusion-producing processes of contemporary civilization. In advertisements, news stories, films, and political campaigns, lumps of unassailable data are implanted in preconceived formats in order to make the entire fabrication credible. Documents waved at hearings by Joseph McCarthy to substantiate his fictive accusations were a version of collage, as is the corpse of Lenin, inserted by Stalin into the Moscow mausoleum to authenticate his own contrived ideology. Twentieth-century fictions are rarely made up of the whole cloth, perhaps because the public has been trained to have faith in "information." Collage is the primary formula of the aesthetics of mystification developed in our time. It is the visual vocabulary of what Walter Benjamin called "the age of mechanical reproduction"; it reflects the absurdity of representing things and images in a universe of forces and energies.

In the vision of collage, the identity of an object is suspended between its practical reality and the conceptual whole in which it is set. A banknote incorporated in a collage has surrendered its simple character as money and undergone aesthetic transformation. A friend of mine was shocked when this principle was violated by burglars who plucked a twenty-dollar bill from a collage hanging on his wall. Collage invites the spectator to respond with a multiple consciousness in which forms, objects, and images are interchangeable. The robbers rejected this invitation by identifying the banknote as exclusively money—a giveaway to the police, thought my friend, that they

Max Ernst, plate from the book *Une Semaine de Bonté*, 1934.
COLLECTION, THE MUSEUM OF MODERN ART, NEW YORK, THE LOUIS E. STERN
COLLECTION

belonged to the lower cultural orders. Like realistic painters, the thieves recognized only the monomorphic realm of appearances solidified by common sense—a realm in which money is a category of its own and is not to be confused with other green rectangles. To cope with sensibilities of this sort, my friend reflected, the artist ought to have used a painted copy of a banknote instead of a genuine one; when the thieves tore it off the canvas, they would have discovered that the back was blank. In his view, people who break into apartments have a special need for the education in the problematic nature of visual experience supplied by collage.

As in other twentieth-century creations, there is a vein of farce in collage: its exposure of the duplicity of art is comparable to the tradition in the theatre, from Pirandello to Genet, of an actor's stepping out of character to remind the audience that "this is a play" and that actors are real people whose profession is pretending to be someone else. Through its interchanging of things and images of them, collage has provided the artist with the means of dissolving reality into endless visual absurdities. The use of these means is most obvious in the collages of Dadaists and Surrealists, such as Ernst, Picabia, and Magritte, but the instruments of farce provided by collage were already fully operative in Picasso's 1913 *Guitar*, in which the navel of a female figure is represented by a tiny circle of newsprint. The current "return to nature" in painting constitutes an abandonment of the comical questioning of appearances that has been the major interest of art since Cubism.

16

Futurism

Futurism, the Milanese art movement born in the years immediately preceding World War I, is the model for later twentieth-century aesthetic vanguards: its fierce criticism of contemporary culture and society aimed to stir up an uneasy self-consciousness, and it incorporated advanced techniques of publicity and showmanship, together with a militant rhetoric difficult for a modern public to ignore. Its message was spiritual stability through living in the present—a program that takes into account modern man's uncertain grasp on the past and the future. Futurism was an aesthetics of action geared to the rhythm of events. Wyndham Lewis, the British painter, novelist, and polemicist, whose Vorticism was a contemporary variant of Futurism, denied that Futurism looked to the future; Severini, whom he called the "foremost" of the Futurists, painted, he pointed out, Paris night spots, and everyone knew there would be no night spots in 1984. "Futurism," said Lewis, "means the Present, with the Past rigidly excluded."

Futurism was not anti-art, but, in rejecting memory and the ideal, it was hostile to the notion of lasting works, and it anticipated that the art of its time, including Futurist art, would rapidly become obsolete and be displaced by new expressions of creative vitality. When Robert Scull dumped his Abstract Expressionist, Pop, and color-field canvases at Sotheby Parke-Bernet, he achieved a realization of the art collector as Futurist. The works he sold—by de Kooning, Newman, Jasper Johns, Rauschenberg, and their contemporaries—had become "Past"; proof of this was their critical acceptance and the high prices they

Giacomo Balla, *Fist of Boccioni—Lines of Force*, 1915, cardboard and wood painted red, 33″ h. x 31″ w. x 12½″ d.

brought at the auction. Only by purging himself of his collection could Scull restore the poise of empty expectancy essential to a fresh confrontation of the new. Perhaps being the proprietor of a fleet of taxicabs was sufficient to inspire him with the spirit of the movement Lewis nicknamed "automobilism." An art critic who denounced the Scull-Sotheby sell-off as "the end of the art world" merely demonstrated, it seems to me, that she had been miseducated in the history of art. It is now sixty-five years since E. F. T. Marinetti, progenitor and guiding brain of Futurism, proclaimed that for art to stay alive it had to keep finding ways of bringing itself to an end. The listlessness in the studios today is undoubtedly due to a decade of artificial stabilization of art and to ongoing efforts by government and private cultural agencies, as well as by the art market, to prevent it from sinking out of sight in the present crisis of society.

Futurism identified art with physical dynamics and effusions of human energy. Futurist paintings, sculptures, and drawings bear such titles as *Path of a Gunshot* and *Fist of Boccioni; Force-Lines of the Fist of Boccioni* (Giacomo Balla); *Sea = Dancer* and *Soldier in Trench* (Gino Severini); *The Night of January 20, 1915, I Dreamed This Picture (Joffre's Angle of Penetration on the Marne Against Two German Cubes)* (Carlo Carrà); *Development of a Bottle in Space (Still Life), Riot in the Gallery,* and *The City Rises* (Umberto Boccioni). In place of static subjects—still-lifes, landscapes, portraits— Futurism found its motifs in various types of motion, whether of birds, winds, or machines, and in forms of risk and struggle, such as auto racing and combat.

The ultimate direction of Futurist activism was political, though Futurism did not specify what kind of politics it advocated. In Italy, under the influence of Marinetti, it became nationalist, militarist, and élitist; in Russia, where Marinetti built a following, it inclined toward the left. In the last analysis, Marinetti found more significance in Futurism than he did in forms of social revolution. "I am delighted to learn," he wrote in 1920, in *Beyond Communism*, "that the Russian Futurists are all Bolsheviks and that for a while Futurist art was the official Russian art. On May Day of last year the Russian cities were decorated with Futurist paintings. Lenin's trains were decorated on the outside with colored dynamic forms very like those of Boccioni, Balla, and Russolo. This does honor to Lenin and cheers us like one of our own victories. . . . Every people had, or still has, its passéism to overthrow."

Futurism revolutionized art by converting it into a field of action. Painting a picture was placed on a par with winning a race or organizing a mass meeting. A well-known photograph of Futurist chiefs on a visit to Paris shows Russolo, Carrà, Marinetti, Boccioni, and Severini in gangster overcoats and derbies staring belligerently into the camera like characters in an early night-club movie. What is interesting is not that tough guys should be artists but that artists should want to look like tough guys. Futurism replaced the artist as bohemian—identified by his guitar, his wine bottle, and his harlequin mask—with the artist as adventurer and cultural agitator; more exactly, with the artist band united by social, philosophical, and aesthetic precepts intended to put them in the van of society as men of the world. A public figure, or one engaged in forcing himself on the public, the artist was no longer so much a source of art objects (Picasso, Matisse) as he was an agonist displaying trophies of victory over society (Duchamp, Warhol).

Futurism had a program before it had paintings and sculptures; in this respect, its works can be seen as illustrations of Futurist doctrine. Moreover, Futurism had a leader who was not himself a painter. Yet Marinetti's concepts, while cohesive enough to give Futurist artists a common direction, were not so narrow as to hem them in. Marinetti was more of a muse than a commissar (the question of the advantages and drawbacks of basing art on ideology still remains to be investigated). Often referred to as the "impresario" of Futurism, Marinetti is an early example of the "artist" without a genre, or of the artist whose genre is used as an instrument in his campaign to transform all genres. He wrote poems, novels, and essays, but his true medium was the manifesto and, later, the boisterous "Futurist evening." This is another way of saying that the major talent of this rhapsodist and poet-anti-poet was for whipping up public attention; the 1960s might have recognized him as a master of "guerrilla theatre." He was adept at demonstrations—not yet even today an acknowledged art form, though it combines spectacle, decoration (banners, uniforms, slogans), rhetoric, noise, music, movement of masses. Marinetti's agitational public performances were to have tremendous reverberations in the Fascist and Communist mass demonstrations of Italy, Russia, and Germany.

Stylistically, Futurism is a derivative of Cubism, an animation of its patterns of visual data—eyes, rows of piano keys—peeping out from among layers of angles and curves. The relation is so close that the

Umberto Boccioni, *Unique Forms of Continuity in Space*, 1913, bronze, 48½″ x 34,″ including base.

two movements are often bracketed as Cubism/Futurism—for instance, in the chapter in *Movements in Modern Art*, by Donald Carroll and Edward Lucie-Smith,* and in the title of a book by Max Kozloff.** In philosophy, mood, and practice, however, Futurism was the direct antithesis of Cubism, and its struggle in painting was mainly directed against this predecessor. Cubism had diluted the formal tradition of European painting and sculpture by injecting into it folk and African elements, but without raising the issue of what was happening to Europe itself. With its concern for the inner logic of form, Cubism is the last grand expression of a kind of laissez-faire, or free commodity production, in art that considers gains in technical and formal resources to be valuable in themselves. Art after the first two decades of this century has, however, never been free of intervention, whether by the state or by the art market. The uprising of Futurism consisted in linking art to history rather than to art history; it imposed upon art the obligation to speak for the times. From Futurism on, the aesthetics of each new advanced art movement—from Dada, Surrealism, Constructivism, and Social Realism to Action painting, anti-Formal art, and Conceptual art—has included a conception of the historical situation and a strategy for dealing with it. There is an inherent agitational element in post-Cubist avant-garde art, which is felt to be present even when the artists involved choose—as in Pop Art—to disavow it.

With the arrival of Futurism, art began to aspire toward a complete conception of life, and, with that, toward a heroic way of living. Dada and Surrealism continued the attack of Futurism on social and cultural forms in the period between the two wars, while Constructivism engaged itself—during the early years of Communist rule—in rebuilding Russia on a rational basis, and the Bauhaus attempted a similar function in Weimar Germany.

That avant-garde paintings and sculptures should have become aspects of ideological striving is of momentous importance in the deciphering of their meaning. (Conceptual art arises from recognizing this ideological essence of contemporary paintings and sculptures, and drawing the conclusion that the works themselves can therefore be dispensed with.) If, despite sympathetic relations between Marinetti and Mussolini, Futurism proved unable to cohabit with Fascism, it was because both were totalitarian; and a similar irreconcilability between

* Donald Carroll and Edward Lucie-Smith, *Movements in Modern Art* (New York: Horizon Press, 1973).
** Max Kozloff, *Cubism and Futurism* (New York: Charterhouse Books, 1973).

a total aesthetic and totalitarian politics undermined the collaboration between Russian Futurism and Bolshevism noted by Marinetti, as well as later attempts of Constructivists and Surrealists to place themselves "in the service of the Revolution" (to quote the title of a Surrealist periodical of the 1930s). Kasimir Malevich—the founder of Suprematism, whose changes from ideology to ideology and from style to style (he was a Futurist from 1911 to 1912) were vividly indicated in a retrospective at the Guggenheim—also arrived, according to the catalogue of his show, at "the idea of art as an independent form of thought, a part of the human conceptual range on a level with religion and materialistic philosophy." But, of course, this view, and Suprematism itself, were unable to resist being crushed by the application of Soviet "doctrinary power."

Futurism has contributed its share to the icons of the twentieth century. Balla's multilegged trotting dog with a bouquet of tails, Severini's dotted armored train, Boccioni's bronze bottle that has the effect of having opened up when it was whirled, and his gladiator striding through time as if it were water streaming behind him are figures in the inner movie of modern visual culture that stand alongside Delaunay's tilted Eiffel Tower and Duchamp's descending nude. Yet the paintings and sculptures of the masters of Futurism are not of first rank in the creations of this century. One reason may be that the movement lasted only a short while; most of its outstanding work was produced in 1911–12. Before the end of World War I, Boccioni, Futurism's most vigorous artist, was dead, and the majority of the artists who had fallen in step with Marinetti, including the prerevolutionary Russians, had moved on to other modes. Wyndham Lewis questioned the creative élan of the Futurists on the ground that they were "too much theorists and propagandists"—a charge that in one form or another has been levelled against all advanced artists since Impressionism. Perhaps contradicting himself, Lewis also declared that "the effervescent, Active-Man of the Futurist imagination [a bit different from a theorist and propagandist] would never be a first-rate artist." My own view is that the profoundest lack in Futurism lay not in being too programmatic or in identifying art with action but in conceiving the "present" in terms of mechanical and technological phenomena—speed, crowds, "forces"—and the thrills of becoming one with them. That, however, was the mood of Futurism, and that is what its historical moment called upon it to embody, and for it excellence in art took second place to intensifying the novel quality of experi-

Umberto Boccioni, *The Bottle in Space*, 1912, bronze, 15″ h. x 24″ w.
THE LYDIA AND HARRY L. WINSTON COLLECTION (MRS. BARNETT MALBIN).

ence in one's own time. In any case, if this brief, overexcited art movement projected stimulating rays throughout modes of creation that came after it, that is so less because of its products than because of the pertinence of its ideas—even when they were wrong—of what it means to be alive in this uniquely unsettling era. For all his reservations about it, Wyndham Lewis praised Futurism by calling it "one of the alternative terms for modern painting."

17
Reginald Marsh:
Decline and Fall

Reginald Marsh belonged to the generation of artists immediately preceding the great modernist upheaval in American painting after the war. In background and career he was in many respects typical of his time. He was born into a financially comfortable family, showed a talent for drawing while he attended Yale, became a professional illustrator (he worked for the *News* and *The New Yorker*), and progressed slowly into painting after a period of study in Paris. I seem to recall similar phases in the biographies of Hopper, Sloan, and other of Marsh's contemporaries. With his illustrator's training and his eagerness to capture the images of the life around him, he sketched without pause until his sudden death in 1954; he even sketched an operation being performed upon him. Drawing was his umbilical link with the outer world, the specialized organ he evolved for absorbing appearances and projecting them onto paper. In his constant copying of nature, he was in the line of American "realism"—of Audubon, Eakins, Homer, Hopper, The Eight. The territory he staked out for himself was the crowds in Coney Island, bums in the Bowery, sailors on leave, burlesque, the circus, locomotives. Above all, he conceived the "Marsh girl." Fruit of his endless anatomical sketching, this self-enamored, full-bodied blond goddess, with spherical breasts and sturdy, beautifully contoured thighs and legs in knee-length flowing skirts, swept like a parade through his slums, posed on the stage of his burlesque theatres, floated sidesaddle on his merry-go-round horses, was ogled by businessmen, by derelicts, and by sailors on shore leave.

The Sketchbooks of Reginald Marsh* by Edward Laning, painter, muralist, and friend, contains two hundred drawings, plus photographs of Marsh at work in various city sites, and a brief but vigorous text that combines aggression (against art historians and modernists), storytelling, warmth, and nostalgia. Laning does not hesitate to inform the reader that in his view Marsh is "the greatest artist of his time"—though he doesn't expect agreement, because things have changed so drastically since Marsh died. Regardless of what one thinks of Marsh's status (in making his claim, Laning is no more frivolous, I suppose, than critics who confer the championship on painters of stripes or vacant canvases), one has no trouble concurring about the depth of difference between his period in art and the present; the difference would have been notable if only in the greater affection among artists of that time for one another. What could Laning possibly have had in mind when he said that Marsh was so great? One of the charms of *The Sketchbooks* is the remoteness to us of the attitudes that painters then took for granted. Marsh studied in Paris in the mid-twenties, but he failed to pay attention not only to the then-dominant Surrealists and the works of Matisse or Picasso, already famous for two decades, but even to the Impressionists. "What he discovered," observes Laning, apparently with approval, "was the Louvre." For six months, Marsh copied Old Masters; reequipped in this way, he returned to the bodies on Coney Island beaches and in the doorways of the Bowery.

Marsh was thus typical of the provincialism of prewar American painting, its ambition to translate local subject matter into the exalted idiom of Europe's masterpieces. This combination may have been what led Laning to decide that Marsh was superior to Picasso. Fortunately, misdirected aims do not prevent works of art from being interesting. Marsh's sketches developed a personal calligraphy that is most eloquent when it is most economical—for example, *Sailors and Girls, Central Park* and the line-and-blot stripper that decorates the back of the book jacket. As Marsh works up his drawings, they tend, like his paintings, to approach the look of sculpture and to acquire a peculiar heaviness. It is evident that Marsh aspired to endow the ephemera of the streets and the midway with the solidity of architectural decorations; his *Girl on Merry-Go-Round*, an opulent semi-nude, is a baroque carving, like the wooden horse on which she is partly poised, and the

---

* Edward Laning, *The Sketchbooks of Reginald Marsh* (New York: New York Graphic Society, 1973).

Reginald Marsh, *Steeplechase*, 1954.

composition as a whole could be the design for a sculptured fountain group. Equally sculptural are the amply proportioned *Two Girls on the Boardwalk*, a drawing in Chinese ink. The spirit of freshness and immediacy of the modernist painters of contemporary life never got through to Marsh.

Laning himself, though in different terms, calls attention to the artificial effect of Marsh's museum-derived aesthetic; "Marsh's omnipresent girl . . . is not real, but merely a projection of Marsh's fantasy." The artists of the pre-modern generation had not the formal means to make contact with the swiftly changing phenomena of the twentieth-century metropolis. Marsh, drawing pad in hand, looks constantly outward and sees only what his Louvre models allow him to recognize as art. The statuesque girls on the boardwalk are blondes, with classical torsos and fine Anglo-Saxon profiles, as are the dryad on the merry-go-round and the hip-grinding nymph on the burlesque stage—all myth-favored fleshy dolls, the artist's ideal sisters and love objects, sanctified by their earlier residence in the museum. A seated figure in a Marsh drawing of a Hudson River pier is an immigrated statue, and even his Coney Island mob scenes are made up of glorified types; I found but one drawing of Jews (an old couple on the beach), none of Italians, only a few of blacks. Laning points out that Marsh's Bowery bums originated in the derelicts he saw under the Pont Neuf, and that his striptease and circus motifs started out from the Folies-Bergère and the Cirque Médrano. Redoing Paris in Americanese was the essence of prewar American art, and it is the absence of the transposed Parisian styles that most sharply separates present-day American art from that of Marsh's generation.

According to Laning, Marsh in his later years had a strong feeling that his environment was fading—"They've torn down the 'L,' the burlesque is gone; I hardly recognize Coney Island anymore"—and when he received the gold medal of the American Academy of Arts and Letters he declared that he was "not a man of this century," a statement that goes to the heart of the matter. Making a thoughtful comparison between Marsh's teeming beaches and movie lobbies and Hopper's empty streets and bedrooms, Laning finds that both represent "a place of death"—love has departed from America, and both the crowd and the single individual are beset by a fatal loneliness. The Marsh girl herself is a death deity—Marsh's Great White Whale. In one of his last paintings she once more rides a wooden horse on a Steeple-chase rail, but now to Laning the horse is a horse of the apocalypse and the British sailor perched behind her fluffy figure is a dead man. Laning sees in Marsh a prophet of the Decline and Fall of the American Empire. Maybe it was the empire that collapsed, or maybe it was the aesthetic dependence that kept American artists out of this century that collapsed. In either case, Laning's elegiac conclusion is testimony that American art had during the war years reached the end of the road and was compelled to find a new starting point.

18

The Profession of Art:
The W.P.A. Art Project

The demonstrations of artists in the thirties, under the banner of "Jobs for All Unemployed Artists," were a kind of charade in which art was presented as an accepted profession in the United States. Even if one ducked the always troubling question of who is an artist, one could not, of course, reasonably expect that all artists would be placed on a payroll. Radical charades were, however, characteristic of the Depression, and intelligent individuals felt no embarrassment in behaving as if "the people" or "the proletariat" had come to power and were prepared to welcome suggestions about arrangements in the new social order. Left-wing theories educated artists to see themselves as the cultural representatives of the masses and as endowed thereby with the privilege of having a say as to how governmental institutions, and even privately endowed ones, ought to be run. A hallucinating assumption of proletarian power was, for example, implicit in the protest of artists against the vandalism committed by the Rockefellers in breaking up Diego Rivera's mural for Rockefeller Center because it contained a likeness of Lenin—after all, the Rockefellers had paid for the mural, and their capitalist loot had been accepted. Cultural combats based on this sort of fanciful supposition that the profit system had been set aside in favor of some higher scale of rights were an everyday component of the life of art in the thirties; they contributed an atmosphere of giddiness in which dreamlike demands, such as the right to remake the world and be paid for doing so, were tiresomely reiterated.

Mr. Lincoln Rothschild, a contributor to *The New Deal Art Projects: An Anthology of Memoirs*, edited by Francis V. O'Connor,* recalls that in the thirties the "announcement of the gift to the nation of Andrew Mellon's great collection of old masters, with funds to build a large museum to house it under government auspices in Washington, D.C., brought forth criticism [from the American Artists' Congress] of the administrative arrangements because of failure to include representation for professional artists in its governing body, and lack of concern for American art and the living American artist in the program of the museum." The protest presupposes that in the United States "professional artists" have become an intellectually coherent quasi-official body entitled to supervise any addition to the nation's cultural life—a body comparable, say, to the Artists' Union in the U.S.S.R. But the American Artists' Congress exposed its lack of seriousness when it declared that the gift of a "great collection of old masters" indicated a "lack of concern for American art and the living American artist." To whom would the availability of masterpieces be of greater "concern" than to artists? Or was it the wish of the Artists' Congress that Mellon should have provided it with funds to buy paintings from its members to hang alongside the Old Masters? Actually, the Artists' Congress was only playing at being a professional organization, just as the union of artists on New Deal projects was only playing at representing a profession or trade when it staged those demonstrations demanding jobs for all unemployed artists. Although it pretended to speak for America's professional artists, it was a political group set up a short time before its statement about the Mellon collection as a unit in a network of homogeneous "fronts," in various cultural fields, through which persons with reputations could lend their prestige to the movement against war and Fascism; it recruited artists who were far apart both in their practice of art and in their conception of it (from Stuart Davis, its executive secretary, to newspaper cartoonists), and its identification with the economic interests of—in Rothschild's phrase—"the professional fine artist" proved to be a façade when it collapsed after the attack on Finland by the Soviet Union as an ally of Nazi Germany.

For all their frivolous aspects, however, the demands of the artists for jobs and for power were part of a drive to affirm a new social basis for art in American society. Painting and sculpture were to be

* Francis V. O'Connor, ed., *The New Deal Art Projects: An Anthology of Memoirs* (Washington, D.C.: Smithsonian Institution Press, 1972).

reconstituted as careers open to all. The effort during the Depression to establish art as a profession was the chief interest of art in the thirties. The theme, apparently unpremeditated, of present and future employment runs through all the reminiscences in Mr. O'Connor's book. The desire of artists for acceptance by society is responsible for the pathos of art in the years before the war and much of the boredom that hung over that period.

Before the thirties, the practice of art in America had been limited to the well-to-do and their protégés, and to artists supporting themselves through commercial work (they included Edward Hopper and John Sloan, to mention the first names that come to mind). The normal prerequisite to being a full-time artist was having an income; in O'Connor's book, Sloan, a veteran member of the early-twentieth-century The Eight, is quoted as offering virtually his entire life's work for "an income of fifty dollars a week, guaranteed for the rest of my life so I can paint." Obviously, Sloan wanted not a job but the means to go his own way as a painter; his was still the traditional idea of the artist as aristocrat: for fifty dollars a week he could be a bohemian—that is, self-elected aristocrat. In the Depression, however, "income" became translated into "job," and the artist was no longer a gentleman, or bohemian pseudo-gentleman, but a socially employed expert. It seemed easy to raise painting to the level of a profession when members of most professions had nothing to do; an artist who cannot sell his paintings is not substantially different from a lawyer without clients. In its lack of earning capacity, art also took on the aspect of a trade whose practitioners were out of work. The Depression brought forth the novel idea of the unemployed artist—a radical revision of the traditional conception, for it implied that it was normal for artists to be hired for fees or wages and that in the absence of commissions they were idle.

In this new version of his relation to his products, the artist was bidden to cease thinking of himself as an adventurer of genius and to believe that what he wanted most was to be put to work. He was no longer to desire freedom through an income, as did Sloan; he was to seek the assurance of a professional rate of pay. Though the Artists' Congress adopted no aesthetic position, its philosophy of how the artist ought to function in society was unambiguous and militant. Rothschild says that the congress organized "what was hoped might be a pilot attempt . . . to broaden economic opportunity for the professional fine artist and to break down the sharp distinction between 'fine and applied' art that had been generated in the nineteenth century by romantic, spiritual pretensions regarding the purpose of the arts. With the cooperation of a friendly manufacturer, a competition was held to obtain novel pictorial designs for gift-wrapping papers." Apparently, "broadened economic opportunity" for "the professional fine artist" consisted in his ceasing to be a fine artist. The liquidation of Romanticism into gift wrappings not only contained the promise of economic stability but had the support of the Leninist conception of the artist as cultural worker, as well as of the neo-Thomist theory of the artist as "maker" or craftsman. Regardless of philosophy or financial status, artists of the thirties were tempted to march to the rhythm of "We Want Jobs!"

The only potential employer of artists en masse was the federal government. Early on, Washington proved willing to include needy artists in its work-relief program. But emergency employment fell short of the ambitions of the new artists' organizations. What they sought from the government was a status equal to that of agencies filling indispensable functions: national defense, forest preservation, mail delivery. The advocates of total employment of artists argued that a public need for art existed, together with a public demand no less real because it had so far failed to express itself. A favorable response to a Works Progress Administration Art Project post-office mural by citizens of a Tennessee town was offered as evidence that the American public was entreating Washington to supply it with art. The Marxism of the 1930s spread the reassuring dogma that an appetite for art is inherent in human nature. On this premise, it was logical for the artist to feel that he was in the company of a cultural vanguard engaged in bringing about the aesthetic self-fulfillment of the masses. To supply him with the means for this transcendental undertaking was the obligation of a government founded on the promise of life, liberty, and the pursuit of happiness.

The New Deal Administration reacted to the notion of the Art Project as the embryo of a future community of art lovers by balancing itself on the ambiguous position of art as the supplier of food (to the artist) and of inspiration (to society). According to Ms. Audrey McMahon, director of the Art Project in New York, "Hopkins [head of the W.P.A.] saw it as a relief setup; Cahill [national director of the W.P.A. Art Project] as a cultural opportunity." Relief meant a job to pay the rent; cultural opportunity meant raising the artist and his public at least to the level of Europe. To avoid deciding which purpose it favored, the W.P.A. incorporated the Art Project into its Professional and Service Division—an evasion of the choice between employing professionals and servicing the unemployed that kept the program in a constant turmoil. Quotas to govern the hiring of non-relief artists— considered essential for high-quality production—kept changing at the whim of officials and the projects were constantly pruned, expanded, then reduced again. The neurasthenia of the government in dealing with art subjected the project artist to a war of nerves, as if a bet had been made as to who would get worn out first. However, the torments of the artists were for the most part the result of the indifference of both high-level officials and the public.

Despite all rebuffs, the prevailing feeling of the thirties consisted in what one of O'Connor's authors characterizes as "the desire [of artists] to participate as dignified citizens with their own creative skills which they wished to bring to the community at large." The aim of reaching the common man resulted in the humiliation of the artists and a costly misdirection of their energies. The Art Project was an important event in American art, but it was not important in regard to style. Critics have blamed the program for the static repetitiousness of the works executed, as if being paid by the government prevented the artists from developing a new sensibility. But the widespread acceptance of the sentimental caricature of the artist as a citizen patronizing his neighbors with his skills was just as great an obstruction to originality as was employment on the project. The standard, economic or political in origin, of what the layman could appreciate was as strictly applied off the project as on it. The new ideology of art for the community cut the link between painting and sculpture in this country and the advanced art of Europe, which Americans had been engaged in absorbing during the twenties. The dullness of project art owed less to bureaucratic regulation than to the artists' fixation about influencing the public. Yet it cannot be denied that the project situation reinforced the social obsession of the artists and was unfavorable to the exploration of new possibilities. Project artists could paint as they chose, but as Peter Busa has complained, "What we did on the Project was colored by our having to do commissioned work." Even when paintings were not actually commissioned, artists felt the presence of a commissioning power. Art that "communicated" with the artist's audience or its representatives was encouraged at the expense of intuition and temperament. One might say that "Projectism" was inherent in the project, in the form of a rational purposefulness in conception and execution, and that this attitude inhibited the arbitrariness, the perversity, and the need to satisfy an I-know-not-what of feeling that goes with creation. Its search for political backing and its eagerness to allocate paintings to schools, libraries, and the offices of congressmen automatically led the project to overstress the public nature of art. Too much importance was placed on the theme of the work and the factual accuracy of details; Edward Laning tells, in the O'Connor symposium, of the difficulty of reaching agreement on whether the first linotype machine was unveiled under an electric bulb or a kerosene lamp. Ideally, the "story" of a project painting and its message would be self-explanatory, as in Laning's *Mergenthaler and the Linotype* and James Newell's *The Evolution of Western Civilization*, but if necessary the project artist stood ready to expound its meaning.

"Distortion of reality"—that is, expressive drawing and color—was kept at a minimum to avoid upsetting the spectator unfamiliar with art or provoking him to damaging wisecracks; the philistine humor of New York's otherwise admired Mayor LaGuardia was particularly menacing on official occasions. The depressing effect of the public presence on the art of the thirties is best exemplified by the mural executed for the Newark Airport by Arshile Gorky. This ten-panel work, *Aviation: Evolution of Forms Under Aerodynamic Limitations*, was conceived by Gorky at about the time of his easel paintings *Enigmatic Combat* and his four versions of *Image in Xhorkom*. The artist, then thirty-two, was approaching a note of his own in his experiments with advanced models (Picasso, Braque, Masson). The contrast in invention, poetic suggestion, and aesthetic quality between the *Xhorkom* compositions and the Newark mural amounts almost to a split personality. *Aviation*, inspired by the project principle of conveying a theme and by Gorky's ambition to be professionally accredited, is an exercise in Cubist-style pattern-making, already current among fashionable portrait painters and designers. By the standard of Gorky's studio paintings, which reach into memory and the unknown, the mural was hackwork. Unfortunately—or luckily, from the standpoint of Gorky's development—even this contrived wall decoration was too "advanced" for the officialdom of the period. Gorky accompanied his mural with an elaborate explanation, in which Cubist theories of two-dimensionality were associated with objects seen from the sky and with the experience of flying, and he cited "the new vision that flight had given to the eyes of man." Gorky's resort

Edward Laning, *Mergenthaler and the Linotype.*

Arshile Gorky at work on *Aviation: Evolution of Forms under Aero-dynamic Limitations*.

to visual and verbal platitudes did not, however, prevent LaGuardia from walking out in the middle of the artist's elucidation of another one of his paintings. Nor did it save *Aviation* from destruction by order of the commanding officer when the Newark Airport was taken over by the military during World War II. One of the great lessons of the thirties is that in our time art cannot educate people, even in art. The "dignified citizen" creating for the "community at large" is a utopian ideal that postulates a society which does not exist and is not likely to.

How shallow were the roots of art as a profession in 1930s America was dramatically demonstrated by the rapid drying up of the Art Project with the start of the defense program and its rapid closing down after Pearl Harbor. Both the presumed people's demand for art and the wholesale satisfaction of that demand by America's newly unveiled reservoir of talent ceased overnight. For the first time, project artists could be said to be genuinely "unemployed." Most found jobs in art-related trades, such as silk-screen printing and map-making, or entered the Army or the war industries. A steady income from painting and sculpture became, as it had been before the Depression, the prerogative of a closed guild whose work enhanced the prestige of the rich and of the politically prominent.

It was the extinction of the illusory market of "art for the people" that brought to light once more an essential dimension of art—I mean art as a vocation practiced for its own sake or to satisfy what the American Artists' Congress had scorned as "spiritual pretensions." The profession of art is actually two professions: one directed toward public taste, the other toward forms of experience embodied only in art and to which creations from all times stand witness. In relating himself and his work to this extended dimension of art, the contemporary artist engages in a mythic vocation, in which, beyond current fashions and social and political problems, he seeks the approval of the masters. In the thirties, this second, "inner" profession, founded on art's values, was centered not in the project and its outstanding ideas and personages but in a handful of young artists—Gorky, de Kooning, Pollock, Gottlieb, Rothko—sensitive to social demands and confused by them, and in the school of Hans Hofmann, which propagated principles of form and feeling derived from the advanced European art movements. Once opportunities for art as employment ended, art for its own sake and for the sake of the inner development of the artist came to

Arshile Gorky, *Xhorkom*, ca. 1936, oil, 40″ x 52″.
COURTESY SIDNEY JANIS GALLERY. PHOTO BY ERIC POLLINER

the fore as a pioneering collective phenomenon. (Perhaps the project, by ceasing to exist, deserves credit for this.) Out of a job, American art forgot its mirage of a respectable social status and dedicated itself to greatness.

Since the emergence, during the past fifteen years, of new categories of customers, private and institutional, for American painting, accompanied by tales of rags to riches in the art world, art has reappeared in the roster of viable professions. With that suddenness with which innovations pop up fully grown in American life, the social potentialities of painting and sculpture (e.g., in banks and office-building lobbies) have presented themselves on a vastly larger scale than they did in the thirties. University training courses in all media, galleries, museums, and grammar-school programs, domestic and international art-appreciation tours—a situation complete with individual and corporate sponsors and tax deductions—have put the New Deal Art Project in the shade. Yet despite this almost magical expansion, the question remains whether art in America can ever stabilize itself as a profession and still qualify as "fine art." Today, an agitation in the manner of the thirties for career opportunities in art is growing more insistent, swelled by demands for equality for blacks, Indians, women. The social issues are complicated by the fact that art does not exist as art without the mythical essence to which social issues are irrelevant.

19

Place Patriotism and the New York Mainstream

Regional painting is usually a matter less of scenery than of polemical contention, maintained with varied degrees of ferocity. The common theme of artists and their spokesmen in Montreal, Albuquerque, Mexico City, Rome, Tokyo is "We have managed (or can manage) to be different." In each instance, the antagonist is New York seen as the center of a global process of art-historical "development" that dooms all other places to belated imitation. An invitation to a New Yorker to discuss New York art and its influence amounts to a provocation; the visitor is expected to offend through bragging and Big Brother condescension. "A good subject would be 'New York, Art Capital of the World,'" an Israeli official suggested sardonically when I was invited to speak at the Jerusalem Museum. If New York is the site from which art history is launched, to be present there would seem indispensable to the creation of an art that matters. One who fails to respond to the cue broadcast from New York is considered to be an exile from both past and future. On the other hand, for the art of a place to differ from that of New York, and to dare to be satisfied with its difference, is to have achieved an identity of its own—a "school" that deserves attention. Regionalism today, in art as in politics, is the revolt of geography against history.

A show in New York of twelve artists from Los Angeles owed less to characteristics of locality than to prevalent aesthetic notions. According to a catalogue foreword by the ubiquitous Maurice Tuchman, of the Los Angeles County Museum of Art, and his associate

Jane Livingston, two tendencies are to be noted among young West Coast artists: art based on art, and an anti-formalist primitivism or ingenuousness. Neither of these preferences is, of course, confined to the West Coast. Art about art is worldwide, and as we shall see, primitivism, ingenuousness, and anti-formalism are also distinguishing features attributed to Chicago "imagism." But if attitudes in Los Angeles art do not derive from that city's pavements, they suffice, nevertheless, according to Tuchman-Livingston, to remove it from the New York orbit and thus to affirm the existence of a "Los Angeles School": "One immediately senses a very great difference in character between this show and comparable gatherings of young New York painters, which [who?] seem by and large more rigidly formalist in the sense of problem-solving and at the same time more delectable." In 1972 Tuchman-Livingston continued to view New York art as the Minimalist abstraction of the sixties, and the departure from this style in Los Angeles was their evidence of regional independence. It is interesting, however, that when, a few years earlier, art in Los Angeles even outdid New York art in being "rigidly formalist," the same strategy of asserting difference was employed to give Los Angeles art a local trademark; an exhibition, by ten Los Angeles artists, of colored plastic boxes and slabs, semi-geometric vacuo-form test tubes, twisted metal bands, and paintings of stripes and chevrons that fitted neatly into New York avant-gardist fashion was sent to Seattle in 1966, accompanied by a catalogue in which John Coplans, organizer of the show, insisted that "style in Los Angeles art, whether conceived of as a characteristic of a collective identity, a sense of place, a mode of procedure, or a shared imagery, is unlike that of New York." He went on to find that painting and sculpture in Los Angeles are an art "ruptured from historical context" and "without affiliation to the central line of development taking place in New York." In sum, to acquire an absolute identity outside the format of art history, the art of a place, regardless of its characteristics, needs only to eradicate the fingerprints of New York.

The new Los Angeles show contained not a single positive feature of locality, whether of mood, lie of the land, surface texture, or way of life; even the takeoffs of film-company insignia by Ed Ruscha and the aggressive shininess of glass and plastics by Larry Bell and Craig Kauffman, prominent in the Seattle exhibition, had been superseded by studio conceits. The later creations are freer in imagination than their predecessors but no less dependent on world-circling modes. Form

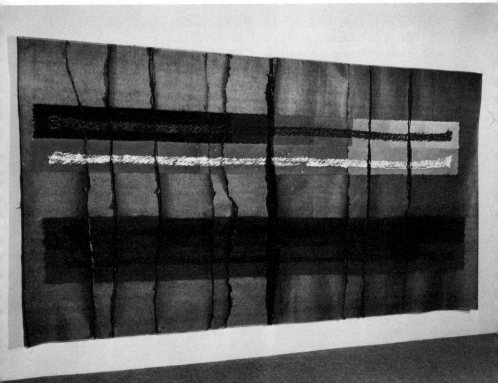

Jack Barth, *Traces #5 (for John McLaughlin)*, 1972, paper, pastels, light-reflective paint, 72″ x 137½″.

was inventively derived from materials in Jack Barth's torn and reconnected heavy paper battings, in Allan McCollum's canvas constructed of tiny painted rectangles, in Scott Grieger's composition of separately suspended painted planes, and in Richard Jackson's construction that exposes the backs of canvases on stretchers. If, as Peter Schjeldahl contended in the *Times*, the Los Angeles creations could not "dispel an air of instant familiarity," this made them neither more nor less art of a place than the work of young artists in Soho, whose works seem equally "familiar." After a hundred years of deepening and stretching each modernist style, there exists a modernist look, or set of looks, so extensive that to find a point of departure outside of it is virtually impossible; the complex of modes can be modified only by work from within them, and the young artist usually has not had enough time to accomplish this. For Schjeldahl, the resemblance between Los Angeles and New York art proved the futility of regional revolt. Like Coplans, he considered New York art the embodiment of art history, but he believed that history was bound to win over place. "It is, finally, perhaps a little foolish to speak of California art *versus* New York art. New York's gravitational field is so strong that any American working in a mainstream (New York) mode will, should he become influential, more or less automatically be 'a New York artist.'" Yet Schjeldahl himself named an exception—Ed Ruscha, whose silk-screen prints of flies and cockroaches on smooth surfaces expressed for Schjeldahl the "sense" of Los Angeles as a place that is "gaga and sinister."

Claes Oldenburg has said that Chicago gives him a "sepulchral feeling" and that it has "a strange metaphysical elegance of death about it"—which is not very far from being "gaga and sinister," like Los Angeles. Franz Schulze, a local art critic and godfather of Chicago Imagist art, who wrote the catalogue for the exhibition of this art at the Museum of Contemporary Art in which Oldenburg is quoted, as well as a book about artists in the show,* is convinced that art in his city reflects a mood distinct from that of any other spot on earth. He describes Chicago paintings with such adjectives as "perverse," "obsessive," "anti-rational," "private," "freakish," "vulgar," "delinquent," all of which become with him terms of praise. Happy the region that harbors a Franz Schulze! He is *for* Chicago art as Dostoevsky was for the Russian peasant: the more repellent the traits, the more precious.

* Franz Schulze, *Fantastic Images: Chicago Art Since 1945* (Chicago: Follett Publishing Company, 1972).

Chicago Imagist art is not regional in the old sense of picturing local settings, history, folkways. Schulze's Chicagoans turn inward, away from Chicago; his key word for them is "introverted." Their art rejects the visible Chicago represented by its lofty buildings in the tradition of Bauhaus rationality. If the paintings and sculptures in the "Chicago Imagist Art" show had anything in common, it was a turn of mind akin to Oldenburg's "metaphysical" element; as in the Los Angeles exhibition, not one work in it had any reference to the visual realities of its point of origin. This is place art by means of exclusion of place.

The best known of Schulze's artists is H. C. Westermann, maker of boxes and cabinets with touches of depravity. At least equally "sepulchral" are Seymour Rosofsky's decayed, epicene figure entitled *Homage* and his *The Unemployment Office*, with its reiterated planes suggestive of a warehouse of coffins. Cosmo Campoli, a veteran modeller of ganglionic birds, pregnant eggs, skulls, and hex effigies, presented his Chicago credentials with the ominous, primitivistic *Birth of Death*. Leon Golub, a New York painter whom I find more wistful than death-dealing, but who claims an ineradicable Chicago coloration, offered evidence of adherence to the Schulze underground with *Burnt Man IV* and his giant wrestlers, who look like figures in antique funeral games. There are charnel intimations, too, in George Cohen's flat, armless woman-shapes and constructions made of mirrors and dismembered dolls, in Irving Petlin's streaked male nudes marching in tense formations, and in the courting of campy gruesomeness in Don Baum's assemblages of dolls attacked by skeletal ravishers. Kerig Pope's *Two Infants Observing Nature* combines the organic and the mechanical in a manner reminiscent of Max Ernst's *Garden Airplane Trap*; Ellen Lanyon achieves similar effects but with fantasy added; Steven Urry has designed wandering visceral sculptures in metal that bring to mind Mickey Mouse. The rowdy element in "Chicago Imagist Art" was supplied by June Leaf, whose puppet theatre of rural types is a cross between Red Grooms's cutouts and Punch and Judy, and by the comic-strip-related grotesqueries cum occasional pornography ("brutish," in Schulze's idiom of flattery) and the color-TV hues of James Nutt, Gladys Nilsson, Ed Paschke, and Karl Wirsum.

"Chicago Imagist Art" was a lively, attractive show. Did the sum of these creations add up, as Schulze contends, to a collective genius of place? Are the nobility of Golub, the reflectiveness of Cohen compatible with the rattiness of the Hairy Who as aspects of a single

June Leaf, *Box Lady*, 1964–65, acrylic on papier-mâché, 17″ x 15½″ x 11″.

Jim Nutt, *It's a Long Way Down*, 1972, acrylic on masonite, 33⅞"
x 24¾".

psychic formation? Among the best items were compositions by Miyoko Ito and Irene Siegel that had no temperamental relation to the theme of the exhibition. As might have been expected after the example of Los Angeles, what passed for Chicago art owed less to positive local traits than to a shared resistance to New York and the "mainstream." "In Chicago," wrote Schulze, "there is not only a proclivity toward literary and imagistic art but a tendency to be defiant of the implications of linear art history. New Yorkers, on the other hand, have a big stake in art history." Like Tuchman-Livingston, Schulze was fighting the formalism of the sixties with which New York is identified in his mind. Of course, anti-"mainstream" shows comparable to that in Chicago could be, and have been, put on in New York, too: the exhibitions of the Rhino Horn group, to mention only one example, constituted a revolt against the "uptown" commissars of formalist art history. Another kind of anti-formalist show would include all the artists in the East Hampton "A Sense of Place" exhibition, plus Abstract Expressionists and Pop artists, from Louise Nevelson to George Segal, who have been battered by the formalist mainstream.

In his eagerness to demonstrate the aesthetic and spiritual difference of Chicago art, Schulze distorts the past of American art since the war by converting artists such as Pollock and Rothko into equivalents of museum curators with a "reverence" for art history. In claiming the appearance of "a definable ideology in art" in Chicago, Schulze is duplicating in reverse the worst feature of his mistaken idea of New York uniformity by substituting a formula for analysis of the actual nature of art in the Second City. Chicago art, it seems, has only to practice a kind of aesthetic know-nothingism and its validity is assured. Yet, devoid both of a grasp of Chicago as a place and of an outlook on art today, the works at the Museum of Contemporary Art failed to convey authority. What was missing in "Chicago Imagist Art" was precisely an aesthetically persuasive image. Instead of asserting how things are either in Chicago or in art, the paintings were displays of personal whims. Lanyon's *Human Head in a Fish Bowl (Singing, Laughing, Talking)* is an instance. To Schulze, this fanciful arbitrariness "represents the tradition of eccentric individualism long associated with the Middle West." But while eccentricity may constitute a tradition when it produces a Model T in the basement, it is not a tradition in art; it is, in fact, the opposite of a tradition. Chicago whimsicality flourishes at the expense of the intellectual element in art, without which painting and sculpture reduce themselves to crafts

Edward Paschke, *Elcina*, 1973, oil on canvas, 60″ x 38″.
COURTESY DESON-ZAKS GALLERY, CHICAGO, AND MUSEUM OF
CONTEMPORARY ART, CHICAGO.

carried on.as a hobby. If the pressure of formalist art history impelled painting and sculpture in the sixties toward a zero of experience, an art of place (and of time) can retrieve richness only through sensibilities activated by new concepts of art. "Primitivism" today is an inherited approach, and for all their "introversion," the images of the Chicago painters rest upon recent styles that have become second nature in placing paint on canvas. Schulze's exhibition was thoroughly "art historical" in its striving for modernist effects.

The reality behind the regional problem is the same everywhere: that all localities have their defectors—there are also defectors from the downtown lofts of New York. Artists in all places struggle with the need to convince themselves that, as Schulze succinctly puts it, "after all, art is possible here," and that artists who took off for greener fields suffered a loss by doing so. What makes art in New York central is that the question "Is art possible *here?*" tends to be transposed into the question "Is art possible?"—a question that has the advantage of touching a deeper cultural disturbance than the limitations of a locality.

20

Trials of Eros

Since art lives by contradicting its immediate past, it was logical throughout the late sixties to expect that the cool, impersonal abstractions, hard-edged or soft, that occupied the galleries would be followed by creations seeking to arouse the strongest feelings. Aesthetics and formal art history would be forced to accommodate themselves to politics, religion (metaphysics), and sex. Of these, sex held the lead, owing to the prevalence of the theme in the work of surviving leaders of Pop Art—for example, Segal's plaster casts of friends making love, Wesselmann's *Great American Nude* series, Warhol's deliberately platitudinous sex symbols (pistols, blurred mouths). As far back as 1966, the Sidney Janis Gallery, continually sifting the moods of the art world for the glitter of a new fashion, opened the season with a display of what it hoped would be pictorial scandals under the forthright title of "Erotic Art." As proof of the catholicity of this theme, the cover of the catalogue was ornamented with images of embracing couples—from the art of the ancient Greeks and Egyptians, through Rembrandt and Poussin, to Brancusi and Delvaux. Another boost to sex in art was the group of cartoons of copulation produced by Picasso as part of his celebrated 1968 series of prints; so graphic was this reaffirmation of the tradition of Eros that the Art Institute of Chicago, where the series was first unveiled, withheld these salacious etchings from the general public. To the photorealists of the turn of the sixties, nudity, reproduced to the last pore and hair curl, ranks with automobiles and storefronts as preferred data of painting and sculpture. The recent international Documenta 5 exhibition in Germany blandly dissolved any surviving distinction between erotic art, obscenity, and pornography by representing sex in all its modes—from sadomasochism, with chains and self-inflicted wounds, to lifelike plastic nudes committed to an eternal round of investigating each other's bodies. A stimulant to the erotic in art is the women-in-the-arts movement, at least in connection with its talk of "female imagery" and the desire of some to even the score with males for their enjoyment of pictures of unclothed ladies by taking the pants off men. Though it may be incorrect to conclude that the erotic has assumed as prominent a role in painting and sculpture as it has in film, the theatre, and fiction, there is no doubt that a strong surge of interest in it has arisen in both new art and the art continuing out of the past.

Two recently published books attempt to give an account of erotic art and to sum up its present situation and its future. Edward Lucie-Smith's *Eroticism in Western Art** begins with glimpses of the exaggerated sexual parts of the prehistoric Venuses and demigods of the caves and the orgiastic perversities of the Greeks of the fifth century B.C. recorded on the rims of cups and vases, takes a side glance at façades in India crowded with coupling gods and their attendants, and after a summary of Renaissance eroticism, arrives at the contributions to visual sexual excitation of the twentieth century, both in and outside of art. *Erotic Art Today*, by Volker Kahmen,** a translation from the German, concentrates on the variegated sexual fantasies of artists of the twentieth century—a subject that has to a large degree been excluded from the consciousness of the American art public by recent criticism, which has trained it to see paintings exclusively in terms of depth and flatness.

Lucie-Smith and Kahmen are both Freudians, but of different types. The first restricts himself to the psychoanalysis that has become a species of folklore, in that some of its concepts have entered into the common vocabulary so that everyone knows that certain objects stand for sexual organs and activity or that torture can be pleasurable not only to the torturer but to his victim as well. Thus Lucie-Smith confines his interpretations to unmistakable symbols; almost all his illustrations are patently erotic—pictures of naked people doing things or

---

* Edward Lucie-Smith, *Eroticism in Western Art* (New York: Praeger Publishers, 1972).
** Volker Kahmen, *Erotic Art Today* (New York: New York Graphic Society, 1972).

Pablo Picasso, L.300, from his suite, *347 Gravures*, 1968, etching, edition 50, 15 x 20 cm.

having things done to them, watching or being watched. In present-day art, he is also concerned with overt sex as it is exemplified by such items as Francis Bacon's *Two Men on a Bed* and George Segal's *Legend of Lot.*

In contrast to Lucie-Smith, Kahmen is a systematic Freudian, to whom all art is erotic at bottom and requires psychoanalytic elucidation—except perhaps pornography, which in his opinion is too engrossed in the physical to be art and—perhaps what amounts to the same thing—requires no interpretation. Any interpenetration, such as of planes by Albers or Vasarely or of chevrons by Noland, stands for an erotic act. In one category or another, such as "concealed erotic stimulus producing works which do not seem erotic" and "sensual tension created through the arrangement of forms," *Erotic Art Today* includes the whole range of twentieth-century art, from lustful graffiti by Picasso, Dali, Bellmer, and Dubuffet to austere abstractions by Mondrian, Newman, Tony Smith, and Larry Bell. Each of Kahmen's three hundred and forty-nine illustrations is subjected to an analysis designed to disclose its erotic content. Thus, sexual desire would appear to be the animating force of art in our time, as it has been in all the centuries since the caves.

In the context of Kahmen's translations of symbols, modern art seems rich in erotic feeling and invention. This impression is, however, deceptive. Many of the works in *Erotic Art Today* are erotic only in the author's Freudian version of them, or in the sense that towers, trees, and lagoons are acknowledged sex symbols, though we are not normally excited by them. In art, at any rate, a distinction must be made between paintings and sculptures whose erotic content is discovered by the analyst and those that arouse erotic feelings by merely being seen. To interpret a Newman abstraction or an Albers geometrical demonstration as erotic is similar to the distortion of imposing a Cubist structure upon a *frottage* by Ernst. The substitution of psychoanalysis for the formalist criticism of the sixties does not promise much of an improvement. A primary attraction of an overtly erotic art work is that it can dispense with interpretation. It delivers its matter directly to the senses: the usual response to it is an interval of worldlessness. In evoking silence, the erotic image provides a model for aesthetic appreciation—one the art world is especially in need of after its long siege of critical overanalysis. For the Freudian, however, works of art are inseparable from his system of symbolic references. Granted that today we are all ideologists of one sort or another, it is all the more important to avoid mistaking concepts for feelings and perceptions.

Besides including images that would excite no one, *Erotic Art Today* unjustifiably expands the quantity of sex imagery in contemporary painting and sculpture by failing to distinguish between erotic art and erotic photographs of art: the photograph of Heizer's trench cut in a lawn bears a resemblance to the sexual furrow of Gerhard Richter's *Female Student*, but the actual earthwork would create no such association. Similarly, the slashed canvas of Fontana's *Concetto Spaziale—Attese*, which in the reduced size and close-up shot of a photograph seems an erotic statement, instead calls to mind (as it is seen on the wall) the spatial concept, suggested by its title, of the picture surface and the rule against violating it.

Kahmen's collection of illustrations leads to the conclusion that an outstanding feature of art in our day, even in its most uninhibited expressions, is an almost total absence of sensuousness. In contrast to the opulent bodies that fill the pages of Lucie-Smith's *Eroticism in Western Art* from the sixteenth through the nineteenth century, sexuality in current erotic art consists for the most part of caricatures, suggestive scrawls, and above all, more or less lewd visual jokes. In Picasso's etchings, the artist charges upon his pinheaded mistress, all breasts and buttocks, with a brush in one hand and a palette in the other, while a wrinkled voyeur, generally taken to be the aged Picasso himself, soberly scrutinizes the performance. Dubuffet does his best to match the nastiness of drawings on fences and in the lavatories of a mental institution. Mario Merz retaliates for the Fall and the fig leaf by placing a patch over the crotch of a tree, and Marisol's *Love* consists of a plaster mask with a Coca-Cola bottle jammed into its mouth.

More than forty years ago, the Surrealists saw that in our civilization the erotic could no longer survive except at night and in the darkness of the unconscious; as soon as it emerged into daylight, it either dissolved or was reduced to physical data. Breton exalted Nadja as the dissolving dream of Eros that manifests itself on a street corner, then vanishes into the traffic; Delvaux's sleepwalking nudes on railroad platforms and boardwalks, and Magritte's faces and bodies, reconstituted as sexual images, retain the idyllic sensuality of the romantic residue of Surrealism. As antithesis, the pulpy humanoids of the Surrealist Bellmer emanate from a quicksand realm where organs grow together in disregard of normal function, so that a pair of legs grafts itself

George Segal, *Legend of Lot*, 1966, plaster, 72″ x 96″ x 108″.
COLLECTION, KAISER WILHELM MUSEUM, KREFELD, GERMANY, COURTESY SIDNEY
JANIS GALLERY, NEW YORK

onto another pair to form a libidinous organism without a trunk or a head. The association of sex with nightmare, indicated in the myths and paintings of aborigines, as in the tragic poetry of Western culture, becomes in Bellmer a threat of biological excrescences, a society of cancers.

Except for the photorealists, sex in contemporary painting and sculpture avoids the visual and emotional forthrightness with which this theme is handled today in novels, movies, and plays. "Sublimation," in the Freudian sense of a disguise of sexuality, is built into the history of art; Lucie-Smith points out that until the Romantic movement sex in painting always required a mythological or satirical "excuse." In some degree, sublimation still persists in fine art, though today the disguise is formal, and not provided by narrative. George Segal's *Legend of Lot,* reproduced by both Kahmen and Lucie-Smith, is a literal enactment of the biblical rape of the sleeping Lot by his maternity-inspired daughters, and the figure of the female nude mounting the recumbent male is almost guaranteed to arouse libidinous feelings. But the effect is substantially reduced by the otherworld whiteness of the artist's characteristic plaster casts and by their rough, unfleshy texture. Here, style is no longer a vehicle with which to stimulate a response to an imagined event; its primary purpose is to affirm itself. Despite the literalism of his approach, Segal sublimates his theme—the total effect of the tableau is one not of illicit sex but of dramatic reverie—through an aesthetic consciousness more extreme and rigorous than is to be found in the current novel, film, or play.

Another "classic" of present-day erotic art, Lindner's *Angel in Me,* also represents an aesthetic sublimation, though of a different order. This huge armored, buckled, and masked giantess, with her private parts exposed, is a Moloch of sexual aggression, frontally poised to overwhelm the spectator. With its hard-edged shapes and flat areas of color, however, the image of the menacing police-state female has actually the effect of an emblem rather than of a bad dream: it stands at a distance, like a poster warning males against being taken into custody and crushed. In *Angel in Me,* the erotic is diluted by memories of art and politics: the painting says more to the mind than to the senses; it awakens emotions attached to problems and ideas, not to bodies. It invites the spectator to reflect on its meaning and to identify its aesthetic mode—a cross between Surrealist fantasy and abstract divisions of the picture plane. In his more recent work, Lindner's erotically

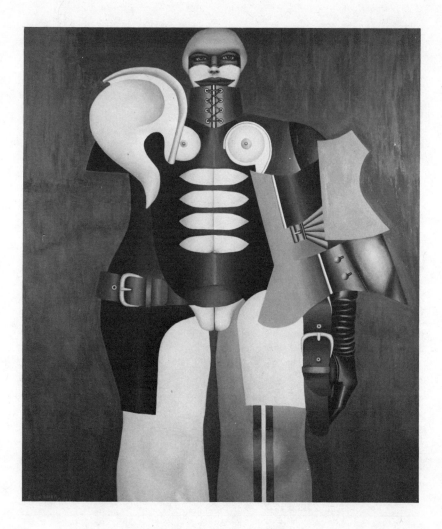

Richard Lindner, *Angel in Me*.

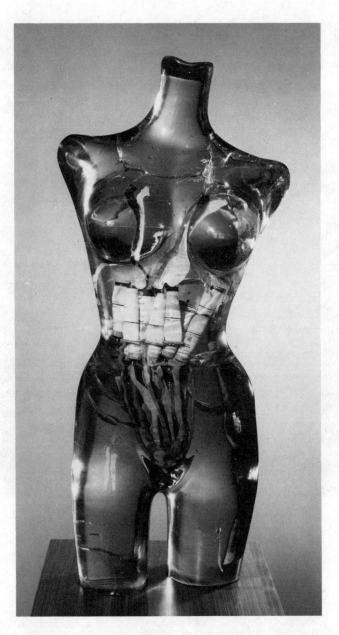

Fernandes Arman, *Le Couleur de Mon Amour*, 1966,
polyester with embedded objects, 35" x 12".
PRIVATE COLLECTION, COURTESY SIDNEY JANIS GALLERY,
NEW YORK. PHOTO BY GEOFFREY CLEMENTS

derived shapes (circles, slits, oval mouths) have developed into an increasingly disembodied alphabet of signs.

Arman's *Le Couleur de Mon Amour*, also reproduced by Kahmen, combines Eros and art to a degree comparable to Picasso's brush-wielding lover. The "color" in the title of this assemblage consists of tubes of paint implanted in the torso of a transparent plastic Venus and pigment from the tubes flowing down into the groin of the nude. Given the shape and size of the paint tubes, Arman's message may be that he makes love with paint. Or perhaps he wishes to convey that paint is his true love, in preference to the cliché glassy goddess through which anyone can see. In any case, in Arman's sculpture art explicitly calls attention to itself as being at least equal to the erotic in interest and vitality. As in traditional art, the impact of the sexual is neutralized, or sublimated, by being subordinated to the aesthetic consciousness. In this respect, Arman, and Segal and Lindner (and Picasso, too), are old-fashioned artists by the measure of the modernist conception that seeks not sublimation but the purging of experience of everything but tangible fact. The aim of "advanced" modernism is not to put reality at a remove through art but to use art to remove barriers to reality. This type of art conceives of the erotic as register-ings of nakedness and sex as is. The most effective medium for such data is not painting or sculpture but film. Film not only restores the illusion of the third dimension banished by modernist painting but enables the nude body and sexual activity to appear as objective visual fact, with the least danger of aesthetic idealization. To the degree that it rejects or ignores the potentialities of art, film can outdo painting and sculpture in simulating actual sexual encounters and setting off the erotic reflex. In comparison with the complex and masterly inventions of Segal, Lindner, and Arman, Watts's close shots of thighs and breasts, Robert Whitman's film strip of a nude in a shower, and Warhol's blurred film visions of a perverse sex act are pathetic in their poverty of emotion and imagination. But in dealing with the erotic, the poverty of unembellished fact is an advantage. As was demonstrated at Documenta 5, the logic of the erotic in film is to move toward pornography:

In *Eroticism in Western Art*, Lucie-Smith arrives at the judgment that, with the competition of photography and the impulse to introduce physical fact into painting and sculpture, "erotic art in the European tradition [is] now apparently coming to an end." And Kahmen, though his reason is not apparent, concludes with a metaphorical prophecy that the erotic itself has become fatally weak. On the other hand, Morse Peckham, in *Art and Pornography*, has confidently proclaimed that "by the twentieth century European culture had created, for good or bad, a pornography, both in literature and the visual arts, which for its imaginativeness and productivity, its savagery and violence, its beauty and charm, its perversity and its normality, is unmatched in human history." Plainly, Lucie-Smith and Kahmen, on the one hand, and Peckham, on the other, are speaking of two different things—and the key to the difference is aesthetic sublimation. To the extent that art modifies sexuality with its own conceits, it is out of tune with the times. By all evidence, this epoch wants its sex straight. The relation of art to this universal subject is thus proof that art has become an esoteric activity whose interests are in conflict with the popular taste; perhaps art ought unequivocally to accept itself as such. It is unlikely that the Museum of Modern Art will ever be able to compete with Times Square.

21

Shall These Bones Live?:
Art Movement Ghosts

When is an art movement dead? When the publicity spotlight has moved off it. "Dead" is synonymous with "out of sight" (and not only in art movements: think of certain public figures, for example). Usually, the darkening of one trend is accompanied by the lighting up of another. Art history in our time is a series of blackouts. The act that is finished leaves no clue to the one to follow. The discontinuity is an effect of the novelty-hunting of the mass media, including the museums. Sometimes, however, all the movements are in the dark and the circle of the spotlight is vacant. This seemed to be the case since 1971. Even the latest trends have become obsolescent, including some that were not actually trends in art. (The real function of the "information" and "software" movements was to supersede all art movements without being art themselves, and they should be classified as curator movements not art movements.) All at once, history has lost its drive. Art has the appearance of standing still. As art-world talk has it, "anything goes." All the past modes are suddenly the same age. Photorealism is as up-to-date, and as out-of-date, as color-field painting and earthworks. Galleries uptown and in Soho exhibit paintings of parked trucks, monumental geometrics in plastic or marble, designs that flare up in Day-Glo or neon, stripes that vanish into creamy grounds, modules, documentary reports of art acts. Never before have there been so many announcements of "first one-man show in New York," mostly of artists who belong to university art faculties and who practice consummately one recent mode or another. They offer a generous supply of objects in all current formats and make it unnecessary to return to the artists who originated these modes.

To the temperamental avant-gardist, the absence of a new trend and the continuous circling around the same models mean that the end of the line has been reached. This does not necessarily convince him that art ought to be given up. In our era of New Lefts, it is customary for the radical will, when faced with a stalemate, to attempt to force the issue of a historical advance. In art, radicalism has invented the aesthetic detour that carries art "beyond" painting and sculpture. To restore the pulse of art demands that art be discarded. "The static, portable indoor art object," writes a leading vanguardist artmaker in *Art Forum*, "can do no more than carry a decorative load that becomes increasingly uninteresting." The art movements have crumbled into countless atoms that are almost uniform, and each movement has left behind its heritage of manner and the possibility of endless variations in form and materials. Granted that decoration is uninteresting except to people interested in decoration, contemporary painting and sculpture may be considered to have nothing more to offer. If this is the case, art can continue only if it becomes something else.

No doubt most of the products of dead art movements are useful merely to fill a space on a wall. But what more is to be expected of art? The question is less likely to arise when new forms keep appearing. Novelty itself is the content of art in our historically conscious culture; Warhol's soup labels need no aesthetic justification. Yet even at the peak of a movement most of the art inspired by it belongs to its manner rather than its substance. Nor is there anything to prevent an observer from reducing the most profound innovations to their decorative aspects. (I suspect that to the *Art Forum* avant-gardist who repudiates painting all twentieth-century canvases are merely "carrying a decorative load.") The prevailing historicism in art accepts as the content of paintings only their contribution to the evolution of forms. Now that art is in the doldrums, even the masterworks of the recent past appear to belong to categories that need not be filled out any further. Recently, Mr. John Canaday of the *Times* reflected the current boredom with painting in a fable in which the various modes of American art from Abstract Expressionism on were "hothouse" products designed for the delectation of Mr. Alfred Barr and the embellishment of that Rockefeller château, the Museum of Modern Art.

Content in art that goes beyond decoration derives not from the

James Brooks, *Solmes*, 1972.

nature of specific art movements but from the relation of artists to them. An art mode, new or old, is for the creative mind essentially a point of beginning. Content is brought into being by the activity through which the artist translates the movement into himself. In such an appropriation, there is no difference between an ongoing movement and one that is finished. During the reign of Minimalism, a painter might realize the new through Impressionism. That art history has a schedule of continuous advances en masse is a fantasy of the historian. The shared syntax of art movements is constantly replaced by the sensibility and practice of individuals. The avant-garde art of yesterday is the only modern equivalent of an aesthetic tradition. *The fading of the ideas of a movement does not mean that it can no longer be a stimulus to creation.* At the very dawn of a movement, the work of its artists commences to replace the concept; instead of Cubism there appear Picasso, Braque, Gris. Compared to the activities to which they give rise, ideas in art have a brief life. In the last analysis, the vitality of art in our time depends on works produced by movements after they have died.

For example, every art student knows that today Abstract Expressionism and Pop Art are dead. Yet Mr. Canaday was able to lift himself out of despair over the shallowness of American painting since the war by a gush of enthusiasm for Red Grooms's Pop Art duplication of a Midwestern discount store. To Canaday, Grooms had eluded America's debilitating art movements and had shot up out of backcountry soil in an efflorescence of simplicity and mental health; Canaday spoke of Grooms as a blooming "sunflower" in contrast to the drooping exotics of the Museum of Modern Art. In reality, of course, nothing could be further from Canaday's ideal of small-town naturalness than Grooms's sophisticated country-boy charade, compounded of an ingenious mixture of naïve art and Pop. Like Oldenburg, Grooms has adapted the visual vocabulary of cartooning, comic strip, and caricature to serve ends of fantasy and social comment not present in the original Pop movement.

As for Abstract Expressionism, the most distinguished exhibitions in the first two months of 1971 were by artists who persisted in this tradition; among them were the Hans Hofmann exhibition at the Emmerich Gallery, Edward Dugmore's paintings at the Green Mountain, Norman Bluhm's show at Martha Jackson, Paul Burlin's at the Museum of Modern Art, Adolph Gottlieb's and William Baziotes's at the Marlborough, and James Brooks's, also at Martha Jackson.

For an artist such as Brooks, whose recent exhibition is the best I have seen of his paintings in twenty years, it is more rewarding to work in the Action-painting mode today than it was in 1950. Then judgments centered on the revolutionary aspects of the new movement and the dramatic personages who were bringing it into being. In that context, Brooks's canvases, consisting of areas of sunken pigment, had the effect of pleasing color patterns. It was plain that he would not have invented Action painting, nor did he personify its characteristic states of being. He lacked the crisis personality of Pollock, de Kooning, or Kline, the exuberance of Hofmann, the nervous self-questioning of Guston. Brooks showed no sign of being attracted to the metaphysical postulates of Action painting or to its aims of penetrating reality or changing the artist's self. It is significant that he approached the new, agitated style by way of Bradley Tomlin—like him, an artist of quiet temperament and primarily concerned with good painting. For Brooks, the new abstract art did not represent a radical break with earlier art that projected the artist's existence into the foreground, in defiance of art values ("I was never interested," said de Kooning, "in how to make a good painting"); it was a way of composing that was aesthetically more effective than Brooks's earlier Cubist-derived approach. Accident, which Brooks adopted in an original manner by experimenting with blottings of pigment, was to him not an aperture opening into a realm of revelation, as it was to Pollock, but the means for an enlarged repertory of decorative possibilities.

The distance that separates Brooks from the originators of Action painting has, however, narrowed considerably with the fading of the movement. Today, the creations of the pioneers fall within a formal canon that was lacking when their works first appeared but which they themselves have helped to create. Art tames itself. And it has become apparent that, whatever secrets the innovators were intent on discovering, they were also intent on creating art. Greatness in art is always a by-product, but of an activity that begins and ends in art. The passions, ideas, insights, and situations that impelled Action painting drop off like spent elements of a space rocket, and there remains the aesthetic. Pollock's mesmeric spillings, de Kooning's smashing brush sweeps become models of a new beauty; to grasp the paintings as they were in the beginning, a new act of creation is required. As Action painting is transformed into nothing but art, the insufficiencies of the painter devoted primarily to art recede. Seen apart from the adventure of innovation, Brooks's paintings have unquestionable merits. From the

William Baziotes, *The Net*, 1953, oil on canvas 19⅞″ x 40″.
ESTATE OF WILLIAM BAZIOTES, COURTESY OF MARLBOROUGH GALLERY, INC., NEW YORK

persistence of his experiments with the "volition" of pigments they derive a uniqueness that is all but organic. His forms repeatedly achieve the impact of unpredictable gestures, his color harmonies are at once daring and luxurious, his rhythms reflect freedom coupled with expertness. At his gradualist pace, Brooks has gained the self-development that was the ultimate aim of Action painting. But whatever Action painting set out to be, Brooks's canvases demonstrate that in the terms established by it it could be the inspirer of good painting.

In regard to creation there is nothing to indicate that a new art movement has any advantage over an obsolescent one; the contrary may well be the case. The movement carries a date, but the art produced in it is not necessarily of the same date. Granted that when a movement dies, some artists are buried with it and others feel obliged to flee the sinking ship, the enthusiastic response to the Cubist Picassos and the Fauvist Matisses when the Stein family collections were shown at the Museum of Modern Art demonstrates that art lives on past its ideological origins, and that the "static, portable indoor art objects" known as paintings have by no means become, as the *Art Forum* writer claims, "increasingly uninteresting." Historicism—the belief in ever-advancing formal phases—insists that only those creations that occupy a foreground position in time are significant. In art, historicism is the philosophy of the spectator in search of novelties that can be proved to be determined by evolution, and of that spectator's intellectual representatives among dealers, curators, and critics.

The reputation of William Baziotes, an outstanding figure among the first-generation Abstract Expressionists, has suffered through his style's lack of historical impact. His art does not go forward from any given point in the art of the recent past or suggest a direction in which art should go. It is lyrical, not epic. Baziotes departed from American painting, with its objectivist and rationalistic leanings, by introducing the idiom of his peculiar poetry. His stylistic connections with Abstract Expressionism are tenuous; his links are equally with Surrealism and Symbolism. The appeal of his canvases is direct; in demanding of the spectator neither knowledge nor theory, they are old-fashioned. A Baziotes arouses a sense of the fabulous, not the consciousness of art history or the impulse to make judgments about art. Yet in its very directness his approach to creation was a most difficult one for a mind of our time, when philosophers speak of "the death of the imagination." His art derived little from appearances, still less from ideas. Nor did he seek suggestions from random marks on the canvas, as did Pollock and Hofmann. Baziotes's compositions have no place for accident. Each of the paintings of his best period is a singular vision created, as it were, whole. This is very hard to do, if one can speak of "doing" a vision. A total image cannot be produced, it must be invoked; its apparition is a kind of happening. Baziotes would, he once told me, walk the streets of New York's West Side staring into the middle distance in the hope of drawing a clue from the unseen—a strange terrain might break through, or a personage: Circe, the one-eyed son of Poseidon, a sea serpent, Ethel Baziotes transformed into a semi-abstraction. The strain of this effort to "see" must have been immense. *Swamp* and *The Net* are examples of the startling absolute-ness achieved by his imagery, as if he were depicting realities that had come forward into the light. His pictures are close to dream, but they are less literal than those of the Surrealists, with the exception of Miró. Moons, suns, eyes, and strange orbs hover in his nights, jungles, and submarine worlds, where invented creatures are netted in zigzag cordages and space is veined with thin lines. Baziotes is almost an artist of symbols; had he continued to live (he died in 1963), he might have converted some of his figures into emblems, in a manner comparable to that of Gottlieb. The psychic difficulties of Baziotes's vision-ary art appear to have intensified over the years. In his later canvases the figurations grow more fragile and sink into soft, muted grounds of gold, pinks, and grays as if seeking protective cover. Any exhibition of his work is a welcome event, but what is needed is a Baziotes retrospective on a fuller scale than was the memorial exhibition at the Guggenheim in 1965.

Dead art movements are the normal life of art; all that can be expected of them is good painting. Even when a new vanguard has appeared, the great majority of artists continue to pursue aesthetic—that is to say, professional—objectives. A valid avant-garde is a *neces-sary* avant-garde—one that arises in response to a crisis that prevents, or reduces to nullity, art that continues to be created in the old man-ner; such were, for example, the Italian Futurists in revolt against a tradition anchored in the ideal, and the postwar Abstract Expressionists who declared their independence in the face of the drying up of the European sources of American art. In the absence of a consciousness of crisis—and what does "anything goes" mean but that there is nothing to overthrow except painting itself?—vanguard movements can origi-nate only in impulses irrelevant to creation. Under these conditions, adherence to a mode that has been superseded is the artist's most effective defense against the novelty obsessions of the mass media and the ambitions of the art world. In his voluntary abnegation of "the inevitable next step" he frees himself from the tyranny of progress in the arts, which by all signs can reach fulfillment only by bringing art to an end.

22

Reality Again: The New Photorealism

The exhibition at the Sidney Janis Gallery entitled "Sharp-Focus Realism" repeated an event staged by the same gallery a decade earlier. The first show, called "New Realists," constituted an announcement that what later came to be known as Pop Art had reached a level of acceptance at which it could challenge the dominance of Abstract Expressionism. The photorealist replay no doubt anticipated a comparable success in displacing the various forms of abstract art favored in the sixties. The signs of a takeover had been multiplying for some time. Contributors to "Sharp-Focus Realism," such as Malcolm Morley, Richard Estes, Duane Hanson, Lowell Nesbitt, Howard Kanovitz, Robert Graham, and Philip Pearlstein, with their ocean liners, shop windows, lifelike effigies, and oversize nudes, had been elbowing abstractionists in uptown galleries, Soho, and the museums for much of the past ten years. The new representational art had also spread out of town; the Chicago Museum of Contemporary Art and adjacent galleries on Ontario Street suddenly filled up with flesh-colored polyester dummies seated at tables or lying crushed and bleeding alongside shattered motorbikes, amid paintings of panel trucks, entrances to diners, closeups of torsos, and photographic segments of landscape. With this gradual buildup, the element of surprise in the "sharp-focus" exhibition was bound to be weaker than Janis' unveiling of Pop. Like its predecessor, it aroused the feeling that history was being made—but that in this instance it was being made rather listlessly. In any case, Pop arrived with a bigger bang. As striptease has demonstrated, no repetition can equal the impact of the first disclosure. Abstract artists whom I met at the opening appeared resigned rather than indignant. Pop had established itself as an art form, and—under the leadership of Warhol, Christo, and other showmen—painting and sculpture had been increasingly amalgamating with the mass media. It was obvious that whatever its future as a reaction against abstract art, photorealism was nothing monstrous but a rational extension of picture-making in popular styles.

Part of the shock of the 1962 exhibition derived from the identification of the Janis Gallery with de Kooning, Pollock, Kline, Guston, Gottlieb. In the creations of the pioneer Abstract Expressionists, a principle was manifest—the avant-garde principle of transforming the self and society. The "objectivity" of Pop was a deliberate abandonment of this principle, and it had the effect of a betrayal. If Pop succeeded, the epoch of art's rebelliousness and secession from society would have come to an end. Today, the consciousness of drastic oppositions has faded from American art; all modes have been legitimated, and preference for one over another, if any, is determined by taste or some theory of art history. With the presence in the sixties of Oldenburg and Segal as Pop stars of the Janis Gallery, "Sharp-Focus Realism" could hardly amount to a confrontation. Nor has the abstract art of the past decade been of a quality to evoke the passionate allegiance aroused by Abstract Expressionism. After years of being presented with displays of stripes, color areas, factory-made cubes, accompanied by sententious museum-catalogue and art-magazine puffs, the art world might well have reached the frame of mind to welcome a supersize colored postcard of a Rose Bowl parade.

The man in shirtsleeves near the gallery entrance was Sidney Janis —except that he was too heavy and too relaxed, and, besides, he was made of plastic by Duane Hanson. Janis was standing in a corner of the next room, but this time he was a painting by Willard Midgette. Through the crowd I saw Janis flit into his office, but he looked too tan and a bit more wizened than I remembered, as if he had been modelled by John De Andrea, creator of two nubile nudes of painted polyester and Fiberglas in another part of the gallery. That vanishing figure, however, was the real Janis. It is difficult to be sure which of the Janises was the most substantial; nothing can match super-realistic art in subverting one's sense of reality. The interval during which a painting is mistaken for the real thing, or a real thing for a painting, is the triumphant moment of trompe-l'oeil art. The artist appears to be

Duane Hanson, *Businessman* (installation view), 1971.

as potent as nature, if not superior to it. Almost immediately, though, the spectator's uncertainty is eliminated by his recognition that the counterfeit is counterfeit. Once the illusion is dissolved, what is left is an object that is interesting not as a work of art but as a successful simulation of something that is not art. The major response to it is curiosity: "How did he do it?" One admires Hanson's *Businessman* neither as a sculpture nor as a concept but as a technical feat that seems a step in advance of the waxworks museum.

Illusionistic art appeals to what the public knows not about art but about things. This ability to brush art aside is the secret of the popularity of illusionism. Ever since the Greeks told of painted grapes being pecked by real birds, wonder at skill in deceiving the eye has moved more people than has appreciation of aesthetic quality. But for art to depend exclusively upon reproducing appearances has the disadvantage of requiring that the painting or sculpture conform to the common perception of things. De Andrea's *Two Women* missed being mistaken for human nudes because they were too small and had hair that looked like a wig. According to the exhibition catalogue, the figures are "life size," but, as I have noted, illusionistic art tends to generate impressions that are not in accord with the facts. Regardless of whether or not they are as large as average women, on the floor, nude, surrounded by a crowd, they are too small to be credible. And while it is true that girls do wear wigs, hair that looks artificial is inappropriate on simulated girls. If, however, De Andrea's women are not "real," even for a moment, what are they? They are pretty figurines, but precisely to the extent that they seem made of flesh, they are a bit grisly in their prettiness, like a beautiful woman known to be suffering from a fatal disease. In their case, the disease is the failure to be alive, even in the spectator's first impression, plus the failure to be art.

Among the other puppets in "Sharp-Focus Realism" was Jann Haworth's *Maid*, a doll that could look human only to those who had forgotten the look of human beings, and this forgetting was prevented by a photograph, in the catalogue, of Miss Haworth seated beside her creation. George Segal's white plaster figures are spectres that recall to onlookers the people from whom the casts were made; in them, obvious artifice holds reality at arm's length and thus keeps it intact. In Haworth's "sharp-focus" maid, the absence of art eliminates reality, too, and leaves only a costumer's stereotype. Robert Graham's miniature nudes, realistic in their anatomy and skin shades, inhabit glass enclosures that are perhaps intended to suggest terrariums in which a new race of tiny human creatures, protected from pollution, is being bred. Of the sculptures in the show, Hanson's *Businessman* came closest to fooling the eye, no doubt through the assistance of authentic posture and clothing; De Andrea's *Sitting Black Boy* was, by being naked, unable to rise to this level of deception.

The most successful visual counterfeits, however, were achieved not with free-standing figures but with paintings of objects against a flat background, as in the simulation by Claudio Bravo of a rectangular package tied with cord. With this type of subject, traditional techniques of Harnett, Peto, Raphaelle Peale, and still earlier illusionists are brought into play: lights and shadows produced by intersecting cords and folds and wrinkles in paper make objects appear to stand forward in space. Stephen Posen's *Purple (Split)* was also a painting of a package, though a more complex one than Bravo's; it simulated a pile of cartons of various sizes and shapes covered by a purple sheet that fell in folds about them, and it seemed to jut out from the wall. Boxes on a wall are a purely arbitrary motif, and Posen no doubt chose it in order to display his virtuosity in painting drapery and creating three-dimensional forms on a flat surface. Marilyn Levine's suitcase and boots in stoneware were translations of objects into a different substance without altering their appearance—essentially, this is conceptual art that brings to the eye nothing not present in nature but instructs the spectator that things may not be what they seem.

In Janis's 1962 exhibition, the new Pop Art was mingled with half a dozen older modes of representational art. As is evident in the works I have been describing, "Sharp-Focus Realism" shaded off similarly into familiar categories of image-making. While Hanson's *Businessman* is naturalism pepped up with new materials, Bravo's lifelike package could have been produced a century ago. Evelyn Taylor's *Untitled* is a Magic Realist canvas in which, as is characteristic of this style, figures and objects stand apart from one another as if they were suspended in an invisible aspic. Paul Staiger's *The Parking Lot at Griffith Planetarium* and Noel Mahaffey's *St. Louis, Missouri* could have come out of an advertising agency's photographic and design departments without the bother of having been translated onto canvas. Philip Pearlstein's *Nude with Outstretched Arms, Green Sofa* is an academic painting that thumbs its nose at academic composition by cropping the model's head just above the eyes and retaining a stray thumb.

The nucleus of novelty in the exhibition was a group of paintings that shared an aggressive glitter precipitated by camera closeups; it is

John De Andrea, *Two Women* (installation view), 1972.
COURTESY SIDNEY JANIS GALLERY, NEW YORK

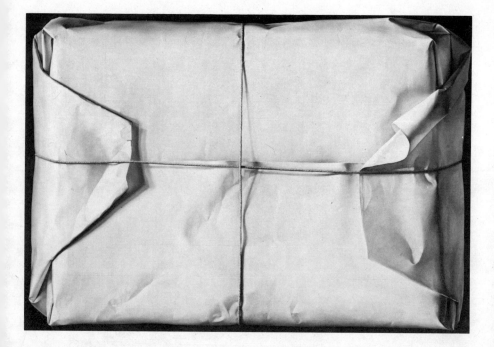

Claudio Bravo, *Untitled*, 1967, chalk, brush, pen and ink, pencil, 29½″ x 43⅜″.

the duplication of photographs upon canvas that constitutes the new realism. They included Richard Estes's *Diner*, Ralph Goings's *Rose Bowl Parade*, David Parish's *Motorcycle*, Tom Blackwell's *'34 Ford Tudor Sedan*, John Salt's *Blue Wreck and Truck*, Malcolm Morley's *Amsterdam in Front of Rotterdam*, Don Eddy's *Showroom Window I*, Robert Cottingham's *Shoe Repair*—businesses, motors, entertainment. Each of the paintings is a composition of shining shapes, reflected lights, and clearly defined details skimmed by the camera lens from surfaces of polished aluminum, steel, and glass, painted fenders, electric signs, crowds, and closely packed buildings photographed from above (Mahaffey's *St. Louis* fits the canon in this respect.) "Sharp-Focus Realism" represents a renewed relation not between art and reality, or nature, but between art and the artifacts of modern industry, including the apparatus of reproduction used by the mass media. The new paintings and sculptures converge with Pop in that both modes, while seeming to base art on life, actually convert it into variations on existing techniques of visual communication. Pop Art fed on the comic strip, grocery labels, news photos, commodities, packaging, billboards. The current "realism" explores such other veins of the media as the photographic travel and publicity poster, the service booklet and the product catalogue, the showroom, the storefront, the picture-weekly glossy—all presided over, one might say, by Hanson's dummy businessman.

Photo-into-art creations are alien to older forms of representation and ought to be exhibited and appreciated apart from them. A painting by Edward Hopper, for instance, embodies the sensibility of a single individual developed over years of looking and drawing, and the same, with all due attention to differences in quality, is true of such contemporaries as Pearlstein, Alice Neel, Lennart Anderson, Gabriel Laderman. In contrast, a sculpture by Hanson or a canvas by Estes or Goings is welded to the objectivity of the camera, and to the extent that photographs of things have become more real to Americans than the things themselves they achieve superior credence precisely through their obvious artificiality. Estes, to my mind, is the most consistently satisfying of these artists in that he candidly treats painting as a photographic problem of reflecting objects as they appear, while composing in series of brightly colored verticals and horizontals. Pop Art introduced a mood of cool neutralism as an antidote to the emotional heat of Abstract Expressionism. This frame of mind has been inherited by photorealism, but without the counterawareness of

Expressionist subjectivity; the new coolness came in from the cold. An outstanding quality of sharp-focus is the absence in it of any tension aroused by the art of the past.

Pictures that copy appearances have been an obsession of American art since the early draftsmen of the exploring expeditions. Current conceptions of art as "information" reinforce this obsession. In copying in paint its photocopies of nature, the present generation of realists seems to feel freer of the demands of art than any of its predecessors. By all evidence, a new stage has been reached in merging painting and sculpture into the mass media. Though William Harnett is a model of the current illusionism, its tutelary spirit is Andy Warhol.

23
Thoughts in Off-Season

A young artist writes—he approves of what I say but not of me; I devote myself too much to older artists and ignore the innovations of the newcomers. In short, he wishes to be discovered, and he believes that it is the job of the critic to unveil him to the art world. I am willing to assume that his studio is loaded with wonders. If I accepted his invitation "to come and look," I could pronounce good and not so good. But judgments of this sort are no longer, it seems to me, of much consequence, and while making them might reassure the artist, it would tend to mislead him about the actual situation of art. Not only have the qualities of art objects become increasingly irrelevant in judging art but the objects themselves are losing their importance. Beauty, skill, touch are still prized in the decorative crafts, but they count for little in works of art. The creation of paintings and sculptures is considered by artists to be a confinement of the creative impulse. "There are already enough objects," says a conceptualist, "and there is no need to add to those that exist." Functioning within a given genre is thought to be the expression of a mind-narrowing egotism, and the better the functioning the more constricting the motive. Avant-garde writings evoke the Dada assumption that everyone is an artist— with the possible exception of those who still choose to be painters and sculptors. Instead of visiting studios, a critic interested in new talent ought logically to conduct a house-to-house search.

In the past, the art object stood between the artist and his public (it could outlast both); in post-object art, the artist and his audience confront each other directly. To be complete, the artist's *act* now

requires to be seen. Contemporary art is inseparable from opinions
about it. Browning's Andrea del Sarto, who,

> painting from myself and to myself,
> Know what I do, am unmoved by men's blame
> Or their praise either

is by today's values a dilettante or a hobbyist, or at best an old-
fashioned Expressionist; in the U.S.S.R. he would be condemned as a
shirker. The last art that could be consummated in the studio was that
of the Action painters, who, lacking a public in any case, converted
painting into a ritual act. The recurrent theme of art since World War
II has been the aesthetics of impermanence, which measures the actual
life of works by their effect on the spectator; a work without spectators would have a duration of zero. Dada art of social confrontation
and Bauhaus art-to-be-used-up have culminated in art as event, factory-made art, art-to-be-thrown-away, conceptual art, art as hearsay
(the actual substance of most "earth" art, inasmuch as the public
rarely sees it). A work in any of these modes performs or happens,
and when it is finished, nothing remains—except possibly salable souvenirs or relics. The revolution of modernism has step by step liberated
the artist from the metaphysical identification of the artisan with his
materials that in the view of nineteenth-century social philosophers
compensated him for a life spent toiling in obscurity while the fruits
of his skill passed to his patron. In Balzac's *The Unknown Masterpiece*,
the fiction of the artist who is at one with his work is perfected by
totally eliminating the spectator. The artist achieves the absolute
through his solitary activity, but the "masterpiece" turns out to be a
mess that matches the artist's feelings from moment to moment; by
attaining freedom from the spectator, he has sacrificed the character
of his work as art.

The illusion that oblivion can be circumvented through the permanence of matter has foundered in the consciousness, no doubt
deepened by Hiroshima, that the physical world, too, is perishable.
Only one thing survives: that which people remember—and they are
more likely to remember the deeds and sayings of people than to
remember things. Duchamp regarded the transience of modern works
as an artist's heroic way of suicide: his opinion reflects, negatively,
the traditional notion of the artist as an object-maker who lives on in
his product. But, with his factory-produced finds, Duchamp himself is
proof that in our time an artist's survival need not depend on objects

fashioned by his hand but can rest on opinions and novel moves that have made their way into art history. The twentieth century is rich in personages—the Bauhaus masters, Gertrude Stein—whose creations are rarely looked at or read.

The romance of the unknown artist who secretes an immortal masterpiece violates fundamental realities of the modern epoch. The downgrading of the art object is an admission that the artist cannot hope to realize himself in solitude. The twentieth century has taught the practical and spiritual urgency of social recognition. To fail to exist publicly is hardly to exist at all. Artists have always loved fame, but satisfying *amour-propre* through fame is trivial in comparison with the compulsion of the contemporary individual to see himself reflected in the external world. A gulf divides those who have appeared on television or been mentioned in the newspapers from the anonymous inhabitants of the universe of mere creatures and things. Recognition need not be much to be everything. History is full of instances—for one, the rescue of intellectuals from Nazi-occupied France—in which to be known or not to be known decided the difference between life and death. The most menacing phrase in the modern lexicon is "the rubbish heap of history," which designates those whose signatures are destined to be obliterated from the register. No revolutionist has appeared in either art or politics who has been willing to go to the extreme of sharing the lot of the eternally nameless. Identity is the ultimate value of this historically conscious epoch. In the U.S.S.R., victims of rigged political trials are considered adequately repaid for their physical extinction if twenty years after their deaths they are "rehabilitated." In granting posthumous reidentification, the Soviet state mimics the process by which society resurrects the forgotten artist or hero. The artist without a reputation is the G.I. of the art world; he provides the countless casualties of the battles of creation. A corner of the sculpture garden at the Museum of Modern Art ought to be set aside as a tomb for the Unknown Artist. But what good is it to be remembered if one is remembered en masse?

The avant-garde concept that everyone is an artist is modified in practice to mean everyone who is looked at and mentioned. Now that skill in making is devalued or in abeyance, the profession of art has been reconstituted to coincide with the art-world roll call. Breathing or moving one's arms and legs is equivalent to executing a fresco—on the condition, however, that the activity is observed and publicly discussed. Whether as object, event, or information, art is now note-

worthy only if it succeeds in agitating the existing art-world aggre-
gation. In its desire to come closer to life, art has enmeshed itself in
public relations. (The sacred word is "communication.") The blending of creation and publicity is one of the "inevitable" trends of
modern mass society. All art now invites "audience participation,"
even if this involves no more than the act of looking. But the corollary
to audience participation is artist participation; the artist undertakes
to lead his public to a collective experience. This continuous interchange between the artist and his audience has destroyed the notion
of "high art" and rendered meaningless the old bohemian anathema
against "selling out." In his polemics of the 1960s against all forms of
seductiveness in painting, Ad Reinhardt attempted to reactivate as a
moral issue the artist's defiance of the spectator, but his reductionism
merely confirmed the insignificance of the art object and itself served
as a form of public relations for the idea of an art stripped of appeal.

The artist today is primarily a maker not of objects but of a public
image of himself. The art world is the stage from which he projects
himself to spectators everywhere. The means he uses to present his
performance are on a par with his art materials and creations;
Duchamp's chess set, featured in news items about him, is as much part
of his *œuvre* as his valise filled with autobiographical relics, which has
been exhibited in museums. Attitudes and artifacts in all categories
have replaced line, color, and form as ingredients of the artwork. But
although the work of art has diminished in importance, there has been
no corresponding decline of public interest in the artist or in the
ambition of individuals to become artists. No profession has been less
embarrassed by the vagueness of its aims. Art now includes works
that are totally overshadowed by the figure of the artist as a celebrated personage. "I wouldn't say," remarks John Cage, elucidator of
avant-gardism for all the arts, "that we are interested in destroying
the barrier between art and life or even blurring it. I would say we are
interested in observing that there is no barrier between the two." But
while art has become one with life—that is, with whatever happens—it
is clear that Cage has created the public effigy of Cage and that this
creation has *not* been left to chance. Regardless of the art status of
his productions, Cage himself is on the art side of the nonexistent
barrier between art and life. In sum, the irreducible reminder of the
idea of art has become the figure of the artist.

The changed relation between the artist and his product has radically altered the situation of art criticism. Critics still pretend to be

moved by aesthetic qualities (the word "delight" keeps recurring in the art columns of the *Times*), but in practice every critic is an ideologist (the *Times* is not immune to bursts of spleen). The critic has a theory about where art is going and a conviction, at times fraught with moral intensity, about where it ought to go; to him, the merit of a work lies in the historical tendency it represents. He appraises artists, young and old, as allies or as enemies. The firmer the critic's outlook the less likely he is to be satisfied with art that has matured without benefit of his collaboration; the young artist who wrote to me ought to be told that contemporary critics are not really interested in discovering original creations. For them, what the artist has accomplished matters less than his potential under new leadership. The critic visits the studio not to appreciate the artist but to enlist him. In inviting him, the artist has implied a readiness to sign up.

The new attitude of the critic toward the artist has been rationalized for me by a leading European art historian who is also an influential critic of current art. It is based on a theory of the division of labor in making art history. The historian, he contends, knows art history and, in fact, creates it; the artist knows only how to do things. Left to himself, the artist is almost certain to do the wrong thing—to deviate from the line of art history and thus to plunge into oblivion. The critic's role is to steer him in the proper direction and advise changes in his technique and subject matter that will coordinate his efforts with the forces of development. Better still, critics should formulate historically valid projects for artists to carry out. That not all critics have the same expectations of the future of art does not, I realize, weaken the cogency of my colleague's argument. The surviving artist would be one who has been lucky enough to pick the winning critic. My own view that art should be left to artists seemed to my mentor both out-of-date and irresponsible; the low-grade art history that would be produced by unassisted artists would only have to be remade later by are historians.

As the art object fades, the critic in the old sense of a connoisseur or judge of qualities fades with it. Like his predecessor, the new critic undertakes to raise artists and works of art into public visibility, but he himself has become an independent power in art—the director of artists in realizing his ideas, their partner and collaborator, their rival for a place in art history. One critic persuades painters to change their style, another proposes irresistible art-world subjects, a third claims to use artists as raw material for his own creations, a fourth coordinates teamwork between artists and business firms. As a conceptualist has said, the critic "no longer reflects on the works themselves" but "is the inciter, the provoker, the tempter." In any case, he melds into the impresario, and in more extreme instances he becomes an artist himself.

In post-object art, criticism has shifted its center of gravity to conform to the shift in emphasis from the product to the performer (a more impressively advanced term would be "programmer"). It is no longer a novelty that paintings and sculptures are given less attention than the theories, costumes, and "human-interest features" of their originators. The boredom that Warhol and Donald Judd have been content to recommend to spectators of their work was not intended to carry over to their persons. If their work is dull, their mode of self-presentation is radical. In traditional art, the canvas is the key to the painter's experience. In post-object art, the artist is the key to what he offers to his audience; in an earthwork, he may be the only factor that distinguishes it from farming or mining.

Now that the art object has been minimalized or eliminated, criticism can no longer apply itself to the artifacts of the studio or workshop. Material exhibits—whether paintings, photographs, or films of an event, or blueprints for a construction—are but data of the persona launched by the artist and his collaborators into the public consciousness. A work by Gorky or Stella or a "systems" artist derives its meaning from the principle personified by its creator; it is art inasmuch as it is an incident in the formation of an art-world protagonist. (In itself, a color pattern by Stella or an information mechanism by Haacke would be as much at home in a commercial-design workshop or in a news center as in a museum.)

The first screening of artist-performers is conducted by dealers and near-dealers (the impresarios and collaborators already mentioned). It is they who choose the cast of characters of the art-world comedy. The critic who wishes to remain a critic ought to give way before these representatives of the mysterious powers of money, fashion, and institutions. The critic who devotes himself to new talent and new artifacts mistakes his cue and gets into the act too soon. The turn of the genuine critic comes after the heroes and comedians have been established in their places. For him, the older artist, whose shape has been defined, has the advantage over the newcomer, in that he represents values injected into art by society. In post-object art, the proper subject matter of criticism is the total performance by which individuals give form to their lives through art and have forms imposed upon them by the culture of the period.

24

What's New:
Ritual Revolution

It is inherent in modernism, in art as in politics, that the desire for an avant-garde persists even when all avant-gardes have vanished or grown tiresome. The lack of a vigorous push in some one direction has been hailed as liberating or "healthy," but it has resulted, as well, in a widespread uneasiness. Art has arrived at the paradox that tradition itself requires the occurrence of radical attacks on tradition. Thus, though it has been apparent for years that the extremist spirit among painters and sculptors has been dwindling, vanguardism continues to be bravely upheld by custodians of tradition—art historians, curators, critics, and editors. Present-day exhibitions, catalogues, and magazine articles tend to outstrip the works with which they deal as they stake out claims in new territory. Even vanguard creations of earlier periods, such as compositions by Monet and Miró, are remodelled by criticism to provide launching platforms for advanced modes. In Germany the art-historian directors of the Documenta 5 exhibition, held in Kassel, took the significant step of collecting objects and images outside of art in order to push the art situation a notch "forward" without help from art or artists. (In the annals of prophecy, when God or History fails to produce anticipated events, the oracles try to force the issue through magic.) In sum, current avant-gardism manifests itself not in new actions, works, or ideas but in items selected and arranged to represent forward movement. This may be a way of saying that vanguardism has been ritualized, and that—independent of the ebb and flow of creation—certain images and phrases function as symbols of advance or of the will to advance.

The art periodical *Opus International*, published in Paris, illustrates how an avant-gardist outlook can sustain itself without an accompanying development in art. Though there is rarely a hint in it of a new style or a new idea, *Opus* manages, issue after issue, to generate the impression that experiment and defiance are flourishing around the globe. This mirage is accomplished by mixing reproductions of Surrealist-inflected paintings and sculptures and occasional Constructivist abstractions with such staples of rebellion as photographs of youths confronting cops, marchers calling for the release of political prisoners, excerpts from minutes of court prosecutions of artists, as well as happenings, the theatre of cruelty, cartoon and comic-strip propaganda, nude behinds, and manifestos that denounce the art market, the consumer society, and the smug self-adulation of art in New York. It might be argued that *Opus* is simply emphasizing visual and intellectual matter that belongs to today—in contrast to American and British art journals in which the concept of the modern is being stretched to include imitations of nineteenth-century landscape paintings, still-lifes, and portraits, as well as actual nineteenth-century paintings and sculptures, not to mention patchwork quilts and Navajo blankets. With increasing speed and with little evidence of resistance, "art of today" is becoming whatever attracts crowds to museums or is sold in galleries. A radical art magazine therefore appears justified in ignoring the flood of art-world fabrications and features in order to evoke a mood in accord with the more bitter realities of the times. But if *Opus* is only trying to keep up with the present, it is ironic that the editors feel impelled to avail themselves of the avant-gardist mannerisms of fifty years ago.

Though in Europe the idea of an aesthetic avant-garde is still linked with social change and political action (even when the link results in nothing but frustrations), American radicalism in art conducts its battles over issues that are formal and metaphysical rather than social. For the past ten years, the advanced sectors of painting and sculpture in the United States have been preoccupied with a quibble about the relation between art and reality. The struggle to merge art with the world of actuality is America's ritual vanguardism, its equivalent of the ritual revolutionism represented by *Opus*. An advance in art is considered to take place to the degree that art divests itself of the characteristics of art. Whatever mode comes closest to a score of zero for the art

VARIABLE PIECE #70 (In Process)
GLOBAL

Throughout the remainder of the artist's lifetime he will photographically document, to the extent of his capacity, the existence of everyone alive in order to produce the most authentic and inclusive representation of the human species that may be assembled in that manner.

Editions of this work will be periodically issued in a variety of topical modes: '100,000 people', '1,000,000 people', '10,000,000 people', 'people personally known by the artist', 'look-alikes', 'over-laps', etc.

Douglas Huebler

November, 1971

In November, 1971 a number of photographs were made in New York City to document various aspects of "everyone alive"; from those one was selected to represent:

MORE THAN ONE PERSON WHOSE SEXUAL FANTASIES
MAY BE ESPECIALLY BIZARRE

That photograph and contact proof print join with this statement to constitute the form of this work: 29/Variable Piece #70: 1971.

November, 1971

Douglas Huebler, *29/Variable Piece #70*, 1971.

Joseph Beuys, *Joseph Beuys' First Trip to the United States*, 1974.
COURTESY RONALD FELDMAN FINE ARTS, INC., NEW YORK

object is assigned the foreground position. Thus, Minimalist creations succeeded Pop as more exact approximations of things that are not art, and they were in turn displaced, seriatim, by Anti-Form art, Earth art, Process art, Conceptualist art, and Information art. The philosophies on which these movements were founded are extremely shaky, at times fatuous, and they have not lasted, but this does not affect the vanguard status of the movements themselves.

Douglas Huebler, for example, is a Conceptualist who imagines that he can accomplish a near-perfect disappearance of art through works made up of varieties of informational data. He does not wish to create art objects, he insists; he wishes, instead, to "state the existence of things in terms of time and/or place." We need not enter into the question of whether existence can be "stated" by the arrangements of photographs, films, maps, and verbal assertions—i.e., the data—that constitute Huebler's "pieces." The rationale for regarding his work as an advancement in art is supplied by Lucy Lippard, an art-historian-critic, whose devotion to avant-gardes of every kind is unwavering. In an article in *Art News*, "Douglas Huebler: Everything About Everything," she expounds Huebler's achievement in abandoning the "physical forms" of art, all of which—even the most recent, such as shaped canvases and sculpture without pedestals—she finds "uninteresting in themselves." It is hard to say whether she is more bored by art or excited by the prospect of its moving ahead. In any case, she contends that the assemblages of everyday fact with which Huebler replaces art can "have all the aesthetic tension which good art must have in order to provoke and then satisfy its maker and its audience." Lippard does not explain how she could have learned what "good art must have" if she did not learn it from art manifested in physical forms. But the point of her analysis is that the essence of art—what she terms "aesthetic form"—can be conveyed through data that are not modified by any formal principle; if this is the case, art has become, to recall the expression featured at Documenta, "superfluous." Nor is it necessary that Huebler's manner of documentation be correct or even make sense, since "one of the most impressive aspects of [his] work," she comments graciously, "is the freedom with which it operates, often independently of the artist." In Lippard's notion of an "aesthetic form" that exists within the spectator in total independence of works of art, the celebrated lists of what art is not (not self-expression, not a copy of nature, not decoration) promulgated by the late Ad Reinhardt culminate in the conclusion that art is not anything. In its place appear works whose medium is reality.

In art, "reality" is a political term, a fighting word: in the process of attacking art as they found it, almost all the art movements of this century raised the banner of "New Realism." Lippard-Huebler's displacement of art by reality must be construed to have agitational objectives in regard not only to art but to society as well. In the United States, revolts tend to be directed against specific situations, rarely against the social structure as a whole. In art, these situations are the gallery system, the techniques of career building, the role of the museums, and so on. The aim of the reality-versus-art vanguard is to liberate the profession of art from the procedures that currently dominate it. The philosophy of extinguishing the art object (or the object as art) represents the conviction that current methods of production and distribution in art ought to be transformed *in toto*. Lippard reveals the social target of current avant-gardist theory when she concludes her exposition of Huebler's (anti-) aesthetics of data and media with a diatribe against the art audience—"five hundred artists and twenty curators and ten critics." In her view, Huebler has transcended the cliché-ridden realm of the art professionals by resorting to the stuff of news and social surveys, which is accessible to everybody "without middle people" (though she is aware that few are likely to find it accessible as art). The clincher in her endorsement of Huebler's avant-gardism is that he lives outside New York and has executed his pieces "in small communities and small schools."

Thus, Lippard-Huebler represent a particular kind of continuation of the avant-garde tradition of aesthetic negation and social revolt. I find this fact more interesting than Huebler's ideas and creations.

Lippard's "Everything About Everything" is paralleled by *The New Avant-Garde: Issues for the Art of the Seventies** by Grégoire Müller, who, like Lippard, is an uncompromising reality-versus-art advocate. Müller holds back from the abyss of the Conceptualists, where reality has melted into varieties of data *about* reality: he wants a work to consist of something physically there. But the thing must be a thing, not art; he is as firm as Lippard is in demanding the exclusion of the art object. Painting is dismissed out of hand, on the ground that the space in a picture is a space conceived by art and subject to

---

* Grégoire Müller, *The New Avant-Garde: Issues for the Art of the Seventies* (New York: Praeger Publishers, 1972).

Walter de Maria, *Star*, 1972, aluminum, solid welded, and polished,
4″ h. x 44″ l. x 50″ w.

Michael Heizer, *Double Negative*, 1969 (reworked 1970), 200,000 ton
displacement in rhyolite and sandstone, Virgin River Mesa, Nevada, 1500' x 50' x 30'.

its conventions, not the actual space occupied by ordinary objects. And Müller rejects sculpture, too, insofar as it consists of material turned into figures or signs. But since a sculpture is a three-dimensional entity, like things in the world, he consents to redefine "sculpture" as the medium of the new vanguardists who work directly on the physical environment.

There is no disputing the radicalism of Müller's approach. If, in demanding that a work possess physical existence, he seems less extreme than Lippard, he goes beyond her by renouncing "aesthetic form" in any sense, whether it is attached to objects or is free-floating within the observer. For him, all aesthetic traditions have become irrelevant; works are to be dealt with directly "in terms of experience." The new work is historical, as opposed to "art-historical"—which is a way of saying that it is an event, not a thing made to satisfy criteria of taste. Art must change fundamentally, Müller contends in order "to compete with a power like Las Vegas," which reminds me of E. E. Cummings's saying that poetry in our time competes with elephants and locomotives. He is consistent with this view when he declares that he chose the works in *The New Avant-Garde* on the basis not of their quality but of their radicalism—radical, that is (since no social or political criteria are mentioned), in discarding painting and sculpture in favor of "actual physical presence of the work in time and in space."

The dozen artists (Huebler is not included) presented in *The New Avant-Garde* have been familiar in New York for at least five years— with the exception of the German activist Joseph Beuys. Among Müller's pacesetters are such museum and gallery favorites as Dan Flavin, Robert Morris, Carl Andre, Walter De Maria, and Michael Heizer—Environmentalists, Earth artists, Anti-Form artists, Process artists. Both the artists and the movements they represent have been discussed at length in the art press, and this is not the place to go into their individual qualities. Having brought his artists together as the avant-garde, Müller in effect denies that they are an avant-garde, except insofar as they embody his idea of art-in-the-real; not one of them, he insists, belongs to any particular school or has any stylistic or ideological relation to the others. More important, Müller destroys even the possibility of an avant-garde by announcing the disappearance of the art context, which is the sole measure of an advanced position. His vanguardism is another instance—together with Documenta, *Opus*, and Lippard—of theory charging ahead of the works on which it purports to base itself. Despite the subtitle of Müller's book, the artists he has chosen present no "issues for the art of the seventies," because those issues have been resolved once and for all by Müller; the art-versus-reality debate has been closed, and no further attention is to be paid to objects that belong to "the realm of artificial space."

Yet beneath the vanguard metaphysics that has won its final victory there remains the real issue for art in this decade: the relation of art to society and to the way art shall be practiced. In the absence of an avant-garde, the professional routines take over, and art becomes an amalgam of petty crafts. In de-arting art, Lippard and Müller reflect the widely felt need to activate art outside the art profession as it is at present constituted—a need intensified periodically by revulsion at big-money promotions and behind-the-scenes museum and gallery deals. Unfortunately, Lippard's and Müller's escape into reality can take place only in theory. In practice, reality-art is no more effective than art-art in removing art from the art world. An artist such as Smithson builds in glamorous solitude (under the eye of the helicopter's camera, naturally) his *Spiral Jetty* in Great Salt Lake, but he fights in art magazines and on lecture platforms in behalf of his reputation as an avant-garde artist. Lippard sums up the matter effectively when she writes that "for obvious reasons, Conceptual art [has] succeeded no better than anything else in subverting the commodity cover that is stifling current art." In its inability to prevent the disappearance of creative exchanges among artists, vanguardism resorts to making theoretical challenges to art. Absurd triumphs are claimed in the over-eagerness to prove that genuine gains have been made, as when Müller explains that "these artists have altered real space in such a way that the spectator literally bumps into pure ideas." Inasmuch as artists are apparently deprived for the present of the possibility of effecting social and cultural change, the avant-garde tradition has become the domain of the art historian-critic. But if being an anti-art artist is difficult, being an anti-art art historian is a hard position indeed. His doctrinal revolutionism brings forth nothing new in art but reenacts upheavals on the symbolic plane of language. It provides the consoling belief that overthrows are occurring as in the past, that barriers to creation are being surmounted, and that art is pursuing a radical purpose, even if it is only the purpose of doing away with itself.

Michael Heizer, *Untitled #4* (red), 1974, polyvinyl latex on canvas, 8′ dia. with two cuts.

COLLECTION OF MR. AND MRS. BURTON TREMAINE, MERIDEN, CONNECTICUT, COURTESY FOURCADE, DROLL, INC., NEW YORK

25

On the Edge:
Documenta 5

In Kassel, two million dollars was spent (in this period of reduced budgets!) on an exhibition investigating a word: "art". Documenta 5, the triumphant German rival of the Venice Biennale, followed the avant-garde tradition of ascertaining how far the concept of art can be stretched. From Matisse to Pollock and from Cubism to earthworks, artists have prompted critics and other artists to cry out that "this time they have gone too far." At Documenta 5, the crossing of boundaries was carried out by a team of curators and art historians instead of by artists—a significant take-over, in that a curator is likely to lack the imaginative and emotional limits of an artist and to go as far as reason will allow. The exhibition in Kassel was undoubtedly the farthest reconnaissance into territory where art has lost its definition, or is prepared to share it with things never before thought of as art. The theme of the show was "Inquiry Into Reality—Today's Imagery," and with this project in mind all aesthetic standards were discarded (as clues to reality, images that possess formal qualities and those that lack them are equally significant). Today's imagery includes, together with what is conventionally accepted as art, anything offered to the eye, from a Woolworth valentine to the printed wisdom of a Conceptualist. This loosening of the notion of what is worth looking at brings a landslide of visual fact into the area once reserved for painting and sculpture. We are made aware that image-making includes news photographs, films, posters, constructions, blueprints, postage stamps, banknotes, costumes, performances, tableaux, comic strips caricatures,

dolls, chessmen, insignia, flags, children's drawings, mantelpiece figurines, armbands, buttons, rubber stamps, garden sculpture, advertisements, emblems, labels, religious chromos, forms produced by wind
and fire. In Documenta 5, individual creations were made subsidiary to
the picture world (*Bilderwelt*) as a whole. This is another way of
saying that categories of visual experience have replaced art criticism.
Harald Szeemann, director of the exhibition, and Jean-Christophe
Ammann, his associate, must have stopped adding items only because
they ran out of space or cash. Had the objection been raised that
some of the exhibits are not art in any sense, Documenta had anticipated it with a huge banner flaunted across the portico of the Fridericianum Museum, the larger of the two buildings in which most of the
exhibition was housed; it announced that "Art Is Superfluous" (*"Kunst
Ist Überflüssig"*).

As a campsite of the far-out, Documenta 5 was an important
stocktaking of international avant-gardism as it existed in 1972, in both
theory and production. The exposure of what has happened to the
tradition of the new was striking. Not only had the notion of creation
disintegrated into "perception" and "information" but the capacity of
art forms to derive new aesthetic modes from earlier ones had petered
out. The most significant feature of Documenta 5 was that in it art
was directionless: it evoked no past (except in the sense of repetition)
and pointed to no future. Art history had been abandoned; the exhibition simply reflected a global mass of opinions and phenomena.
According to Dr. Ammann, the planners of Documenta 5 began with
the observation that, in contrast to the years of the first four Documentas (the series was inaugurated in 1955), in the 1970s no art movement is dominant and all postwar styles enjoy equal prestige. Since art
is no longer forging "ahead," it was decided to replace art as an
independent realm of activity with selections of imagery classified in
terms of the "ideologies" reflected in it. Presumably, the spectator was
to become aware that advertisements for cola drinks and the body
movements of a blindfolded performer constitute "an interrelated structure of social realities."

The effect of this program was to give the theories of the organizers
of Documenta precedence over the works on display; in the language
of one of Documenta's numerous documents, "an abstract grating of
ideas is placed before physical observation." The primary substance to
be apprehended in this "inquiry into reality" is hypotheses and conclusions. The close formal scrutiny of paintings practiced by art criticism

in the sixties had been rendered obsolete by exhibits that need have been looked at only long enough to grasp the sociological reason they were there. Art, non-art, and sub-art can be pushed into the same pigeonholes.

Some American artists felt that this was a demotion and resented it; Robert Morris, it is reported, withdrew from the exhibition with the complaint that he did not "wish to have my work used to illustrate misguided sociological principles." However, his objection to having an ideology imposed on his art by the context in which it is exhibited arrived a bit late. Since the last war, it has become increasingly usual for directors of exhibitions to use works of art as tags for their "themes"—technical, aesthetic, and/or historical. For example, in 1969 Morris participated in an exhibition organized by the same Harald Szeemann, then director of the Kunsthalle in Bern, in which Morris's strips of felt were presented as an example of what happens "when attitude becomes form" and as a work of art that is "almost entirely the result of manipulation of material." (Isn't all art "the result of manipulation of material"?) Had art in the past fifteen years not been "used to illustrate misguided sociological principles," much of it would never have seen the light. The take-over of art by ideological showmen has been a steadily expanding process; in Documenta 5, the fusion of art and words, repeatedly noted in these reports, had been openly acknowledged without fear of scandal. Adrift on the measureless ocean of "today's imagery," paintings, gestures, environments relied on inflatable cushions of phrases to rescue them from oblivion.

Documenta 5 pioneered in providing a theoretical basis for the dependence of art on ideology: it consists in the belief that art in our time fails in meaning unless it is assisted by interpretation, and that in the context of ideas non-art can be equally meaningful, as in the example of deep readings of comic strips or of bedroom behavior. The bite of the slogan "Art Is Superfluous" is its implication of the emptiness of art in the absence of an added idea. Thus the exhibition directors' categories push forward, the museum hands take over, and the subjection of art to sociology proclaims that, above all, the *artist* is superfluous. The grand principle of avant-gardism has become "Liquidate art, liquidate yourselves."

At the Neue Galerie, which shared most of Documenta with the Fridericianum, the outstanding attraction was Claes Oldenburg's *Maus Museum*, a Documenta in microcosm. Named for its design, which is based on a geometric version of Mickey Mouse, it is an assemblage of found objects as is, found objects altered, and leftovers of object-making—in sum, an intermixture that presents art as lingering on in the form of objects, such as rubber frankfurters, trick cigars, souvenir Washington Monuments, that awaken analogies with art or are art by accident or by identification with the artist as a public personage.

The Neue Galerie was the backward-looking portion of Documenta 5, in that it contained most of the paintings and sculptures in the exhibition, chiefly American photorealist canvases and Edward Kienholz's punningly entitled tableau of the castration of a black man, *Five Car Stud*, plus advertising posters and a large display of home-decoration and ecclesiastical kitsch. At the Fridericianum, the major exhibits were people—Joseph Beuys, like Bella Abzug, identified by a never-absent hat; Ben Vautier, usually designated as "Ben"; Vito Acconci, whose pulse and perspiration have been measured in art galleries; and Vettor Pisani, whose art medium is a nude lady-in-chains reputed to be his wife—all of whom stage themselves as works of art. Each has his "act," though one that belongs not to drama or entertainment but to pantomime designed to demonstrate one idea—that the avant-garde tradition has left the rails of painting and sculpture and run aground in physical, psychological, and social data.

So art was dismissed or underwent metamorphosis. Yet it was art, often as no more than the word, that held Documenta 5 together. Indeed, nowhere on earth did the idea of art and the artist carry more potent magic or seem more profoundly linked with momentous trends in world civilization than in this hippodrome of art's superfluity. As befits sociological inquiry, seriousness was the note. In this exhibition there were no smiles on the faces of artists or spectators: an oversize deadpan by Chuck Close presided over Documenta 5, and the desperate, bellicose dedication of Beuys, Ben, Acconci, and Pisani constituted the atmosphere of *Selbstdarstellung* in Kassel. In the museum directors' investigation of reality, their first move, as the custodians of art, was to assert art's intellectual centrality, including contemporary doubts and negations of its traditional mediums.

"What makes Beuys's distributing political leaflets at the Fridericianum art?" I asked Ammann.

"He, his office, the stacks of papers," was the not unexpected reply, "constitute a sculpture."

Edward Kienholz, *Five-Car Stud*, 1972.
PHOTO BY BERND KRACKE

"Granted," I conceded, "that any three-dimensional enclosure of space can be regarded as a sculpture, what is gained by imposing the idea of art, complex and indefinite as it is, on what Beuys is doing?"

"In the museum," responded Ammann, "distributing political leaflets is art. In Beuys's office in Düsseldorf, it is politics."

If Documenta 5 dissipated art by translating it into social ideas, it restored the balance by accepting as art anything placed in the frame of the Museum. The different ideologies implicit in comic books, paintings, happenings converge at bottom into one ideology—that of the museum engaged in accrediting objects as art or as acceptable art substitutes. Critics who say that Documenta is anti-art fail to understand that its sovereign principle was attachment to the idea of art and the desire to see it recognized in all aspects of life. A fierce onslaught of words kept attention focused on art as an issue. On the walls and columns of the Fridericianum, posters challenged the spectator with such questions as "Why art?" "Is art for happiness?" "Must man change mankind in order to change art?" (Anyone not obsessed with art would have put this last question in reverse.) The concern with, if not for, art often reached an intensity that was oppressive. Ben, who was featured near the entrance of both the Fridericianum and the Neue Galerie, and was the author of the questions just quoted, indulged himself in apparently inexhaustible sputterings and charades on the theme of "*L'art, c'est moi.*" His "environment" was a roomful of apothegms, slogans, and photographs, among them a Parisian art-gallery poster announcing that "Ben does not exhibit" and a snapshot of Ben sitting on a stool in the middle of traffic holding a sign saying that he is a work of art. Ben's exhibit also involved a platform on which those lucky enough to come at the right time could see the artist sleep. A new genre seems to have evolved out of the mating of art and words —objects, events, and performances that become art by throwing out hints about art and non-art. It is its persistent adherence to the theme of art that differentiated Documenta from a combination of Coney Island side shows, a flea market, and booths at a fair. Whatever their visual or physical matter, its exhibits were ultimately either statements about art or art about statements about art. Documenta's preoccupation with the art world was symbolized by its catalogue, which weighed eight pounds, consisted of fifteen hundred pages, cost sixty-five DMs (upward of twenty dollars), and supplied exhaustive lists of gallery showings and art-magazine reviews of each of its exhibitors.

With their sociological approach and no new art movement to

worry about, the directors of Documenta could have included in "today's imagery" any paintings and sculptures shown in art galleries or reproduced in the press, from Greek mosaics to a collage by Schwitters. In its display of dateless art, such as the beer mugs and folk dolls, in its "trivial realism," or kitsch, section, Documenta took advantage of this freedom. But the choices in painting and sculpture demonstrated that the social philosophizing of exhibition directors occurs within the orbit of art-world fashion and publicity. If the Documenta theme-makers saw nothing new in art today, they were highly conscious of what was old; it included art in all modes, from Abstract Expressionism to Minimalism, that had been featured in earlier Documentas and other international exhibitions. In art, therefore, Documenta 5 fell back on the new art of yesterday—photorealism, conceptualism, and body art, most of it thoroughly familiar in the United States, though perhaps less so in Europe. Once again, America was the front runner; its entries were about equal in number to those of all other countries combined. (Japan and Latin America, I was told, lagged so far behind in invention that they did not deserve inclusion; presumably, their lack of "today's imagery" made their "reality" uninteresting.) Thus, though art history as the latest thing was verbally repudiated, it won after all in the selection of the exhibits. The paintings and sculptures were the newest available, even if they were oldish-new.

For Americans, Documenta 5 was overpoweringly *déjà vu*, to say nothing of already heard. One met again *'61 Pontiac*, by Robert Bechtle, sidewalk "casualties" by Duane Hanson, Paul Sarkisian's gigantic junk-loaded rural back porch, a nude couple in plastic making love on the floor, Richard Estes' telephone booths, Malcolm Morley's race track, all of which had had their day in New York and Chicago. Reminiscences of color painting survived in works of Brice Marden, Robert Ryman, and Robert Mangold. Nancy Graves, whose hanging sculpture has a claim to be new but is too individual to constitute a "movement," had been summoned up out of Soho; and for no visible reason, Al Jensen and Joseph Cornell were remembered. In its liberation from art history, Documenta 5 enveloped itself in nostalgia for what was last to be new.

Other ideologies aside, both the art and the sub-art exhibits were divided between Expressionist and Objectivist creations. Under the headings of "Individual Mythologies" and "Selbstdarstellung," much

Nancy Graves, *Schamane*, 1970.
PHOTO BY WERNER LENGEMANN

Paul Thek, *Trauminsel: Pyramide und Arche*, 1972.
PHOTO BY WERNER LENGEMANN

of Documenta 5 was given over to bodily presences, actual or filmed, by performers such as Ben, Acconci, and Lucas Samaras, who seemed to want to be smelled. Paul Thek's crummy grotto of earth, packing-case coffins, and walls lined with old newspapers, and Michael Buthe's Art Nouveau cave, *Homage to the Sun*, represented ad-hoc religions. "Individual Mythologies" reached into paintings by psychotics; included was an extraordinary three-foot-high pile of illustrated diaries by an inmate of a Swiss mental hospital, who had also formed a "museum" of works by fellow patients that was obtained by Documenta. Genuine schizophrenia shaded off into "artistic" or drug-induced imitations in galleries of photographic horrors involving fish heads, genitalia, evisceration, blood-stained religious vestments, and crude crucifixes, plus photographic portraits of the artist gagged, gashed, and split in two. This group of repulsive fantasies fitted into the scheme of the exhibition as instances of self-expression through images. It may be time for avant-gardist reasoning to discover that if aesthetic standards are dissolved it becomes necessary to replace them with moral ones. On a different plane of self-projection, Beuys's agitation for direct democracy through plebiscite could also be regarded as an individual mythology; Beuys, who has been called a "saint" (perhaps Sartre's *Saint Genet* is responsible), at that time had given up drawing but was considered, I was told, the most important influence in German art.

Parallel with these personifications of disorder, uneasiness, and dream —on the whole, the Europeans seem more tense and disturbed than the Americans—were the clean, static presences of the "living statues," Gilbert and George, previously seen and heard on West Broadway; the impersonal harshly lit panoramas of the West Coast Sharp-Focus Realists; the Dadaist inventions of technocrats, such as Panamarenko's dirigible and Robert Filliou's *Das Poipoïdrom*; twig sculptures by Charles Arnoldi and cord-and-bead compositions by Nathalie Bieser (in Documenta's setting, any original art was especially attractive); and, mysteriously, Hard-Edge geometrical abstractions done twenty years ago by Auguste Herbin. Individual passion and objective conception met in out-of-doors constructions carrying political messages: a pavilion hailing Red China; a wall plastered with pronouncements and slogans of Artists' Liberation, a British group; a reproduction of a devastated, trash-covered hill in Vietnam; a block-long row of political posters of the past forty years.

In its totality (and because of the familiarity of the exhibits it was the totality that determined the final impression), Documenta 5 was an extended argument about what constitutes art today—an argument that occasionally broke down into obscenities and violence (the slasher photographs, Pisani's nude in chains). To underline its purpose, the exhibition ought to have included a round-the-clock panel discussion, with hecklers from the floor and periodic fist fights. (Near the end of the exhibition, a stabbing might have been arranged to symbolize the demand that Documenta's reality be made more real.) It was reported that the opening was aswarm with demonstrations and leaflets directed against the exhibition, but by midsummer these had disappeared. True, Documenta heckled itself, but with two million to spend, steps could have been taken to incorporate outside opposition; why limit radical speculation about art and society to a handful of curators and professors? Though politically Beuys's program of participatory democracy is utopian, there is no reason why it could not be the basis for organizing the next Documenta. There is something disturbing about seeing students in beards and long hair wandering through the galleries with their mouths shut. Documenta is an educational venture (besides being, of course, a regional promotion), and dialogue is fundamental to it.

Beyond continuing the modernist questioning of art "as a social institution," Documenta 5 had no significant message. Certainly, no exhibition on this scale was needed to bring the news that people today are introverted, dreamy, prurient, vulgar, mentally unbalanced, and superficial (kitsch-loving), or to take sides with Mao or urge ending the war in Vietnam. The gist of Documenta 5 consisted in indicating the phase now reached by the traditional shuffling of vanguard art between denying its existence and claiming to illuminate reality. For all the protests of purists and champions of "quality," this shuffling, at times coming close to chicanery, belongs to the essence of modernist creation, since original art is both art and non-art at a single glance. For art to maintain its intellectual interest, avant-gardist questioning must continue to pursue its own self-cancelling logic, even when, as now, art itself has come to a standstill. In Documenta 5, despite inner contradictions, this questioning attained a new level of inclusiveness (thanks to the two million) and a theoretical force approaching brutality.

Joseph Beuys, *Actions*, 1972.
PHOTO BY WERNER LENGEMANN

26

Adding Up: The Reign of the Art Market

Recent adventures of art have been concentrated in the auction rooms. I am not unmindful of the dramatic installation of Christo's orange hanging near Rifle, Colorado. But his *Valley Curtain* was an incident *in* art, whereas the bidding at Sotheby Parke-Bernet's has had an impact, perhaps decisive, on the whole structure of art itself. At the auctions, the present has doubled back on itself to recover styles and personages passed over in the forward rush of the avant-gardes. Throughout the sixties, the art world had grown accustomed to leaping prices for Pollocks, Rothkos, de Koonings, Johnses, Lichtensteins. The idea of the new as value had been zealously promoted by critics, art historians, and curators. But what principle is behind the interest in Kuniyoshi? Feininger? Joseph Stella? By the latest evidence of the art market, the ideal of novelty seems simply to have faded away. The necessity for an avant-garde has been replaced by the whimsicalities of competitive bidding. One effect has been the putting aside of not only the dubious notion of progress in the arts but the century-old tradition that identifies art with the creation of new forms and places a premium on the pioneers. In the seventies, the suspicion has been deepening that a cultural epoch may be in the process of coming to a close. Whatever trends still remain discernible have ceased to arouse expectancy. One idea in art seems as good as another, and no idea best of all. Artists have been reaching out in all directions, but mostly backward. In an exhibition I attended recently, two former abstractionists had turned, respectively, to portraits and to drawings of sunflowers, and a newcomer was unhesitatingly introducing herself with still-lifes of fruits and bouquets. Obviously, the new was no longer a tradition that needed to be respected even in appearance.

Recognition of the arrest of motion has taken form in the softening of ideological prejudices and in a tolerance that extends equally to sculptures that consist of suspended strips of plastic, paintings of moody landscapes, portrait groups of friends and Conceptualist placards. The "new-talent" exhibitions with which member galleries of the Art Dealers Association of America now close the New York art season, in June, evince, by the orthodoxy of their choices, not so much the anticipation of unveiling any original direction among artists as the hope of discovering susceptibilities in the art public to thitherto unfamiliar artistic personalities. But "personality" was precisely the quality that, along with the intention and outlook of the artist, had been discouraged by the Minimalist aesthetics of the preceding decade on the ground that it is irrelevant to the art object. A critical context had been created which demanded that works be stripped of individual or social identifying marks. With anonymity as the ideal, exemplified in the uniform-sized square black paintings of Ad Reinhardt and the expanded scaleless patterns of Kenneth Noland and Frank Stella, nothing remained of meaning in art but what could be derived from the fact of art's own existence. Art history became the sole judge of the legitimate concerns of painting and sculpture, and its decisions were enforced by the institutional embodiment of art history, the museum. In the sixties, the remark that began as a wisecrack—"Art is whatever goes into the museum"—was at length elevated into an axiom.

Cynosure of dealers, collectors, and artists on the make, the museum did not take long to disqualify itself as the ultimate art critic. The desire to enlarge its public led it in the direction of the mass media (by means of items acquired and exhibitions programmed for the purpose of attracting crowds), and competition for audiences and financial support put showmanship ahead of scholarly endeavor. Moreover, its new position of power led the museum to develop its own versions of bureaucratic corruption: favoritism in buying and showing, falsification of recent art history, using museum prestige to enhance investments by trustees, secret deals in the acquisition and sale of museum properties. The scandals surrounding the Metropolitan represent the culmination of practices spread across the entire horizon of the museum world.

Since the rise of art history, in the nineteenth century, art historians have been directly linked with market prices of paintings and sculptures because of their authority in deciding attributions. By the 1970s, art history, having achieved the leading role in the day-to-day life of art, had overgrown all its theoretical boundaries and gone to seed; it was now prepared to put the stamp of value on anything, not excluding publicized fakes. For example, conventional nineteenth-century American landscapes and conversation pieces by forgotten craftsmen have been systematically exhumed from attics and courthouse corridors, catalogued with explanations of their place in art history, and accorded high-level promotion by aggressive galleries. The annual award to an outstanding art historian, set up two years ago by the Art Dealers Association, openly acknowledges the indebtedness of the art business to art scholars, and the choice of Alfred Barr to be the recipient of the initial award gave notice that the sphere of common interest includes the museum. According to Russell Lynes, in *Good Old Modern: An Intimate Portrait of the Museum of Modern Art*,* the interweaving of the educational and collecting transactions of this museum and the financial interests of its trustees has for a long time been taking place slightly below the public eye level. "There has always," says Lynes, known for his mildness, "hung over the Museum, and therefore over Barr, the cloud of commercial manipulation, the accusation that it was in business to support the dollar values of its trustees' collections, that it exerted an exaggerated and unhealthy influence over the art market." The merchandising role of the MOMA was officially acknowledged by its advertisement in *Business Week* offering an "Art Advisory Service which provides curatorial consultation to corporations and individuals who wish to acquire contemporary works of art in all media for private and public spaces."

The texture of collaboration between dealers, collectors, and exhibitors has become increasingly dense, to the point at which the artist is confronted by a solid wall of opinion and fashion forecasts constructed, essentially, out of the data of the art market. The presence of this potent professional establishment has radically affected the relation, once largely regulated by the taste of patrons, of the artist to society and to his own product. He has been forced to recognize that the market-centered complex which determines values in art is a realm of chance, since the standards it sets are often influenced by condi-

---

* Russell Lynes, *Good Old Modern: An Intimate Portrait of the Museum of Modern Art* (New York: Atheneum Publishers, 1973).

tions having nothing to do with art—for example, by the rise and fall of currencies—and that therefore success as an artist is both fortuitous and transitory (formulated in Warhol's celebrated remark about everyone's being famous for fifteen minutes). Thus, in regard to status, the artist is a gambler, but he cannot, as in the past, hope to win through gaining the respect of colleagues or through the future relevance of his creations. Both respect and intellectual relevance are blocked off by the mysterious processes of the international art exchange. (Efforts to explicate these processes in newsletters devoted to art as investment have so far been utterly amateurish.)

The final blow to any illusion regarding the operation of objective values in art was delivered by the apparently arbitrary behavior of the yen on the art market. The Japanese bid of nearly a quarter of a million dollars for a Kuniyoshi had the effect of a bewildering finale to the claims of advanced styles and ideas to represent the significant art of our time. The very idea of significance dissolved when, as Anita Feldman reported in *Art News*, "Yuzo Saeki, a local imitator of Vlaminck, sells for more than Vlaminck"; if, she added, a painting by Toulouse-Lautrec "did not appear in the movie *Moulin Rouge*, no self-respecting buyer seems to want it around." Thenceforth, no individual vision or mode of creation could be accorded precedence over any other. An artist's struggle for quality and meaning would be carried on only as the result of gratuitous decisions of the will—an expression of an ethical or aesthetic obsession unrelated to any external standard or desired effect. In contrast, the norm would be for the artist to duplicate in various mediums and genres (drawings, reliefs, tapestries, prints) whatever motif had achieved marketability.

In the reign of the market, the intellectual role of the artist, in which is embodied his social or philosophical motive for painting, is cancelled, and his public existence is restricted to the objects he has fabricated. A list could be drawn up of important human aims that animated painting and sculpture in the first half of this century: it would include efforts by Futurists, Social Realists, and Constructivists to inaugurate a new social order; by Symbolists, Suprematists, and Abstract Expressionists to attain a sign language of rare psychic states; by Dadaists to expose the absurdities of reason in daily life; by Surrealists to draw myths out of the unconscious; and so on. The history of modern vanguardism is the history of ideas through which, in each instance, art was given new importance. By its illumination of aspects of the physical world, of social moods, of the human condition, art in our time has continually redefined itself as a factor in contemporary intellectual culture. Its transcendence of the market motive has constituted a running critique of capitalist incentive. Modernism echoes with alternatives to industrialist modes of production; it derives inspiration from the rituals of earlier cultures, aristocratic disciplines, dream-structured games, and alchemical formulas, as well as from the illogic of technology and from communal experiments in brotherhood.

But as Conceptualists have insisted, ideas in art are plagued by their relation to the artwork as object. Social acceptance of the style of a painting sets in motion the process of extinguishing its concept: the evolution of Neo-Plasticism liquidates the politics and metaphysics of Mondrian; admiration for the Abstract Expressionist handling of space dissolves the pantheistic enthusiasms of Pollock and Hofmann. Once a manner has established itself, its ideological caul is cast off, and the artist-thinker emerges as the proprietor of an inventory of decorative artifacts. Creations in the same mode continue to be produced by the artist or his followers without attention to their originating idea. It now no longer matters whether the art was intended to heckle tyrants or to capture the colors of Morocco. The intention or "message" of the artist (e.g., Duchamp's anti-art) becomes a means for publicizing his heritage of objects, not a force to bring about a change in beliefs (e.g., the growing awareness of Duchamp's denigration of art results in a rising market value of his readymades, rather than in a lowered respect for art). The politics of Picasso's *Guernica* contributes to veneration of this painting as a fabulous creation of the twentieth century, but it no longer generates antagonism toward Franco's Spain or even distaste by Franco toward the painting.

Thus, each of the advanced art movements has crumbled because of the success of its aesthetics, leaving behind creations more or less formally related to one another. The legatee of the radical insights and creative innovations of twentieth-century art has been art history and its neutralized consciousness. In this context, past art, whatever its purpose, has been reinterpreted as an aspect of cultural education. With the rise in the market value and popular prestige of art in the sixties, ideas in art have correspondingly depreciated. The Minimalism of the sixties closed the book on the art movements of the preceding hundred years by repudiating the meanings they had attempted to instill into art. The Minimalist theory of "objecthood" reflected within art itself that stripping of paintings and sculptures of considerations of intention, feeling, and attitude which is inherent in formalist art history and the market mentality. Evaluation of artworks could thus be based on their status as objects, unaffected by the response of spectators.

Today, art exists, but it lacks a reason for existing, except as a medium of exchange, a species of money. Art as a commodity does not even exist for art's sake, since that implies existence for the sake of aesthetic pleasure. That the present spectacle of art consists of depersonalized works seeking their level on the market produces a nostalgia for paintings and sculptures motivated by human purposes—a quest that is stronger at the fringes of the art world than in its professional center. A recent number of the University of Wisconsin quarterly *Arts in Society* raises the issue of a "humanist" art, which means figurative paintings and sculptures that communicate a social or philosophical message. In this symposium, John Berger, the British art critic and novelist, expresses the crisis-feeling that in art today "none of the reasons found in the past for being an artist exist anymore," and he warns that "new reasons have to be found, or art should be abandoned." To call for a new approach to art under the threat of art's coming to an end is the traditional avant-garde response to cultural change.

The new cannot, however, be delivered to order, and considering the art-historical destiny of styles emanating from the "reasons" of earlier vanguards, the rise of a successor potent enough to survive existing market mechanisms seems highly unlikely. The crisis of art in our time is a permanent one: art is always on the verge of ending—if not actually, then as a subject of serious intellectual interest. Probably the best motive for being an artist is, as noted by Rimbaud, the odiousness of other métiers, including being counselor to Presidents. Certainly art will not end as long as it is a trade in which it is possible, at no matter what odds, to do well. The market has its own mysteries and an accompanying glamour: an object made by hand which fetches more than five million dollars is a sacred entity in a money-venerating society and deserves to be worshiped for that reason alone; the crowds that line up for blocks at the doors of a museum to get a glimpse of a newly acquired masterpiece priced in the newspapers bear witness to a profound truth of our time. The convertibility of a van Gogh or a Rembrandt into cash represents the essence of contemporary feeling about it. It may be that it is time to abandon not art but art criticism, which has anyway become little more than a shopping guide. To study the uses of art in our society, including its political and religious uses, would appear to be more rewarding. As for the artist, his intellectual need is not to find new reasons for being an artist (the tradition of investigating reality still holds) but to understand the forces that are pressing upon creation within the present novel situation.

27

The Old Age
of Modernism

Directing a museum has become an uneasy occupation, not unlike being a White House assistant. Though the survival of his institution may not be threatened, the director lacks assurance that the program he was employed to conduct will be allowed to continue. The chief problem is, of course, financial. This season, not a single museum was able to mount a major exhibition without contributions from the National Endowment for the Arts and a sponsoring business corporation—plus in many cases a grant from a State Arts Council. Even purchases of inexpensive drawings by "younger artists" have depended upon government grants and matching donations. As is the case with universities, the centrality of fund-raising in the daily life of museums has begun to determine the qualifications of those who head them; in several notable instances art historians have been replaced by professional administrators.

Still, as important as the problem of money—if not more important in the long run—are the problems of principle that confront museums today in relation to art, the artist, and the art public. That American museums have been floundering in such matters as policies of acquisition and of sell-off, or dealing in stolen or smuggled objects, has been much publicized in the last few years. A more complex issue, and one more directly affecting the influence of the museum on the life of art in this country and the response of the public to it, is the museum's position in regard to contemporary creations. So long as cash was plentiful, the problem could be met by "experiment"—a concept that enables the typical intellectual floundering of the museums to assume the guise of open-minded hospitality to the new. Throughout the 1960s, thematic exhibitions and retrospectives were organized on the flimsiest premises. The unfortunate role of the museum in contemporary art has been well summed up by Thomas Albright in an article for the San Francisco *Chronicle*, although the article itself champions museum showings of new creations: they have, he acknowledges, "contributed to the promotional apparatus that has managed to convert even the most powerful works of contemporary art into commodities and conversation pieces." The museums' record of destructive activities makes them all the more vulnerable to the current pressure from trustees, potential donors, community representatives, artists' groups, and conservative legislators, educators, and editorial writers. It is a sign of the seriousness of the situation that the Association of Art Museum Directors, at its last annual conference, invited an artist, an art dealer, and a critic to speak on the museum as "Seen from the Outside." For professionals to solicit appraisal from outsiders rarely signifies less than a sense of approaching storm.

The dilemma of the museum in regard to present-day art is not new, nor is it easy to resolve; the very term "modern art" has always been a troublesome one. All periods, criticism of the term points out, were modern for those who lived in them. In describing its art as modern, our epoch implies that its today will last forever. Implicit in "modern" is the notion of a "continuing present," a denial of the validity of both yesterday and tomorrow. To be modern is basically to be timeless, to look not toward a future but toward Utopia, toward, as Rimbaud said, "the happiness that none escapes," a higher condition of man, the "revolution in permanence," that still living dream conceived by the nineteenth century. "Modern" has never been simply the label of a period, like "Renaissance" or "Baroque." It is inherently polemical; it declares the obsolescence of the heritage of earlier times, and even forecasts its own obsolescence in the present that is to come. Rimbaud took a pledge to be "absolutely modern" as if he were stiffening himself for an ordeal; can anyone have resolved to be "absolutely Romanesque" or "absolutely Rococo"? Some modern art is already a hundred years old, yet modernism as a concept overlaps upon the art of today. So it seems natural for museums of modern art to include art that is current, and demands by artists that they do so are difficult to reject. A cut-off point that brings modern art to an end somewhere in the past is necessarily arbitrary.

Yet the subject of the museum *is* the past; its collections are the embodiment of art history. It is as art history that the museum is on solid ground, in respect to both its function and its competence. But only as art history; the closer the museum approaches to the present the shakier becomes the foundation on which it operates. How far from the present the past is thus becomes a decisive question. Art of last year? Of five years ago? A generation? Do this painting, that object have an authentic place in art history, or are they being admitted provisionally—at the expense of the budget and the trust of all the artists who have been excluded—to satisfy demands stimulated by fashion or publicity? Museum decisions that come forward into present-day art project into the future. And when the past is left behind, the museum's historical supports dissolve. What is expertise in regard to the art of the past becomes gambling with respect to the art of today. Training in art history, which is the basis of the museum profession, is made "inoperative," as they say in Washington, once the object of the museum has become the sorting out of existing works and trends.

Institutions do not like to gamble, still less to admit that they do so. Nor are they likely to have the talent for successful betting. There are no courses for museum directors and curators that will equip them to beat the odds. Most museum excursions into the present have been disasters, intellectually as well as in their effects on artists, the public, and the reputations of the museums themselves. Worst of all, when institutions gamble they prefer not to know that they are gambling. Thrown into the present, museum directors mess with art history, seeking phantom analogies with past art to buttress their responses to new phenomena, from Pop to Conceptualism. As a result, a system of deceit and self-deceit is automatically generated, and its results are presented as public education. The current demoralization of the art world is attributable at least in part to museum interference, ideological and practical, with ongoing creation in art. One of the most catastrophic effects has been the dissemination among artists of the belief, by no means misconceived, that merit has no relation to recognition, that thought and imagination are, if not outlawed, secondary to "what's cooking," that at the top of the art world the cards are mysteriously stacked by arrangements between museum people, dealers, critics, and tax-benefiting collectors. So the choice for the artist is either to devote himself to getting into the game or to wither in obscurity for having missed the boat.

Following upon years of disappointing interventions in the field by museums, opinion seems to be turning in a direction that threatens the whole enterprise of modernism in art. A basis for this is the apparent exhaustion of the premises of modernism in the studios—an exhaustion now mentioned as a matter of course in the art magazines. To John Canaday, the end of this road has manifested itself in the glow of a wish fulfillment. "Perhaps a wonderful thing is happening," he exclaimed, in his bounciest, most wide-eyed art-appreciation manner, "and Americans are beginning to realize that this search [for meaning in works of art] can work backward now that there is nowhere forward to go." From this moment on, we can delight our eyes with ancient Chinese scrolls and forget about the condition of man as expressed in contemporary art. Canaday's sprightly farewell to the twentieth century is paralleled by the reorganization of the Pasadena Museum of Modern Art (until recently a stronghold of the national avant-garde exhibition circuit) in order to eliminate shows of contemporary art and to devote the major portion of its space to Norton Simon's collection of Renaissance and Impressionist works.

A similar "deemphasizing of contemporary art programming," as a newspaper of the region describes it, is under way in Berkeley at the University Art Museum, the construction of which, in the late sixties, was stimulated by a large gift of paintings and cash by Hans Hofmann, and which until last year was a showcase for advanced developments in world and local art, as they were conceived by its director, Peter Selz, formerly a curator at the Museum of Modern Art. Reports of the impending change charged that university art historians opposed to modern art had gained control of the museum and were planning to convert it into a teaching instrument of their and other campus courses. This charge has been denied, although it is conceded that the museum is "pulling back from some contemporary art," and in turn Selz has been accused in the press of "administrative imperialism and open misuse of power [which] enraged everyone, from the regents to most contemporary artists." The situation is still unclear, and the conflict between pro- and anti-moderns has focused on a search committee appointed to nominate a new director. However the matter comes out, it is to be expected that contemporary-art activities in Berkeley's museum will henceforth take place under less than friendly scrutiny. A statement in the newly arrived issue of *Arts-Canada* applies equally to San Francisco: "Presumably, the art community of Toronto feels endangered by a possible anti-contemporary-art trend in the area. Such a trend, if it is building up, should not be underestimated."

The riposte to the hardening aesthetic conservatism takes the form of traditional vanguardist reflexes. Ambitious curators continue to favor new technology (photo-realism, videotape) and Conceptual art, apparently for no better reason than that they represent "younger artists"—which, of course, they do not, any more than does figure-drawing or pottery-making. The repetition of obsolescent gestures of defiance becomes increasingly farcical as attacks on the museums—for example, Dubuffet's "anti-cultural" retrospectives—are conducted under the sanction of art-historical precedents. The latest episode is the case of Mr. Jean Toche, arrested, at the instigation of the Metropolitan Museum, for mailing out an open letter urging the kidnapping of museum trustees and officials. Toche, whose genre as an artist is com-posing manifestos and letters of protest, accused the Museum of Mod-ern Art of vandalism because it had removed an inscription sprayed by a visitor from a paint can on Picasso's *Guernica*; in retribution, Toche decreed that officials of all museums be seized and held for trial by a "people's court." This burlesque of the history of artists' protests and of insurrectionary politics, instead of being attacked as a slur on the social radicalism of modernist art movements, has already received the support of more than a hundred artists, art teachers, crit-ics, historians, curators, dealers, collectors, and editors in the United States and abroad, who have denounced "the political arrest of artist Jean Toche" and affirmed his right to "freedom of artistic expression" (which presumably includes the right to muss up masterpieces). On the list of protesters I recognized veteran painters to whom the notion that art can consist in writing open letters is beyond doubt profes-sionally abhorrent but who apparently felt obliged to rally to Toche out of fidelity to vanguardist clichés.

The defense adduced in behalf of Toche rests entirely on art his-tory; it is contrived of the identical arguments used by museums to justify their selections of new work. Even Toche's lawyers have adopted the position that his "protest letters . . . are his art form," and that his incitement to violence should be taken not literally but as a composition in the tradition of Dada and Surrealism. Half a dozen pro-Toche historians play variations on this theme. Lucy Lippard, mention-ing her "collection" of Conceptual artworks (open letters) by Toche,

sees his activities as a continuation of Dada that carries the blessings of
Duchamp, Cocteau (yes!), Max Ernst, and George Grosz. A curator
at the Metropolitan considers Toche's kidnapping call not a threat to
anyone but an appropriate "literary close" to an emotional expression
regarding museums. A City University art professor identifies Toche's
letter as a "Dadaist gesture" that the Metropolitan failed to comprehend; a contributing editor of *Arts* interprets it as "a conceptual art
process" that, since it is a work of art, can have no connection with
violence. The art critic of *Newsweek* refers to the "long and deep
roots in art history" of Toche's act as evidence that it should be considered to be not a menace but a "metaphor." Another defense volun-
teer claims to possess a "vast archive" documenting Dada/Surrealist
behavior, and cites persons and statements once considered scandalous
and now safely ensconced in art history, with books being written
about them. Finally, James Harithas, director of the Everson Museum,
for whom, too, Toche's "proposal" is a work of Conceptual art, dis-
cerns in the incident a factor that can be taken seriously—the existence
of a perilous tension between museums and artists.

It appears never to have occurred to the aesthetes who hail Toche's
recycled Dadaism that they have provided reasons for denouncing him
as a plagiarist. Their defense of Toche is a collective testimonial that
aesthetic militancy today is haunted by *déjà vu*. A vanguardism of
ritual phrases invokes the past without regard to any absurdity or
mental cheating involved. In the Toche case, the roles of the avant-
garde and the museum are reversed: while Toche's champions appeal
to art history for authority to destroy the museum and its contents,
the museum reacts radically—i.e., with forceful assurance—to the contemporary fact of kidnapping. The view of the vanguard "art community" that an act should not be taken seriously if it can be classified
as art but that art should be taken seriously is a repudiation of the
belief of Futurists, Dadaists, Surrealists, and Constructivists that art
can change the world. And in taking the view that an art event should
not be evaluated in and for itself but should be highly regarded
because of its ancestry in art movements of half a century ago, the
avant-garde faces rearward while pretending to advance. The sum of
the situation is that the art world today is unable to distinguish
between genuine acts of defiance or nonconformity and farcical mim-
icking of subversion that discredits the radical past of modernism.
Toche's "crime" is actually not an attack on the museum but a conventional effort to be included in it. The contention that his kidnap

note is a work of art leads to the conclusion that the Metropolitan should have collected it instead of having the F.B.I. collect its author.

American museums today are trapped between the battle lines of an empty and passé verbal radicalism and an academic conservatism that has yet to reconcile itself to an art of its own time. To stabilize their position, the museums must settle their intellectual accounts with modernism—not as a slogan but as historical fact. In our day, what used to be vanguard art has become a tradition. For better or worse, it is the aesthetic past of the generations now living; to be ignorant of it is to remain unconscious of aspects of oneself and one's environment. The vital role of the museum in America is to extend and deepen knowledge of this tradition, transplanted here by the Armory Show in 1913. It was as a tradition that the Museum of Modern Art brought the works of the vanguard to artists, students, and the public in the thirties and made possible the surge of American painting in the first postwar years. In the thirties, it is worth noting, modernism was to all appearances part of the past, suppressed by force in Moscow, Berlin, Rome, silenced in Paris by the conflict between the political right and left. In that decade, a spectator in New York was looking *back* to modern art; new as they seemed, the exhibits at the Museum of Modern Art belonged to art movements that were already extinct. Precisely for this reason, the thirties were the period when this museum made its most decisive impact on American culture; later, when the American postwar vanguard appeared, the museum did far less well.

Time in the world of the museum is slower than it is outside. Regardless of semantics, modern art is art of the past, a period style, with its masterpieces, heroes, and legends. In the museum, modern art is no longer a process of realizing new possibilities; it is the province of historians and curators engaged in the classification and preservation of artifacts. Promotion of innovations, if there are to be any, had better be left to risk-taking dealers, collectors, and critics.

28

The Peaceable Kingdom: American Folk Art

Like African and pre-Columbian sculpture, children's drawings, and works by Sunday painters and institutionalized novices, American folk art owes its current prestige to the modernist overthrow in taste. For the academically trained sensibility that dominated nineteenth-century American art, the limnings, cartoonlike tableaux, and stiff, anatomically distorted figure carvings by itinerant craftsmen in the Colonies and the early Republic were simply effusions of technical incompetence. The aesthetic virtues of American folk art were not discovered until the early 1920s; that is, a few years after the Armory Show and the taking hold of modernism in American painting and sculpture. Since then, with each subsequent victory of advanced styles and concepts, folk art has gained ground. In the thirties, a strong surge of enthusiasm for the aesthetic artifacts produced by farmers, carpenters, tombstone carvers, sailors, and housewives was stimulated by political ideas concerning the innate creativity of "the people"; the decade could be named "The People, Yes" Decade, after the poem by Carl Sandburg. Finally, boosted by the acceptance of such "naïve" painters as Rousseau, Bombois, and Vivin as classics of European modernism, American folk art has achieved equality with other modes in museums and art galleries and publications. Its academic antagonist, with his demands for correct proportion, modelling, and perspective, has ceased to have any voice, at least in the art world, and new aesthetic premises have made it possible to attribute excellence to woodenly composed portraits and family groups and landscapes with misshapen cows—on the grounds of originality, directness, and spontaneity of color and design.

In sum, folk art of whatever date has become "modern" art. Yet folk art escapes the handicaps that plague modernism; it is particularly free of the nervous consciousness of art-historical "trends" that characterize modernist art movements. Folk art was an ingredient of modernism from the beginning without being aware of it, and has continued to infuse advanced painting and sculpture with its energies. Baudelaire found himself moved by the red and green stripes of a café, presumably the self-expression of a local house painter, and Rimbaud emphasized that the junky poetry of street art had a major part in his "alchemy of the word." There are folk and folk-art forms in Chagall and in early Kandinsky and Malevich, Dada, the constructions of Schwitters, the paint handling of Magritte, the doodles of Klee, the abstractions of Arshile Gorky and Stuart Davis, the flags and targets of Jasper Johns, the carved caricatures of Marisol.

Introduced into sophisticated art, with its overtone of historical analogy, folk elements, whether native or borrowed from foreign cultures (e.g., African), awaken envious comparisons with a simpler past now lost both in art and in life, and cast doubt upon the future of the Western tradition in art. Folk art in its pure state, however, raises no problems but induces a mood of relaxed enjoyment. At "The Flowering of American Folk Art 1776–1876" exhibition at the Whitney Museum, it was noted that spectators seem unusually "happy" for an art-gallery crowd of the seventies; perhaps the absence of the need to decide where they ought to place the exhibits on the calendar of originality and influences made the viewers feel carefree. In folk art, everybody is original and everybody came first, even if he was first only in copying an illustration in a manual. Obviously, the paintings and carvings at the Whitney belonged to a period that differs from ours. But in the environment of tin peacocks, cigar-store Indians, wedding quilts, mustachioed whirligigs, and Edward Hicks's biblical utopias, members of today's frenetic art world found themselves reassured about the ultimate worth of art objects, independent of their aesthetico-historical rationale. The time when these objects were made does not assert itself in them and hardly seems to matter, nor does their place of origin. In their haphazard relation to historically identifiable styles—for example, eighteenth-century British portraiture—the folk creations are unlocated in time to a degree that makes a Conceptual exhibition in Soho seem dated.

Folk art stands still. It neither aspires upward, like academic painting, nor advances forward, like the inventions of the modernist art
movements. The lions of Hicks are not ancestors of the lions of Rousseau. No one is anyone else's forerunner, and the question of who did
it first, which breeds hypertension among contemporary artists and
critics, does not arise. All works of folk art exist simultaneously in the
peaceable kingdom of individual imaginings and skill. In reference to
folk art, the word "modern" loses its temporal meaning of "belonging
to the present" and stands for the absence of any date, a kind of permanent "now," or eternity. One commentator found the chief trait of
folk art to be youthfulness.

In theory, folk and high art belong to separate aesthetic categories,
of which high art alone is legitimate. Several years ago, for example,
the Metropolitan Museum presented an exhibition of nineteenth-century painting, sculpture, and house furnishings which strictly excluded
folk art from what Mr. Hoving called "America the Beautiful." But
while folk art can be distinguished from academic art, its boundaries
are as difficult to define as those of sanity. The old approach (presumably in control at the Met) was to determine what folk art is by
the negative measure of academic standards. But these standards no
longer carry any weight in the evaluation of painting and sculpture;
indeed, they seem to be prevalent now only in discussions of folk art.
In her introduction to the catalogue of "The Flowering," Alice Winchester, a veteran folk-art advocate, tried to separate folk from fine
art on the basis of the "artistic innocence" of the first and its "obvious
ineptitudes and distortions." But the folk artists are innocent and inept
only by the rules of academic art, which also found Cézanne, Matisse,
and Picasso inept. Alice Winchester recognized that her definition was
faulty, but apparently no better one was available—how could one be
when art itself redefines what it is from innovation to innovation?
More to the point was her observation that "as folk art has become
increasingly popular in recent years, its limits have grown more and
more indistinct." The wood sculpture of Henry Ward Beecher at the
Whitney, or the oil painting with simulated frame called *Ann Gould
Crane and Granddaughter Jennette*, would not be out of place in a
first-rate exhibition of contemporary art of the human figure.

Even though one might not know what folk art is, one could find
some works at the Whitney folkier than others. *The Prodigal Son
Reveling with Harlots*, a watercolor in which *two* male revellers
(who revels by himself?) are suspended in profile in front of high-

Artist unknown, *The Prodigal Son Revelling with Harlots*, ca. 1790,
watercolor on paper.

backed dining-table chairs while the accompanying temptresses, clothed from neck to ankle, ply them with cups of perdition, seems not only "artistically innocent" but based on no more experience in the ways of the world than a five-year-old farm boy's. Yet this painting, with its combination of stripes, solid colors, and odd, dotted areas (the stockings of the prodigals and the clothing of the harlots), becomes less a mere amateur scrawl and more aesthetically complex the longer one looks at it; ten years from now, it may serve as a model for a new Red Grooms. In contrast, *The Quilting Party*, copied in oil on wood from an academic engraving in a magazine, fails to suggest "ineptitude" even temporarily, and could fall into place as a social-realist composition of the thirties.

Folk art separates itself from officially accepted art on the basis not of the artist's *degree* of skill but of the *kind* of skill (improvised or traditional) and the social environment in which the skill is applied (farmhouse portraits, inn signs versus drawing-room pictures). Rufus Porter, a nineteenth-century itinerant wall decorator, had more painting tricks up his sleeve than were dreamed of in half a dozen academic life classes. He invented techniques of stencilling, stamping, and painting elements of country scenes on plaster walls, and built up what in fine art might have amounted to a school of followers—except that (a typical happening in the story of folk art) a new factory-made cheap wallpaper put an end to his trade. Even in the reign of academic standards, there was nothing to prevent a limner or sign painter from crossing over into the ranks of the fine artists by surrendering his techniques for theirs—an exchange that is no longer automatically regarded as an improvement; today, it is common for Copley's British portraiture to be described as a decline from his more primitive New England style. In the opposite direction, an academically trained professional might develop the "awkwardness" that comes from making style subservient to an obsessive vision or idea, as was the case with Washington Allston, Ryder, and de Kooning. In America, the push in the direction of made-up modes of art—a characteristic of folk art—has been provided by the notion of the American as a "new man," and of America as the "new land" and a "new secular order."

In the past, folk art existed as a manifestation of social hierarchy; folk painting and sculpture were low-class accompaniments of respect-inspiring creations, analogous to comic rustics in serious dramas. To the old academic regime, the folk were culturally identical with savages—strangers from below instead of from the outside. The label for both was "barbarian," with its dual connotation of innocence (noble savage) and ineptitude. Now the arts of all classes and castes are intermixed (even those of the intellectual avant-garde) and are undergoing assimilation into a global aesthetic that already comprises the arts of formerly alien cultures, high and low. Apparently, history has decreed that what was once anthropology shall now be art, and what was once in ethnological and folk museums—from American Indian and Eskimo art to scrimshaw carvings—shall now be lodged in the art museum. By a process seemingly irreversible, onetime cultural outsiders and undersiders are being lifted into visibility. *This movement may well turn out to be the most radical art accomplishment of the twentieth century.*

The largest survey to date of American folk art—the show at the Whitney—came at a time when art-historically oriented fine art has lost its direction. Advanced painting and sculpture have been increasingly subsumed under their conceptual aspect, until the logical unfolding of their reasoning has isolated their ideas from art and left them empty of content. In the February 1974 issue of *Art Forum*, an essay on the British Art and Language movement emphasizes that this latest effort toward a new conception of art is "exclusive of 'normal' art practices and attitudes" because "normal" art is "so contradictory, compromised, and anomalous that any return to it [is] impossible." Having reached this extreme of ideas without works, art may now need to enter a period of works without ideas—at least without ideas centered on the art-historical question of what is proper for "art in the seventies." To an art dependent on such calculations, folk art is the direct antithesis; its outstanding feature is its freedom from any doctrine of the "evolution of forms." Its naïveté is a reflection of its single-minded obedience to temperament—that of the artist and of his immediate public. In its skilled use of unskill, it is the model for an uninhibited making of works: the leading folk-style artist of the postwar period is Dubuffet, whose eye on his clientele is unwavering.

Folk art did not, of course, come to an end in 1876; the dates enclosing the Whitney display were admittedly chosen to constitute a package for the American Bicentennial. Folk art lives on in numerous local trades as well as in forms generated by the modernist art movements; making traditional and "experimental" pictures and objects is encouraged by Sunday-magazine sections and by supermarket periodicals, and there are untutored versions of Dada collages, color-field compositions, mathematical trompe-l'oeil, even Conceptual diagrams.

Rufus Porter, *Steamship Victory*, 1838, wall mural.
COLLECTION OF LOUIS F. DIGIOVANNI, COURTESY WHITNEY MUSEUM OF AMERICAN
ART. PHOTO BY GEOFFREY CLEMENTS

The graffiti in New York subways are probably the largest spontaneous mass outpouring and group showing of folk art that have ever taken place.

Folk painting, carving, ironwork, stitchery, and so on represent the indestructible aspect of art, the love of materials and of making, and the desire to please. A passage in the Whitney catalogue sums up the motive of the folk artist: "People like my work, and I like to paint for them." Folk art does not solve the problem of meaning or confront the ordeal of the modern historical consciousness. Very likely, it is not of primary importance in contemporary affairs. On the other hand, this may be a time that calls for modesty. It may be unwise for art today to try to assume the burden of man's future—at least, to try to assume it alone.

Index